Europe's Reformations, 1450–1650

Critical Issues in History

Europe's Reformations, 1450–1650: Doctrine, Politics, and Community

Second Edition

James D. Tracy

ROWMAN & LITTLEFIELD PUBLISHERS, INC.
Lanham • Boulder • New York • Toronto • Oxford

ROWMAN & LITTLEFIELD PUBLISHERS, INC.

Published in the United States of America
by Rowman & Littlefield Publishers, Inc.
A wholly owned subsidary of The Rowman & Littlefield Publishing Group, Inc.
4501 Forbes Boulevard, Suite 200, Lanham, Maryland 20706
www.rowmanlittlefield.com

P.O. Box 317, Oxford OX2 9RU, UK

British Library Cataloguing in Publication Information Available

Library of Congress Cataloging-in-Publication Data

Tracy, James D.
  Europe's reformations, 1450–1650 : doctrine, politics, and community /
James D. Tracy. — 2nd ed.
    p. cm. — (Critical issues in history)
  Includes bibliographical references and index.
  ISBN-13: 978-0-7425-3788-0 (hardcover : alk. paper)
  ISBN-13: 978-0-7425-3789-7 (pbk. : alk. paper)
  ISBN-10: 0-7425-3788-9 (hardcover : alk. paper)
  ISBN-10: 0-7425-3789-7 (pbk. : alk. paper)
  1. Reformation. 2. Europe—Church history—15th century. 3. Europe—
Church history. I. Title. II. Series.
BR290.T73 2006
274'.06—dc22

2005009336

Printed in the United States of America

♾ ™The paper used in this publication meets the minimum requirements of
American National Standard for Information Sciences—Permanence of Paper for
Printed Library Materials, ANSI/NISO Z39.48–1992.

For Sue

Contents

Figures

ix

Note Regarding Glossary and Bibliography

Readers encountering names or terms that are not familiar—or not familiar enough—are invited to consult the glossary beginning on page 311. References to fuller discussion of matters treated here are found in the bibliography. There are also general works of reference that should be mentioned. The *Oxford Encyclopedia of the Reformation*, edited by Hans J. Hillerbrand (4 vols., Oxford University Press, 1995), has capsule summaries for important figures, ideas, and events, up to about 1600. Readers interested in the flavor of debate among scholars may turn to the forty essays (many on themes relevant to this book) contained in the *Handbook of European History during the Late Middle Ages, Renaissance, and Reformation, 1400–1600*, edited by Heiko A. Oberman, Thomas A. Brady, Jr., and James D. Tracy (2 vols., Leiden, 1994; paperback edition Grand Rapids, Mich., 1995). To get a sense of scholarship as it takes shape, the most helpful scholarly journals are *Archiv für Reformationsgeschichte / Archive for Reformation History* (articles in English and German) and the *Sixteenth Century Journal*.

Acknowledgments

This book is a weaving together of the ideas of many scholars, whose complicated arguments I have ventured to compress into paragraphs or even sentences. I owe special thanks to my graduate student, Troy Osborne, who identified illustrations for the text; my friend and colleague David Kieft; and my father-in-law, Robert Soman, for judicious, nonspecialist readings of the manuscript. This book will be a success if it conveys something of the sustained intellectual pleasure I have had from forty years of professional association with the colleagues whose works are cited in the bibliography.

Europe, ca. 1530

Details of the area labeled "The Empire" are presented on p. xviii.

The Holy Roman Empire
ca. 1550

Legend:
- Imperial Cities
- Habsburg Territories
- Boundary of the Empire
- *Liège* — Major Ecclesiastical Principalities

Bodies of water: Baltic Sea, North Sea

Regions and territories: PRUSSIA, POLAND, DENMARK, HOLSTEIN, BRANDENBURG, ANHALT, LUSATIA, MORAVIA, BOHEMIA, AUSTRIA, STYRIA, CARINTHIA, CARNIOLA, ELECTORATE OF SAXONY, DUCHY OF SAXONY, BAVARIA, TYROL, *Salzburg*, HESSE, *Würzburg*, *Bamberg*, *Mainz*, PALATINATE, WÜRTTEMBERG, *Magdeburg*, *Bremen*, *Osnabrück*, *Münster*, *Paderborn*, WESTPHALIA, *Cologne*, *Liège*, BRABANT, LUXEMBURG, HOLLAND, ZEELAND, FLANDERS, LORRAINE, FRANCHE COMTÉ, SWISS CONFEDERATION

Rivers: Vistula R., Warthe R., Oder R., Moldau R., Danube R., Inn R., Elbe R., Rhine R., Weser R., Meuse R., Haase R.

Cities: Danzig, Cracow, Berlin, Legnica, Brünn, Vienna, Graz, Klagenfurt, Laibach, Wittenberg, Dresden, Leipzig, Prague, Regensburg, Klosterneuburg... Brixen, Trent, Innsbruck, Munich, Augsburg, Ingolstadt, Nördlingen, Donauwörth, Ulm, Konstanz, Zurich, Basel, Bern, Neuchâtel, Besançon, Geneva, Lübeck, Hamburg, Schleswig, Bremen, Hamburg, Chemnitz, Zwickau, Jena, Erfurt, Eisenach, Schmalkalden, Nürnberg, Frankfurt, Mainz, Worms, Speyer, Heidelberg, Stuttgart, Strasbourg, Metz, Trier, Lorraine, Cologne, Bonn, Liège, Amsterdam, Haarlem, Leiden, Utrecht, Rotterdam

I | INTRODUCTION

In 1517, Latin Christendom was a larger society made up of a nearly endless multitude of corporate bodies, each ready and willing to defend its lawful turf against all comers. The one thing most people had in common in this rather contentious world was their belief in the Holy Catholic Church. But in that year Martin Luther unwittingly began what was to become the Protestant Reformation when he proposed a public debate on certain aspects of church practice regarding the forgiveness of sins. By the time of Luther's death (1546), there were many churches, not just one, and "Lutherans" were battling the followers of Geneva's John Calvin (d. 1564), among others, for the loyalty of new converts. Most of the new religious bodies were backed by governments that had armies as well as printing presses to defend their beliefs. Thus religious loyalties now cut across all the others, dividing brother from sister, villager from villager, parishioner from parishioner, guild brother from guild brother. Many Europeans drew spiritual consolation and a more confident view of life from the new religious communities, including the Catholic Church, which found new vigor in facing the Protestant challenge. Others found in the spaces created by open conflict among the contending forms of Christianity greater freedom not to practice any religion at all. Religious rivalry also became a potent additive to the normal stew of political conflict that bred incessant warfare among Europe's many states. Thus the Reformation created a new world in Europe, one recognizably similar in some ways to the pluralistic world that we ourselves inhabit. This book tells the story of what Europe was like before the Reformation, how the Reformation itself developed, and how Europe was changed by it. In this introductory section, chapter 1 explains the premises of my own approach to the Reformation. Chapter 2 briefly discusses some of the Reformation's more distinctive features in the overall context of European history.

1 | Premises

The chronology and organization of this book are based on two premises. The first is that we can best understand the historical significance of the Protestant movement by viewing it not as unprecedented, but as the high point in a series of "reformations" that convulsed the Latin or Western half of Christendom from the eleventh to the eighteenth centuries. The second and more general premise is that religious belief is a motive force in history, but only one among many, so that the outcome of a religious movement can never be explained solely on the basis of religion.

When Martin Luther sent off copies of the *Ninety-five Theses* to church authorities (31 October 1517), "reformation" was a familiar word. In southern France in the tenth century, the monastery of Cluny spearheaded a *reformatio* of the Benedictine order based on a return to its original discipline and austerity of life. Pope Gregory VII (d. 1085) launched an effort to reform the church as a whole by attacking the regnant political system of the Holy Roman Empire. Since bishops were chosen from families loyal to the emperor, emperors found it convenient to have these spiritual rulers exercise secular power in their territories as well. In a ceremony known as investiture or "clothing" with the symbols of office, "prince-bishops" received both their spiritual and their temporal authority from the emperor.

This was the arrangement Pope Gregory now denounced as corrupt, demanding that it cease immediately. The emperor, not surprisingly, took a different view. After nearly fifty years, a struggle that convulsed much of Europe ended in compromise: Bishops would still be "invested" by the emperor or his representative as temporal rulers, but they would henceforth be "invested" with spiritual authority by the pope or by other bishops. In retrospect, this acceptance on both sides of a clear distinction between spiritual and secular authority can be seen as a necessary precondition for the much later (and distinctively European) idea of a separation between church and state. At the time, however, neither party was satisfied by the compromise, and tension between the claims of pope and emperor continued. Beginning around 1150, the focal point of conflict shifted to efforts by the emperors to gain control over the populous towns of northern Italy, close to the Papal States, a band of territory stretching from Rome north to the Adriatic Sea. This struggle ended only when Emperor Frederick II, bitterly opposed by several successive popes, died without a legitimate heir (1250).

Meanwhile, a many-sided movement largely under lay leadership sought to reform the church by urging that men of God must imitate the poverty of Christ and his apostles, rather than living in the lavish style favored by popes and prince-bishops. In southeastern France during the twelfth century, a merchant named Peter Waldo sought permission to travel from town to town preaching the gospel, as the apostles had done. But when local bishops were unyielding (church law, canon law, provided that only ordained clergymen could preach), Waldo and his followers rejected church authority and formed by their preaching a growing underground movement, until royal officials joined with the church in a campaign of suppression. In remote Alpine valleys seldom seen by the king's men, Waldensians survived to welcome the Protestant Reformation of the sixteenth century.

Other branches of the broad apostolic poverty movement remained within the church. Francis of Assisi in Italy (d. 1226) and Dominic de Guzman in Spain (d. 1221) cast off all trappings of wealth and begged in the streets for their food (fig 1.1). Their followers, Franciscans and Dominicans, came to be known as begging brothers, or mendicant friars. They made it their mission to preach to the inhabitants of Europe's now burgeoning cities. But as people flocked to the new mendicant churches, resentment grew among the secular or parish clergy, who defended their spiritual turf with lawsuits and even fisticuffs. Moreover, as the new mendicant orders accumulated property through the donations of pious folk, the Franciscans especially quarreled bitterly among themselves about how strictly the rule of poverty must be observed. To some, it seemed true reform was farther away than ever.

The problems of the papacy in the late Middle Ages brought new demands for reform. When popes resided at Avignon in southern France (1304–1378), the papacy seemed to be under the thumb of the French king. Then came the papal schism from 1378 to 1414, when two factions of cardinals (backed by rival rulers) maintained two lines of claimants to the papal

Figure 1.1. St. Francis of Assisi renounces his father's wealth. Francis's father, a cloth merchant, holds the clothes his son has renounced. Giotto di Bondone (1266–1336), "St. Francis renounces his worldly goods." Church of San Francesco, Assisi. *Alinari/Art Resource, NY.*

throne, one in Rome, the other at Avignon. To deal with this dilemma, some professors of theology and canon law rejected the idea that the pope alone wielded final authority, arguing that an ecumenical council could depose a wayward pope. Conciliarism, as this doctrine was called, seemed to triumph when Holy Roman Emperor Sigismund I summoned the bishops of Latin Christendom to the German city of Constance. The Council of Constance (1414–1417) ended the schism, elected a new pope, and proclaimed the right of future councils to govern the church. But hopes for lasting change were again thwarted. The next council bogged down in squabbles between bishops from territories whose rulers were at war. The pope once again became sole head of the church, but by default, since many theologians and canon lawyers north of the Alps still advocated a conciliar doctrine of church authority.

Meanwhile, the Council of Constance had touched off a war by its treatment of a Czech preacher and theology professor named Jan Hus. Hus taught (among other things) that lay people were unjustly deprived of their right to receive in the sacrament of the eucharist, or communion, not just the host (the bread) consecrated by the priest at mass but also the wine, now consumed only by the priest. Hus's appeal to the spiritual dignity of lay people was extremely popular in Prague, notably among fellow Czechs, who chafed under control of the city and the university by Prague's German-speaking minority. Charged with heresy on various points by German professors at the university, Hus accepted a safe-conduct from the council, meaning he could return safely after having been heard. But having determined that some of his opinions were indeed heretical, and that he violated the terms of his safe-conduct by preaching to the populace in Constance, the council had Hus burned at the stake (fig. 1.2). The reaction in Czech-speaking lands shows the explosive power of two sentiments that will also be visible in the Reformation: (1) lay resentment of clerical privilege and (2) national pride. Czech-speaking priests and nobles led a rebellion against Bohemia's king, forming a new polity backed by a strong citizen army. Over time, the Hussites, or Utraquists, in Bohemia split into competing parties. One reconciled with the papacy, retaining the right for lay people to receive the consecrated wine. But a more radical faction survived, like the Alpine Waldensians, to greet the new dawn proclaimed by Protestant Reformers.

Martin Luther's instant and enormous popularity easily matches the enthusiasm for Hus in Bohemia a century earlier. Luther was not a martyr, unlike Hus, but the printing press made him virtually an overnight sensation all across the German-speaking lands of Central and Eastern Europe (see chapter 4). But this broad movement of support for a new understanding of the gospel showed internal fissures almost immediately. Huldrych Zwingli in Zurich and then John Calvin in Geneva laid the foundations for what his-

Figure 1.2. The burning of Jan Hus. The Czech preacher and theologian Jan Hus, burned at the stake in 1414 by order of the Council of Constance (right) and the Holy Roman Emperor (left): Diebold Schilling, "Berner Chronik." *Burgerbibliothek Bern, Mss. h.h. I 1, p. 367.*

torians call Reformed Protestantism, as distinct from the Lutheranism that bears Luther's name (see chapter 6). Still others concluded that the Catholic Church must once and for all reform itself. Charles V, Holy Roman Emperor from 1519 to 1556, would have preferred to see Luther burned as a heretic, like Hus. But Charles had little control over the German heartland of his empire, where authority rested with local rulers such as Luther's prince and protector, the elector of Saxony. Beginning in the 1520s, a growing number among the empire's many cities and territories decreed uniform adoption of the Reformation, forcing stubborn Catholics to choose between conformity or exile and placing in doubt the very survival of Catholicism in Germany. After many false starts, the pope; Charles V; and the emperor's great rival, the king of France, set aside their quarrels long enough to permit convening a desperately needed ecumenical council at Trent (in Latin, *Tridentum*). Meeting at intervals over a period of years, the Council (1545–1563) clarified Catholic doctrine on points challenged by the Reformers and laid the groundwork for creating a better-educated and better-disciplined parish clergy to compete with the new Protestant pastorate.

Meanwhile, a different kind of Catholic reform was already underway in Spain and Italy, through the emergence of new religious orders, in particular the Society of Jesus, or Jesuits, founded by a Basque nobleman, Ignatius of Loyola (d. 1556), and the Capuchins, begun as a reform movement among the Franciscan friars. As Jesuits and Capuchins labored to regain for Catholicism territories that had largely been lost to Protestantism, their zeal imparted a new sense of hope to dispirited Catholics in Germany. When preaching alone failed to achieve the objective, Jesuits counseled ardent Catholic rulers on a judicious use of princely power to make stubborn Protestants choose between conformity and exile.

Was the Catholic resurgence that began around 1550 an attempt to roll back the advance of Protestantism, or an outgrowth of new forms of Catholic spirituality? Clearly, it was both a "Counter-Reformation" and a "Catholic Reformation" at the same time. Current scholarship, leaving this older debate aside, focuses on the many similarities between Tridentine Catholicism and the new state churches of Protestant lands—Lutheran in much of Germany and Scandinavia, Reformed in Switzerland and several other areas, Anglican in England.

Leaders of the favored confession worked closely with government officials toward three objectives. First, there must be a well-educated clergy, solidly grounded in correct or orthodox doctrine. Second, all inhabitants of the territory must learn at least the rudiments of true doctrine, through sound preaching, the establishment of primary schools, and Sunday catechism classes for the young. Last, there must be a betterment of popular behavior and belief, particularly an improvement of the sexual mores that all reformers now saw as intolerably lax, and an all-out assault on resort by the people to a whole spectrum of practices seen as superstitious or diabolical, ranging from magical incantations to outright witchcraft.

Inducing ordinary folk to change the ways their ancestors had lived and thought for centuries was no easy task. Scholars debate whether the desired transformation was accomplished or not (see part IV). But it is clear that, despite the obvious differences in doctrine, the rival churches breathed a shared atmosphere and struggled to move forward along a similar path. This time, the reformation of Christian society was going to be made to stick.

Yet the call for reformation was not stilled even by the apparent success of the new churches. For one thing, small sects that lacked all the trappings of wealth and authority roundly condemned churches that had made their compromises with state power in order to become established. For another, each of the established churches harbored zealous believers not satisfied by changes they saw as half-hearted. Under Queen Elizabeth I (d. 1603), England's Puritans called for removal of "popish" elements still to be seen in Anglican worship. In the Lutheran churches of Germany in the seventeenth century, a long struggle to define the true, orthodox, meaning of Luther's teaching was followed by a Pietist movement that aimed to get away from dry doctrinal formulas, back to the personal experience of God's forgiveness described in Luther's writings. Rather than forming a new church, Pietists met in small groups to pray and read scripture, like devout dissidents elsewhere, such as the Jansenists of Counter-Reformation France and the Collegiants of the officially Calvinist Dutch Republic. In the following century Lutheran Pietism grew stronger, while Jansenism survived as an underground movement, despite persecution by the French king. In England, John Wesley's preaching launched a spiritual revival that led to a separate Methodist Church, echoed by the Great Awakening in far-off America.

These reform movements form a continuum, but in this book we need only include enough of that continuum to provide a proper framing for the events of the sixteenth century. Each part of the book will begin with a chapter on "late medieval background" (fourteenth and fifteenth centuries), followed by chapters on the main lines of development down to about the middle of the seventeenth century. My treatment of the sixteenth century will include the Catholic Reformation while emphasizing Protestantism.

Until about forty years ago, most scholars understood the Protestant Reformation as the proclamation of a leading idea that took concrete form in social, political, and economic institutions. In German universities, scholars influenced by an idealist philosophy of history pored over the doctrines of the principal Reformers, especially Martin Luther and John Calvin. One scholar argued that doctrinal syntheses had been forged at various times during the history of Latin Christendom, each one pointing toward a form of government and society that represented its logical outcome. Thus, the scholastic theology of medieval university professors, epitomized in the natural law doctrine of St. Thomas Aquinas (d. 1274), legitimized the rights of subjects and pointed to a monarchy in which the king's power was limited by a parliament. But Luther's sharp distinction between the realm of faith and the realm of power undercut any religious justification for active resistance to rulers, and thus pointed to the absolute or unlimited monarchy some seventeenth-century rulers claimed to exercise. By contrast, Calvin's rejection of episcopacy (the office of bishops) in favor of a quasi-republican form of church government, together with his followers' defiance of Catholic monarchs in France and elsewhere, pointed toward the eventual emergence of democracy.

In North America, the Reformation was until fairly recently a topic of interest mainly for students in Protestant theological seminaries and denominational colleges. Courses on Reformation history did not become common on state university campuses until the 1960s. In the common Protestant view, Martin Luther, by his courageous protest, had freed ordinary believers from the domination of a corrupt and greedy clergy. Centuries of superstition, imposed on a gullible people by the Catholic Church, had melted away when Luther proclaimed that scripture was the sole source of authority and that lay men and women were free to read the Bible and interpret it for themselves. Thus, the Reformation was the dawn of an era when, for the first time, individuals were encouraged to think for themselves.

Meanwhile, in Catholic seminaries and denominational colleges, scholars idealized the high Middle Ages, especially the thirteenth century, when universities flourished and virtuous rulers and urban guilds worked to lay the foundations of a just social order. From this perspective, when Luther made his personal religious experience the measure of Christian faith, he loosed upon the world a destructive individualism, a wanton tearing down of beliefs and institutions laboriously built up over the centuries—as in the case of Protestant iconoclasts (image breakers) who smashed to pieces the religious art cherished by their ancestors. Interestingly, the competing denominational interpretations both emphasized the emergence in the Reformation of a modern form of individualism, for good or for ill.

The historical-materialist interpretation of the Reformation, first put forward by Karl Marx (d. 1883) and Friedrich Engels (d. 1895), was in more recent times cultivated in the German Democratic Republic (1945–1989). The Communist state required scholars to work within the parameters of official ideology, but East German historians found ways of making the argument interesting. In this view, the Reformation was an "early bourgeois revolution," that is, an attempt by the burghers of Germany's many towns to overthrow the power of an aristocracy of feudal nobles, rooted in their control of agricultural land and peasant labor. The movement was premature, since the burghers were not yet strong enough to seize control of state power, but it was a revolution nonetheless, because Luther's attack on the authority of the church undermined the religious respect for the status quo that propped up the power structure of feudal society.

In this great struggle, loyalties followed class interests. The most prestigious urban families—the so-called patricians—favored the old religion. Up-and-coming merchants, not yet part of the ruling elite, rallied to Luther's cause. Lower down the economic scale, members of the craft guilds endorsed the more thoroughgoing rejection of Catholic belief and practice preached by Huldrych Zwingli in Zurich and later by John Calvin in Geneva. Marx's proletarians—unskilled laborers, often recent migrants from the countryside—showed themselves the true revolutionaries by embracing the most radical of theological options, that of Anabaptist preachers who were often of humble origin themselves.

In the last four or five decades, proponents of these three very different lines of interpretation—idealist, denominational, and materialist—have criticized but also borrowed from one another's work, resulting in a great melting pot of opinions that makes for a much richer understanding of the Reformation. The ecumenical movement among Christians has enabled scholars working in the context of a faith community to set aside hostile stereotypes. Meanwhile, the growing interest among historians at large in the lives and beliefs of ordinary men and women has generated new questions about how the teachings of the Reformers—or of the pre-Reformation Catholic Church—were understood and practiced in daily life. Finally, and especially in the Germany that was until recently two distinct countries, scholars from East and West initiated multiple contacts that softened earlier dichotomies. Those starting from a materialist perspective began to recognize religious ideas as having a motive force of their own not strictly derived from class interests. Those starting from a theological perspective began to recognize that the religious choices of sixteenth-century men and women were not completely individualistic, because religion—and religious change—also had a social dimension.

From this dazzling variety of possible ingredients for an interpretative stew, each historian will cook up his or her own recipe. I confess an attraction to a principle first stated by the German philosopher Georg W. F. Hegel: the great movements of history involve a convergence of ideal principles and selfish interests, woven together in such a way that those involved often cannot tell one from the other. In general, Hegel's principle means that while ideas have a definite impact on history, it is never the impact expected by their proponents. As applied to the Reformation, it means that men and women will not willingly die a martyr's death for material interests, but neither will they in great numbers willingly disrupt the normal inertia of their daily lives solely for the sake of religious principles.

The Reformations of the sixteenth century thus represent a confluence of distinct developments, each having its own trajectory. This multilayered process cannot be captured by a single narrative line. Hence the rest of this book is divided into three topical sections, each showing a different strand of the same story: part II, "Doctrine to Live By" (what the reformers taught); part III, "Politics" (how princely governments and their rivalries shaped the outcome of various Reformations); and part IV, "Society and Community" (the antagonisms within society, considered as a problem that each of the Reformations sought to overcome). Each part begins with a chapter on pertinent late medieval background, followed by chapters on the Reformations in the German and Swiss lands and then in other parts of Europe.

This three-stranded narrative—rather like a novel or a film that recounts the same events more than once, each time from the perspective of a different character—may leave the reader with questions that are not answered until a later section. But if we are to give both ideal and material motivation in history the respect that each deserves, we must be willing to follow each along its own path of development. My hope is that with each successive strand the overall picture will become a bit clearer, so that readers will gain, in the end, a cumulative understanding of that complex process we call Europe's Reformations.

2 | The Reformation in European Perspective

It is precisely by looking at the Protestant movement in the wider chronological framework suggested in the previous chapter that one can best discern its distinctive features. I believe there are six: (1) *sola scriptura*, the Protestant insistence on the sole authority of scripture; (2) *sola fide*, the doctrine of salvation or justification "by faith alone"; (3) the doctrine of the priesthood of all believers; (4) the confessional state, meaning that rulers use their powers to promote the true Christian confession; (5) the holy community, meaning that for a genuine reformation the town or village as a whole must conform itself to God's law; and (6) the reform of worship and religious practice, focusing attention on the sermon rather than on ritual action. Each of these points involves a message preached by the Reformers, reactions to that message from various levels of society, and outcomes that neither the Reformers nor their Catholic opponents could have predicted.

1. *Sola scriptura.* At medieval universities, theologians-in-training lectured on the writings of earlier scholars before being allowed to lecture on the Bible. Theologians who organized their findings into massive *Summae* (Summaries), like St. Thomas, sifted the Bible for answers to all their questions. To be sure, they consulted other authorities as well—Church Fathers like St. Augustine (d. 430) and pagan philosophers like Aristotle—but the Bible came first. Theologians offered their own interpretations of scripture, but only the church pronounced with authority, through the decrees of ecumenical councils or the papal pronouncements held by some theologians to be infallible. Luther, though trained as a scholastic theologian, challenged this tradition on two fundamental points. First, scripture to him was not a repository of answers to all questions. Rather, it was a single message of overpowering clarity, an answer to the one question that mattered most: How can sinful human beings be saved from the everlasting fires of hell? Second, he rejected the church's claim to control interpretation. By 1519, he

13

was convinced that one could not rely on ecumenical councils or the Fathers, not even St. Augustine, from whom he himself had learned a great deal. "Scripture alone" (*sola scriptura*) had saving truth—all else was mere "human opinion."

Luther's conviction that the Bible was only now being understood, after centuries of darkness, parallels the views of humanists like Erasmus of Rotterdam (d. 1536). Italian humanists of the fifteenth century learned Greek from refugee Byzantine scholars, thus gaining direct access to works previously known only in translation. One Venetian humanist now argued that the scholastics had not even understood Aristotle, their great hero, because of reliance on faulty Latin texts. Scripture was open to the same kind of study. Pope Nicholas V commissioned Lorenzo Valla (d. 1457) to compare Vatican Library manuscripts of the Greek New Testament with the Vulgate translation, used for centuries in the Latin liturgy. Inspired by Valla's work, Erasmus published the first Greek New Testament in 1516, with copious notes on how the precious original differed from the Vulgate. Though not a humanist by training, Luther learned New Testament Greek and, going Erasmus one better, the Hebrew of the Old Testament as well. Erasmus saw the original New Testament text as a "fountain" of pure truth from which Christians could now drink in the plain meaning of the gospel, obscured for so many centuries by the errors of copyists and translators. This was Luther's belief too, even though he and Erasmus did not read the Gospels the same way (see chapter 5).

Most people in Europe were peasants, and few peasants could read in their own language, much less Latin or Greek. Yet Luther's contrast between "scripture alone" and "mere human opinion" had an astonishing resonance in many a humble household. The printing press provides part of the answer to this puzzle—short pamphlets featured cartoons setting forth "scripture alone" in terms that anyone could understand (fig. 2.1). But there was also a great hunger for preaching in late medieval Germany, which led to the building of so-called hall-churches, free of the interior pillars that made it hard to see the pulpit. This hunger for preaching was a hunger for God's Word. Between the Gutenberg Bible of 1455 (in Latin) and the beginning of the Reformation, printers in Germany published more than one hundred partial or full translations of the Bible in numerous German dialects. Events of the 1520s make it clear that people who could not read harbored deep-seated beliefs about the meaning of scripture. To them, God's Word must have answers not just to the question of salvation, but also to social and economic injustices pressing in on their daily lives. Luther was to find, to his dismay, that German peasants who rallied to the cause of God's Word understood "scripture alone" quite differently than he did.

Figure 2.1. Luther outbowls his foes. The reason Luther (in his garb as an Augustinian friar) bowls so well—to the dismay of pope and cardinals to the right—is that his bowling ball is labeled "Holy Scripture": Otto Clemen, Flugschriften aus der ersten Jahren der Reformation (4 vols., Leipzig: R. Haupt, 1907–1911), vol. 3. *Courtesy of University Libraries, University of Minnesota, Minneapolis.*

2. *Sola fide*. Justification "by faith alone." The common opinion among medieval theologians was that sinners are "justified" when they freely accept the grace or favor that God extends to them and do the "good works" that God's commandments require. For Luther, this belief in the competence of human free will obscured the one truth on which the very salvation of humankind depended. From his own struggle to live as a pious monk, and from his study of St. Paul's Epistles, he was convinced that man is saved not by any work or act of will, but solely by grace. God's law

commands unselfish love, but no human being can overcome his inborn selfishness. The true purpose of the commandments is to convince the sinner of his utter impotence, opening the door to an unqualified faith or trust that a gracious God will freely grant a forgiveness he does not deserve. Thus "Christian liberty" means that the sinner who experiences the joy of faith is freed from the dread of God's punishment that necessarily shadows all who vainly imagine they must achieve His forgiveness by their own good actions. It is by this faith alone that one can be saved.

In the cloister, fellow monks saw Luther (fig. 2.2) as a "scrupulous" brother—a touch too anxious about averting God's wrath. The very notion of "scrupulosity" does not appear in monastic literature until after about 1300, suggesting a heightened sense of sin among men and women who, like Luther, had vowed their lives to God. Meanwhile, theologians placed more and more stress on what man must do to attain his own salvation, and preachers constantly warned their congregations of the pains of hell, urging layfolk to imitate the devotion of monks and nuns in doing good works and avoiding sin. Manifestations of popular anxiety to ward off the wrath of God suggest that such sermons were not falling on deaf ears. Some pious folk adopted the practice of scourging themselves in a token of penance for their sins (fig. 2.3), others joined confraternities of flagellants who scourged one another in the same spirit. Indeed, it seems the medieval centuries were marked by a process of "guiltification"—raising in believers a consciousness of their own sinfulness—which for some had reached a breaking point by Luther's time. A number of his followers left personal accounts of the deliverance from the burden of anxiety they too found in the Christian liberty of which he spoke.

But followers of John Calvin, who also condemned justification by works, believed that God's grace served a purpose beyond the spiritual consolation of the individual: it guided believers in truly good works to glorify His name. Adherents of the Catholic Reformation sought to live out a doctrine of good works that was essentially medieval, yet purged of excesses and adapted to new circumstances. Thus if Luther's scrupulosity disclosed a larger crisis in the religious sensibility of Latin Christendom, his solution was but one of several that believers found meaningful.

3. *The priesthood of all believers.* From ancient times priests and members of religious orders enjoyed freedom from taxation and other special privileges, seen by the clergy as proof of their God-given preeminence in Christian society. In the clerical conception of the church, lay people had but a passive role. But as towns and villages gained a measure of political autonomy, lay boards (the English term for them was "churchwardens") took over management of the church building and other parish property. As urban craftsmen formed guilds to govern their own trades, men and

Figure 2.2. Luther as an Augustinian friar. Lucas Cranach the Younger (1515–1586), "Martin Luther as a Monk," 1520. *The Metropolitan Museum of Art, gift of Felix M. Warburg, 1920 (20.64.21), photograph. All rights reserved, Metropolitan Museum of Art.*

women formed religious confraternities whose aims were usually devotional and sometimes social, like founding a hospital. As literacy among the laity slowly increased, especially in urbanized regions like northern Italy and the Low Countries, dealers in manuscript books had a brisk trade in pious treatises in the languages of the people.

The clergy of the late Middle Ages were not particularly corrupt—by and large, priests fulfilled their duties in celebrating mass and administering the sacraments. But as lay people grew more active in the life of the church, they

Figure 2.3. The spirit of penance. Albrecht Dürer (1471–1528), "The Penitent." ©
Copyright The Trustees of the British Museum.

held the clergy to a higher standard. For many, it was no longer acceptable
if parish priests, despite the church's rule on celibacy, had women who were
wives in everything but name, or if the Franciscan friars claimed for their
taverns exemption from the beer tax that other innkeepers had to pay.
Anticlericalism—resentment of the wealth and privileges of the clergy—
was widely diffused among lay people in the late Middle Ages, though more
in some parts of Europe than others. Bohemia's Hussite revolution was one
expression of this resentment; the Reformation was another.

Here, too, Luther touched off feelings more explosive than he realized. He appealed to the laity's sense of spiritual worth in his idea of the "priesthood of all believers"—every Christian man and woman has a priestly dignity in the sight of God; ministers of God's Word are only delegated to exercise an authority vested in all. But Luther wanted monasteries to be dissolved in an orderly fashion by town governments, not sacked by angry mobs, as sometimes happened. He wanted new preachers of the Word, trained in the biblical languages, to wield an authority not unlike what most of them had been used to as former Catholic priests. But Anabaptist preachers drew crowds when they proclaimed that the Bible was fully accessible to humble folk in the vernacular, never mind book-learning or priestly authority (fig. 2.4). Owing to his distinctive doctrine of church governance, John Calvin made a further concession to the dignity of the laity by including lay elders in church decisions. Yet it was in Calvinist towns that one heard complaints that the new ministers were displaying all the arrogance of the old priests.

In the end, Lutheran and Calvinist pastors did consolidate their authority, but only with the backing of town and territorial governments (see points 4 and 5). Meanwhile, in Catholic lands, the first goal of reformers (again with state support) was to form a parish clergy that could regain, among lay people, the respect that had been lost. Thus, if the Reformation's initial effect in the 1520s was to shatter the prestige of the clergy, the next century or so was occupied with competing strategies for rebuilding it.

4. The confessional state. The legislation of Emperor Constantine (d. 337) and his successors gave the Catholic Church a privileged place in the late Roman world. There was now only one path to salvation and one true doctrine to guide people along the way. Over time, Christians professing what the church identified as false doctrine came to be liable for prosecution by secular judges for the civil crime of heresy. What may be called the principle of intolerance—that no one person may be allowed to endanger the spiritual well-being of the community—was forged in this early period and would remain the common belief of Latin Christian Europe down through the seventeenth century. Those who confessed true doctrine formed a single great family in the sight of God, the *corpus Christianum* (Christian body) or Christendom. It was not entirely clear, however, who was the earthly head of this Christian body—Was it the pope in Rome or the Holy Roman Emperor in Germany?

In fact, struggles between temporal and spiritual authority were not limited to the conflicts between papacy and empire noted in chapter 1. Each major ruler made demands that were not acceptable to Rome, especially regarding control over appointments to key ecclesiastical posts in his

Figure 2.4. Anabaptist meeting. Persecuted by town and territorial governments alike, Anabaptists were sometimes captured in the midst of worship: "Nocturnal Anabaptist Gathering Taken by Surprise." *Wick Collection, Zentralbibliothek Zurich.*

realm—the bishoprics and the important monasteries—as well as the right to tax the income from the landed endowments by which they were supported. During the centuries when the papacy was weakened first by its years of exile in Avignon and then by the schism of 1378–1414, strong monarchs in France, England, and Castile (in Spain) gained effective control over ecclesiastical appointments as well as the taxation of church wealth. Popes were allowed to levy their own taxes on the income of bishops and abbots in these lands, but within limits, and only if they sanctioned the king's right to do likewise.

In Germany, by contrast, the relatively strong monarchy of earlier centuries, weakened in part by conflicts with the papacy, gave way after 1250 to an ineffective central government. Emperors of the late Middle Ages were not strong enough to interpose themselves between the papacy and the German church. Moreover, since Germany's prince-bishops were in the unique position of being able to pass the burdens of papal taxation on to the subjects whom they ruled as temporal princes, the flow of revenues to Rome became a political issue here as nowhere else. Germany, so went a common refrain, was "the pope's cow." Of all the reasons why the obscure monk who challenged papal authority became a hero in Germany almost overnight, this national resentment of papal control of the German church was probably the most important. Punning on a Greek word, Luther's German humanist supporters dubbed him not *Lutherus*, but *Eleutherius*, the "liberator" of Germany from "papal tyranny."

It might seem that the teachings of the Reformers were hostile to prevailing notions about the unity of church and state in one Christian body. Luther's early writings condemned coercion of any kind in matters of faith, whether by the pope or by the secular ruler. John Calvin held that the church must have a government of its own, lest princes or town councils be tempted to meddle in affairs that did not properly concern them. In practice, however, the Reformers could not accept the possibility that pastors might teach the new doctrines or not, as they saw fit, and neither rulers nor their subjects could accept a permanent religious division among Christians living in the same city or territory.

Only one doctrine could be the true form of Christianity, and in the common belief, the ruler who tolerated falsehood risked calling down upon his land the wrath of God. Thus it was state power, at the town or territorial level, that cleared the churches of clergy who refused to accept the new teachings and state power again that forced ordinary men and women to choose between accepting what was now deemed the correct confession of faith or finding a new place of residence. Having control over the religious life of his territory was of course an asset to the prince. Well-educated preachers were good at reminding people of their solemn duty of obedience to the prince and useful for keeping the baptism and marriage registers that made it easier to assess the taxable wealth of the prince's subjects. Still, we should be wary of imputing overly calculating motives to princes and their councillors. They too were caught up in a spirit of enthusiasm for the great enterprise of making a more godly world.

This dependence of reform movements on state power had a further implication. Preachers of all eras stressed that a prince's highest duty was to govern his subjects well, but in fact the "honor and reputation" of a prince came from his success in making war. Thus as confessional regimes based on hostile creeds emerged in states that were neighbors but not good neighbors, garden-variety territorial rivalries came to be infused with a new religious intensity. Among the autonomous cantons of the Swiss Confederation, for example, long-standing rivalry divided the so-called forest cantons of the Alpine meadows, founders of the Confederation, from town-centered cantons a bit to the north. Hence, when the town-centered cantons eagerly embraced the Reformation, the forest cantons enthusiastically proclaimed their loyalty to Catholicism. Conflict between the two confessional parties led to the first of the Reformation era's religious wars in 1531, only fourteen years after Luther had circulated his *Ninety-five Theses* (see chapter 6).

Friction between Emperor Charles V and Germany's Protestant princes, papered over in numerous compromises, broke out into war in 1547, again from 1552 to 1555. Soon thereafter France fell into a series of civil wars pitting one religious faction against another, lasting from 1562 to 1598. Religious issues were also important in the long rebellion of the Low Countries provinces against their sovereign, the king of Spain (1572–1648), in the Thirty Years' War in Germany (1618–1648), and in the civil war in England between adherents of the crown and of Parliament (1641–1660). This conjunction between war and religion is an important part of our story. In many cases, a territory's ultimate religious identity depended not on what the people seem to have wanted, or what the preachers preached, but on who won the last battle.

5. *The holy community.* Between approximately 1050 and 1400, towns all over Western and Central Europe organized themselves as "communities." This meant having a body of officials whose decisions were binding on all. There would be a mayor or mayors, aldermen (to use the English term) who served as a court for certain kinds of cases, as well as a legislative council, and a sheriff. Often surrounded by high protective walls built by the burghers themselves, town communities were proud of their distinctiveness in a society dominated by agriculture and by the estates of noble families (fig. 2.5). After about 1300, villages too began organizing as communities, in part to protect their interests against towns

Figure 2.5. The free imperial city of Nuremberg. Early sixteenth-century artists often exaggerated the distinction between town and countryside by showing cities (as here) free of suburban development beyond the walls: "Nuremberg in the Reichswald," 1516. *Germanisches Museum, Nuremberg.*

that sought to control trade in agricultural products. Sheriffs were usually appointed by the territorial ruler, but mayors and aldermen served by election in villages as well as towns, and despite oligarchical election procedures, those chosen were keenly aware of having to answer to fellow citizens.

While mayors and aldermen sitting jointly spoke as "the community" in making decisions in behalf of all, "the community" also meant everybody— especially the so-called common man, the small farmer, or, in towns, the members of craft guilds. This dual meaning of "community" reflects the gulf that separated the great majority, struggling to earn their bread day by day, from the wealthy stratum that monopolized the more important local offices. In many parts of Europe, some time between roughly 1200 and 1400, merchant and artisan guilds in the towns demanded and got a share of power, giving the common man a voice in public affairs. But whether local governments were broad or narrow in their social composition, they all had the same problem: making the community in name a community in fact, in which people focused on interests that united them against the outside world, rather than on the economic and family rivalries that pitted burgher against burgher, villager against villager.

Since the idea of community had a moral connotation, it was to be expected that local governments took an interest in religion and morality. From about 1300, towns began imposing civil penalties for offenses like adultery, blaspheming the name of God, drunken brawling, or engaging in prostitution outside the special districts now created. Many issues relating to worship were beyond the reach of magistrates, since the right to appoint the pastor of a town's parish church was often held by a monastery or noble family outside the walls. But towns exercised what influence they could to procure the appointment of native sons. They also sought to foster public devotion by taking over the management of local religious institutions—convents, hospitals, schools—and by enacting laws that prohibited taverns from opening their doors on Sunday mornings, when mass was being celebrated. In the minds of sixteenth-century men and women, the community was a corporate body not just according to human law, but also in the sight of God.

This sense of standing as a community under God's judgment helps explain the appeal of Reformation doctrine. For if the true doctrine was now being preached for the first time, one could hope for the formation, at last, of a true community, holy and pleasing in the eyes of the Lord. This yearning for a more godly manner of life seems to have been felt most keenly by folk who toiled in their artisan shops or tilled modest parcels in the countryside. These men and women saw themselves as persons of honor, not like the wandering rabble whose only thought was of their next meal, nor like the rich and powerful, who allowed themselves to be tempted by the idea that God's rules were more lenient for important people.

Yet patrician ruling families were now demanding to be addressed as "lords" of the city, like noble lords ruling their country properties. Fearful for their own position, they also tended to be very cautious about approving any radical change in a town's form of worship. From the standpoint of the common man, if the self-styled better sort of people were not minded to follow the call of God's Word, then perhaps it was time for a change in the way the community governed itself. In not a few towns, the triumph of the Reformation was coterminous with efforts to achieve broader participation of the citizenry in local government. More generally, across Europe, in Lutheran, Catholic, and Reformed areas, hard-working people from the lower-to-middling sector of the population gave strong support for raising the standards of behavior in public, compelling sons and daughters to be more obedient of parental wishes (especially in the important matter of marriages where property was involved), and rooting out altogether the diabolical evil of witchcraft.

6. *The reform of worship.* Protestantism was founded on a new understanding of God's Word, proclaimed from the pulpit by preachers learned in Greek and Hebrew. For the literate minority, this religion of the Word built on existing pious practices, for the private reading of scripture now encouraged was not all that different from the private

Figure 2.6. Books of hours. Late medieval patrons often had themselves represented (as here) praying from a book of canonical hours: Jan van Eyck (1390–1441), "The Madonna of Chancellor Rolin." *Réunion des Musées Nationaux, Art Resource, NY.*

reading of books of canonical hours that had long been common among devout lay people, especially women (fig. 2.6). Worship services in the language of the people, not the Latin that few of the laity understood, bridged the gap between those who could read and those who could not, as did the vernacular hymns, rare in Catholic worship, that helped rally people to the new faith.

Yet the traditional religious culture of the illiterate, especially in the countryside, had a life and power of its own. Worshipers usually did not receive communion more than once or twice a year, and in country parishes, where priests had little education, there was not always a Sunday sermon. The most solemn moment of Sunday mass came when the priest held aloft the consecrated host for the veneration of all (fig. 2.7). Also important were the processions in which the whole parish participated: around the boundaries of the parish, to invoke God's blessing on the crops; on the feast day of the parish's patron saint, usually the chief festival of the village year; and in the torch-lit funeral corteges, held at dusk to convey

Figure 2.7. Elevation of the Host. Richard Muther, Die deutsche Bücherillustration der Gotik und Frührenaissance (Munich: G. Hirth, 1922), p. 240. *Courtesy of University Libraries, University of Minnesota, Minneapolis.*

the faithful departed to the next life at the very hour that daylight gave way to darkness. People also took comfort in the familiar sacred furnishings of the church interior, statues and stained glass windows, many of them endowed by prominent families or, in towns, by the guilds. Statues in particular were a focal point for personal devotion. Moreover, statues and relics of the saints could work miracles, as attested by stories circulating in almost every vicinity. Thus, for the majority of Europe's Christians, religion meant participating in the solemn public rituals by which one gained access to heavenly protection.

In Luther's German liturgy, the sermon became the highlight of the service, and country people were confronted, often for the first time, with learned orations from men trained in university theology faculties. With the aid of Luther's *Small Catechism,* youngsters were to master the main points of doctrine, either in newly established village schools or in Sunday afternoon catechism classes. But the order of the worship service and for a time even the priestly vestments were kept as before. Luther saw religious images as encouragements to piety, and in many churches that became Lutheran all statues and paintings remained in place.

Zwingli and Calvin made no such concessions to tradition. In their view popular belief was nothing but a rank growth of idolatry and superstition to be torn up by its roots: no more saints, no religious images of any kind, no funeral processions, no more festivals that blended Christian themes with worldly celebration, like the parish saint's day or Christmas, with its popular carols. Even more than in Lutheran territories, the sermon was the main event of the service. In the Great Church of Zurich, where Zwingli had preached, the altar was removed, the communion table that replaced it was kept to one side; later on, at the front of the church, a large pulpit was built supported by braces anchored in the wall. Nowhere is the new religion of the Word more graphically expressed. Thus, the Reformation also involved something like a cultural war between university-trained preachers grimly resolved to raise their ignorant flocks to a higher level of religious consciousness, and a mute, largely illiterate peasantry whose capacity for resisting unwanted innovations is only now beginning to be appreciated.

The six points highlighted here have to do not just with questions of religious belief, but also with power politics and conflicts of various kinds within European society. The Reformations of the sixteenth century represent a confluence of distinct developments, each having its own trajectory. This multilayered process cannot be captured by a chronological narrative. Hence the three topical sections of the book that follow aim to show

how different strands of the story came together, rather as in a novel or a film that recounts the same events more than once, each time from the perspective of a different character. The doctrinal issues presented in part II, "Doctrine to Live By," include *sola scriptura* (point 1) and *sola fide* (point 2). Part III, "Politics," considers, as in point 4 (the confessional state), how princely governments and their rivalries shaped the outcome of the various Reformations. Part IV, "Society and Community," treats the antagonisms within society (between different lay groups and between laity and clergy, as in point 3) as a problem that each of the Reformations sought to overcome through reforming worship and building a true Christian community (as in points 5 and 6). Each part will begin with a chapter on pertinent late medieval background, followed by chapters on the Reformations in the German and Swiss lands and then in other parts of Europe.

II DOCTRINE TO LIVE BY

Doctrine has always been the way Christians explain who they are. In early centuries, the Latin word *doctrina* meant a "teaching" that formed the hearts of believers as well as instructing their minds in the "right" or orthodox understanding of God's dealings with humankind. This is not to say that religion begins with doctrine. According to an ancient Christian maxim, "the rule of prayer is the rule of belief"; formal statements of faith represent an articulation of what people mean when they worship in a certain way. But doctrine was also the expression of a person's principles; if certain Christians professed false doctrine, there must be something wrong also with how they lived and worshiped. For sixteenth-century Christians the question was, which is the orthodox doctrine—the teaching that had been accepted for so many centuries or the new doctrine that was (so its proponents claimed) the good, old doctrine of the ancient church, and thus not really new at all? Historical scholarship shows that doctrine itself was not the only issue—the political and social tensions that divided sixteenth-century Christians are also reflected in their newfound differences on matters of belief. But one must begin by taking seriously the understanding that contemporaries had of their own experience. As far as is possible, the discussion in chapters 3–7 will focus on matters of doctrine, reserving discussion of the pertinent political and social issues to parts III and IV.

3 | Doctrine

Late Medieval Background

People in fourteenth- and fifteenth-century Europe were religious, but not in the way readers may think. Surrounded by the technological sophistication of the twenty-first century, we find it hard to grasp the raw insecurity of life in earlier ages. Plagues that carried off whole families appeared seemingly from nowhere, as did the flooding and adverse weather conditions that made for a poor harvest and the famine that almost inevitably followed. The fact that the causes of human disease and plant blight were so poorly understood added to the psychological insecurity of an era when Christian folk commonly ascribed such things to evil spells cast by one's enemies or to machinations of the perfidious Jews. Ordinary people were also at risk in time of war. Commanders deemed it risky to accept battle with the enemy's army and safer to punish his towns, or at least his villages, since the towns were often surrounded by stout walls. Humble men and women could take some satisfaction in the fact—as expressed by the "wheel of fortune" image popular in the fifteenth century (fig. 3.1)—that not even the powerful were secure. Great nobles could be ruined by intrigues at court, rich merchants by sudden price changes in far-off lands.

Medieval Europeans did not suffer these afflictions passively. Their strategies for making life more predictable included new farming methods that increased yield, extensive dikes and drainage canals to contain waters, regular correspondence among merchants about commodity prices, and stockpiles of grain by city governments to hold prices down during a scarcity. Over time these multiple improvements fed into a technological revolution that, by the eighteenth century, put Europe well in advance of other areas of the globe. Yet no one cherished the illusion that man by his puny efforts could bend the power of nature, or the will of God.

In pre-Christian times, the peoples of Europe, like peoples everywhere, practiced various rituals to invoke the blessing of the gods and ward off

Figure 3.1. Dame Fortune and the wheel of fortune. Dame Fortune and her wheel, from a manuscript translation (1503) of Francesco Petrarca's De Remediis Utriusque Fortunae ("On the Remedies for Good and Bad Fortune"). *Bibliothèque nationale de France.*

the power of evil spirits. Traces of this ancient paganism persisted long after the peoples of Europe were Christianized. For example, Bernardino of Siena (d. 1444), a famous Franciscan preacher later canonized as a saint, found in one midsize Italian city the custom of attempting to cure eye afflictions with water from "the spring of Apollo," named after one of the ancient gods. When he demanded that the source of such frank paganism be stopped up, he was told to take his preaching elsewhere. He came back some years later and had his followers destroy the superstructures, proposing that the spring itself be incorporated into a church to be dedicated to the Virgin Mary, under the title of Our Lady of the Favors. Since they would still have their healing waters, now under Christian auspices, the townsfolk agreed.

This one incident may stand for thousands over a span of centuries, as Europeans came to accept a monotheistic religion. Christianity focused on eternal salvation but was never a religion of the spirit alone, for the God of biblical faith is Lord of the universe, and His power extends to storms and plagues and battles. Ordinary people believed in the promise of life eternal, but they attached at least as much importance to the promise of God's protection in their daily lives, including protection against the evil spirits that in a Christian view of the world were now seen as devils, minions of Satan. Like Bernardino, preachers had to frame their message so as to appeal to listeners who had priorities of their own. This chapter traces the interaction between Christian teaching, promulgated by learned men of the fourteenth and fifteenth centuries, and the religious inclinations of ordinary folk.

Each bishop was responsible for the teaching of true doctrine in his diocese, and for the warding off of false doctrine, or heresy. Theology—the formal study of scripture and the Fathers—was cultivated at first by the bishops themselves, later by monastic scholars. With the rise of universities, this function of reflecting on doctrine was claimed by professors at the new faculties of theology, masters of arts, and doctors of theology. Theologians like Thomas Aquinas (d. 1274) and John Duns Scotus (d. 1308), whose training in the arts centered on Aristotle's philosophy, sought to reconcile biblical faith with the findings of human reason. They maintained that certain truths of faith (like the existence of God) could be demonstrated by human reason and that others were at least compatible with truths discoverable by reason, even though Aristotle, the greatest of philosophers, had held certain opinions contrary to faith.

Aquinas and Scotus founded "schools" of thought that continued, but the philosophy and theology of the next two centuries took a different turn, known to contemporaries as "the modern way" and to historians as nominalism. Aquinas and Scotus believed that the human mind can grasp in a general way the principles by which God has ordered the world. Take, for example, the Ten Commandments God gave to Moses on Mount Sinai (Exod. 20:1–17) or the summary of the commandments cited by Jesus in the Gospels: to love God above all things and to love one's neighbor as oneself (Mark 12:28–34). We may infer, Aquinas and Scotus argued, that these are the precepts that God in his wisdom knows will best enable us to fulfill our true nature as human beings. But any such claim to discern the mind of God seemed to many subsequent theologians an attempt to confine the awesome power of God within limits devised by human reason. The tendency of the "modern way" was to scale back reason's claims and make room for the sovereign freedom of God's impenetrable will. Concerning the commandments, "modernists" held that we know only that these are the precepts God commands, nothing more; any speculation as to why He may have given us these commands and not others is unwarranted by reason and dangerous to the faith.

The "modern" emphasis on the sovereignty of God's will developed in two strikingly distinct ways. The more common trend was to exalt the freedom of the human will. Just as God was free to accept a person's "merits" or good works as the basis for salvation, man was able, by strenuous effort, to achieve a degree of conformity with the commandments that God would find acceptable. Gabriel Biel (d. 1495), the leading German theologian of his day, put the matter succinctly: "do what is in you" and God's grace will supply whatever may be lacking for salvation.

But other "modernists," especially among the order of Augustinian friars, came to very different conclusions on the basis of their study of the writings of St. Augustine. That Church Father spent his later years in controversy with followers of a British monk named Pelagius, who believed (as Augustine thought) that man could attain salvation by his own efforts, without any need for God's grace. Augustine believed that owing to the "original sin" of Adam and Eve in the Garden of Eden, man's whole nature is steeped in selfishness, alienated from God, and of its own power utterly incapable of fulfilling God's law. Only God's freely given grace frees man from the shackles of sinfulness. But God grants his grace only to those whom He chooses, for reasons that no man may know. Moreover, it is false to say (as Augustine himself had said in earlier writings) that man is free to accept or reject the grace of God, for God's choice brooks no resistance. Taking up a term used in the Epistles of St. Paul, Augustine maintained that those chosen for salvation are "predestined" from all eternity, according to God's inscrutable will.

Thus the two branches of the "modern way" reached diametrically opposed conclusions about how human beings can be saved from damnation. In the person of Martin Luther, the clash between these two theological tendencies would become a clash within the mind and heart of a single man. As an Augustinian friar, he was predisposed to favor Augustine's teaching. But as a theology student at the University of Wittenberg he was taught by a professor who had been Gabriel Biel's pupil.

Luther was unusual among professors of theology in that he also had an appointment as a preacher. Preaching to the laity was not a high-status activity among the clergy, and university professors or canons of cathedral chapters who preached regularly were considered an oddity. The famous preachers of the late Middle Ages were almost all members of the orders of mendicant friars that took preaching as their special mission, the Franciscans (like Bernardino of Siena), the Dominicans, and also Luther's Augustinian friars. Friars had chairs of theology reserved for their orders in university faculties, but they also had churches of their own in the towns and made circuits of pulpits in outlying parishes. Because of what was called "pluralism" in the holding of church offices, many a parish was staffed by a low-paid vicar, not by the pastor himself. In urban parish churches, staffed by the secular clergy, the pastor himself (even if resident) usually did not preach. In the larger German towns of the fifteenth century, this task was increasingly taken over by holders of endowed preacherships, established by pious donations. The better-known urban preachers, friars, or secular priests frequently had university degrees in theology. But in small towns and especially in the countryside, there was often no one to preach but the pastor or (especially in rural areas) the vicar who took his place. Most vicars had never seen the inside of a university, and if they preached at all (some did not) they might read aloud to their congregations from manuals of listener-friendly sermons prepared by someone higher up in the chain of learning and prestige.

Preachers knew from experience that among common people the accepted way of proving a point was by telling a story. Hence, sermons were full of stories—incidents from scripture or from the lives of the saints, accounts of local miracles, or tales of how God raised up the lowly and cast down the proud. Sermons were meant to point out a moral; introducing a theological argument was more difficult. This leads to a second observation: preachers concentrated on morals and had relatively little to say about doctrine. To be sure, church leaders expected even simple believers to be able to recite two basic prayers, the Our Father and the Hail Mary, as well as the Apostles' Creed. There is precious little information about whether people knew their prayers, but knowledge of doctrine at this rudimentary level was in fact diffused in many ways, perhaps most effectively through popular devotions like the Angelus and the rosary, common from the fifteenth century. Pulpit rhetoric tended to focus on how people ought to live. To be a good Catholic was to love God, obey the commandments of God and the commandments of the church, and to live at peace with one's neighbors.

No doubt many people lived more or less in this way. But Satan and his minions were abroad in the world setting snares for unwary souls—neither the preachers nor their listeners had the slightest doubt on this point. Vice was not just a moral failing; it was evidence of the power of the devil in the human heart, and preachers saw it as their sacred duty not to mince words in denouncing sin. Accordingly, their sermons depict a world obsessed by sexual license, boundless greed, and lust for the blood of one's enemies. The seeming contrast between the norms of Christian life and how people actually lived (as described in sermons) becomes even sharper if one considers the importance of monastic ideals.

Lay Christians had long imitated the example of monks and nuns in one way or another. For example, they gave time and effort to what were called the corporal and spiritual works of mercy (fig. 3.2). The "Tables of the Holy Spirit" that first appeared in city parishes in France during the twelfth century provided food for the urban poor, just as monasteries provided for the rural poor. But now that many of the leading urban preachers were themselves members of religious orders—mendicant friars—sermons often held up the simplicity and austerity of monastic life to be emulated by individual lay people. In increasing numbers, ordinary men and women joined "third orders" for the laity, attended services at which the canonical hours were sung, or left instructions in their wills that they be buried in the habit of a religious order. But the appeal to monastic ideals also implied a higher moral standard for the laity, consistent with the monastic practice of carefully examining one's conscience for sins against God and one's neighbor. By this measure a layman must find himself guilty of adultery if he merely desired another man's wife or guilty of the grave sin of hatred if he but fervently wished ill to his enemies.

This raising of moral consciousness or "guiltification" leads to a final observation. There was, after all, a theology implicit in late medieval preaching, one that resembled the "free will" school of the modern way. It was not that all preachers had studied the works of theologians like Gabriel Biel, though some had. Rather, preachers had to get through to the hardened sinners they saw before them, and many found no better way of doing so than by hammering home the fear of God. At the same time, lest they leave listeners wallowing in despair, preachers also emphasized the concrete steps sinners could take—indeed must—to save themselves from the wrath of God. Paradoxically, the same centuries that witnessed a revival among some theologians of Augustine's doctrine of predestination were marked by a tradition of preaching that stressed, more than ever, human free will and the good works by which men aided in their salvation.

Figure 3.2. Feeding the hungry in Alkmaar, province of Holland, 1504. Feeding the hungry, one of seven panels on "The Corporal Works of Mercy" by the anonymous Master of Alkmaar (province of Holland), ca. 1504. Note that Christ himself stands among the poor (cf. Matt. 25:35). *Rijksmuseum—Stichting, Amsterdam.*

How listeners reacted to sermons is not easy to reconstruct. Some people ignored the church altogether, as many as 10 to 15 percent in one area that has been studied; they simply never went to Sunday mass. But there is also evidence of a higher level of religious engagement on the part of devout laity. Treatises on how to achieve a sense of personal union with God through prayer were written not just for lay people but by lay people, like England's Richard Rolle (d. 1349) and Margery Kempe (d. 1440). The fourteenth and fifteenth centuries saw few new religious orders but a number of lay brotherhoods and sisterhoods that emulated monastic life without binding vows. The Beguines, communities of unmarried women and widows, lived in enclosed courtyards carved out of crowded urban centers, each woman contributing to the common chest through a craft like spinning, and each free to leave and marry as she wished. The Brothers of the Common Life sometimes operated schools aimed at recruiting boys for the priesthood. Although the most famous document of their spiritual outlook, *The Imitation of Christ* (1476), was written by a priest-member, most Brothers were laymen who, like the Beguines, could leave and marry if they wished.

Most people fell somewhere between the two extremes—the irreligious and the devout. For those who had enough property to make a bequest, wills offer a window on religious attitudes. Many bequests went for pious purposes, sometimes more than half the total, and two types of such gifts are of special interest here: the endowing of masses for the release of one's soul from purgatory and donations to charitable foundations. Formalizing the suggestions of earlier Christian writers, theologians of the eleventh century proposed that many souls at the point of death, perhaps most, will not be found worthy either of admission to God's presence in heaven or of condemnation to an eternity of punishment in hell; there must therefore be an intermediate state, a place of purgation where souls are cleansed of the dross of sin and so prepared for admission to paradise. The doctrine of purgatory was quickly accepted by the church, and wealthy clergy and members of the aristocracy began leaving sums in their wills to endow masses to be said for their souls as a way of speeding their release from purgatory. Belief in purgatory was immortalized in the middle section of the greatest of medieval poems, the *Divine Comedy* of Dante Alighieri (1265–1321).

In Dante's lifetime, the practice of endowing soul masses was democratized, as men and women even of modest means began designating proportional sums in their wills for this purpose. Indeed, the custom came to be so widespread that a whole class of "chantry priests" were able to make a living, barely, by saying masses for various testators and collecting the small fees provided by their wills. Late medieval wills also reflect the emphasis of preachers on good works, particularly works of charity. Merchant testators often earmarked bequests to the poor to atone for the sin of usury. Wealthy persons also left funds to build hospitals for the sick or enclosed courtyards with small dwellings to house the poor or the aged. The largest foundation of this kind, endowed in 1519 by the great merchant-banker of Augsburg, Jakob Fugger, still exists, operating according to rules established by the benefactor (fig. 3.3). Many other testators made smaller bequests to one or more of their city's charitable foundations.

For people who did not have money enough to leave a will, the evidence available points in the same general direction. Ordinary believers of the late Middle Ages set great store by indulgences, promises by the church

Figure 3.3. The Fuggerei in Augsburg. The row-houses on this section of a late sixteenth-century map of Augsburg mark Jacob Fugger's city for the poor, built in 1519: from G. Braun and F. Hogenberg, Civitates Orbis Terrarum, as abridged in Adrien Romain, Parvum Theatrum Urbium Praecipuarum Totius Orbis Terrarum (Frankfurt, 1595). *Courtesy of University Libraries, University of Minnesota, Minneapolis.*

that all who met certain conditions could have stated periods of punishment in purgatory remitted, either for themselves or for their deceased kinfolk. Churches where an indulgence was to be obtained on a particular day might have to open their doors at four or five in the morning to accommodate the crowd.

Especially in the cities, people also joined in great numbers the religious fellowships known as confraternities. These came in many kinds: for men, for women, for both sexes, some headed by priests, most by lay people. Each had a common devotion, gathering on a certain day in a certain church for particular prayers, but many also had charitable aims: giving alms to the poor, raising funds for dowries for poor but honorable girls, or operating a hospital. Some confraternities even took on the vital but life-threatening task of burying the victims in times of plague. All of these practices varied considerably with time and place. For example, the endowing of soul masses waned in fifteenth-century Italy but waxed in sixteenth-century Spain. It also became more common for confraternities to concern themselves with preparation for a good death, including a last confession of one's sins to a priest, or praying for the souls in purgatory. Charitable bequests increased in some parts of Europe but decreased in others. In Germany, indulgences were distinctly less popular if the monies donated were sent across the Alps to papal Rome rather than going to local churches. But the overall pattern of religious activity among the laity does seem to reflect the constant stress of preachers on the fires of hell and on the good works man must do to attain his own salvation.

Lay people also had concerns that were uniquely their own. The custom of processing along the boundaries of the parish, to invoke God's blessing and cast out any devils that might be infesting the area, long established in the countryside, was adopted by urban parishes as well. There might even be a fight if groups from two different parishes met along the boundary, each suspecting the other of driving its demons into their parish. According to a belief condemned by some clergy as superstitious but actively promoted by others, anyone who gazed upon the consecrated host would not die that day. Hence, in some areas the priest at daily mass took to elevating the host not just once, as the rubrics prescribed, but twice, for the benefit of those who came late. Parish boards began commissioning craftsmen to create elaborate golden "monstrances" with glass windows, so that the host might be carried aloft in procession and seen by all. During the fifteenth century, the church authorized a new feast, that of "Corpus Christi" (the Body of Christ), a day on which people from all of a town's parishes followed the monstrance in solemn procession, invoking God's blessing on the whole city. The confraternities, always founded for purposes of prayer and charitable works, seem to have functioned for their members as a surrogate extended family, creating bonds that were social as well as spiritual. Rules were often vague about prayers to be said at meetings but detailed and precise about support for the families of deceased members and prayers for their souls.

Thus, if the clergy were getting through to the laity, lay people were using practices sanctioned by the church for their own purposes. This does not mean that lay people did not grumble about the power and privileges of the clergy—in fact such resentment seems to have been growing (see part IV). But to grasp the religious life of the late Middle Ages, one must recognize that Christians high and low, theology professors and illiterate peasants, shared to a significant degree a common understanding of doctrine. Theologians of the "free will" modernist school wrote learned treatises on what each person must do to be saved; preachers expounded a similar message in plain language; and lay people recited their prayers, gave to the poor, endowed masses for their souls, and joined confraternities, all in the earnest hope of doing what was needed for God's blessing in this life and the next.

At a more speculative level, one may wonder whether participants in this good-works Catholicism of the late Middle Ages had something else in common, a pattern of thought that encouraged repetitious behavior. Scholastic philosophers and theologians continued to multiply their subtle distinctions in a language that was increasingly technical. Preachers introduced more and more subcategories into their catalogues of the various types of sin that good Christians must be careful to avoid. Ordinary believers could not have enough of a good thing, whether it be the endowing of thousands of soul masses by some, an endless collection of indulgences by others, or the proliferation of confraternities, thirty or more in not a few urban parishes. This pattern of activity may also be compared to the "flamboyant" Gothic architecture of the same period, with its arches within arches and traceries within traceries (fig. 3.4). Scholars who make such comparisons have suggested—plausibly, I think—that this repetitious behavior, this topping-up of good works with yet more good works, betrays a certain underlying anxiety, a fear that by doing as much as possible one still might not be doing enough.

Meanwhile, the authority that university professors of theology claimed in matters of doctrine was coming under challenge from the devotees of a new kind of learning. In Italy there were still traces of ancient Roman educational practices, based not on logic but on rhetoric, the art of speaking and writing eloquently. Small schools run by teachers of oratory offered an alternative to the university liberal arts curriculum based on Aristotle's logic. Around 1300, Italian teachers of rhetoric began modeling their instruction on what is now called classical Latin, dating from the era of authors like Cicero

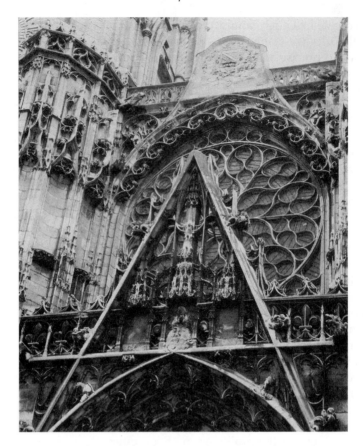

Figure 3.4. Flamboyant Gothic (mid-15th century). West façade, Cathedral of Saints Peter and Paul, Troyes, France. *Bridgeman Art Library.*

(d. 43 B.C.) and Livy (d. 17 A.D.). They also contended that poetry, history, and moral philosophy—what Cicero had called "the studies of humanity"— were the best preparation for an orator. Accordingly, as teachers of these subjects gained a foothold in universities, students nicknamed them "humanists." Mastering the classical style required knowing the history of the Latin language and, if possible, Greek as well, a language well known to classical Latin authors. Some humanists proved the value of their craft by acting as textual detectives, showing, for example, that a particular document, for reasons of style, could not possibly be assigned to the author or period to which it was ascribed.

Thus was born philology, the scientific study of texts. Armed with the new philological method of inquiry, humanists like Lorenzo Valla (d.

1457) challenged the monopoly over the interpretation of texts claimed by university professors. Working as an independent scholar, Valla showed that law professors misunderstood the texts of ancient Roman law because they tried to take them apart according to the rules of scholastic logic, instead of setting them into their proper historical context. Working for the king of Naples, he demonstrated beyond reasonable doubt that a text used by the popes to buttress their territorial claims against Naples was a crude forgery. Working for a humanist pope, and making use of Latin and Greek manuscripts housed in the Vatican Library, he showed that the Vulgate Latin New Testament was riddled with mistranslations, some of which distorted the meaning of the Greek original.

In Italy, where most universities were of recent origin, debates between humanist scholars like Valla and university professors steeped in scholastic logic were conducted with civility. But a real battle was joined when, by about 1500, humanist scholarly methods began to penetrate northern universities, where the privileges of the professoriate were deeply entrenched. Erasmus of Rotterdam (1469–1536) was the standard-bearer of humanist scholarship in this more combative era. The illegitimate son of a priest, Erasmus (by his telling) entered a monastery for lack of a better way of continuing the life of study he had chosen. There he chafed under constraints real or imagined, above all the superstitious fear that Christians might be contaminated by contact with pagan Latin poets of the classical era, like his beloved Horace (d. 8 B.C.). Given the chance to serve as Latin secretary to a local bishop, Erasmus "escaped" from his monastery and never went back. After years of scrounging support from semiliterate patrons, he gained the attention of the learned world through his collection of *Adages,* or pithy sayings from Greek and Latin authors , especially in the second edition of 1508.

His real passion was for "ancient theology," that is, the vision of Christian life propounded by the Fathers of the Church, and closely based on scripture. The Fathers were themselves trained in the art of rhetoric, not logic, and Erasmus admired their way of weaving scripture into their works and writing so as to reach the heart, making readers better Christians. He set himself to master Greek, even though no teacher was available, and thus gained access to the Greek Fathers, especially Origen (d. 255), a sophisticated thinker and biblical scholar. When he found a manuscript of Valla's unpublished treatise on the New Testament (1505), Erasmus also found his calling. It took eleven years to prepare the first-ever printed edition of the Greek New Testament that appeared in 1516, to be followed by four subsequent editions. Each was accompanied by copious notes discussing the Greek and Latin manuscripts he had examined and, where manuscripts or quotations of the New Testament by the Fathers offered different readings,

Figure 3.5. Christ's charge to Peter. St. Peter kneels before Christ dressed as a priest, while another apostle holds his papal tiara. This ahistorical view of the papacy would be challenged by humanists and Reformers alike. Fernando Gallego and assistants, *retablo* from the cathedral of Ciudad Rodrigo, Spain. *Collection of the University of Arizona Museum of Art, Tucson. Gift of Samuel H. Kress Foundation (61.13.36).*

explaining why he had chosen one rather than another. As a New Testament philologist, Erasmus was a scholar of unparalleled brilliance, improvising as he went along interpretative techniques that would not be recognized as standard procedure until 150 years after his death, like the principle of the "harder reading."

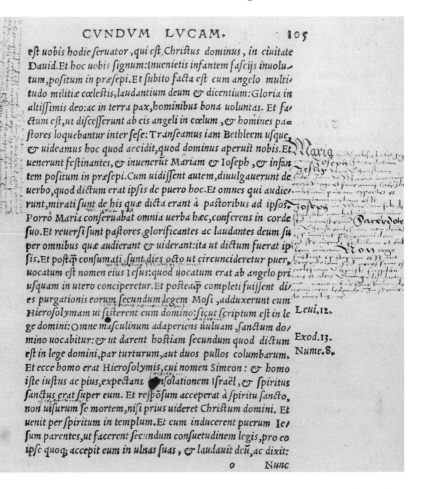

Figure 3.6. Studying the scriptures. An unknown sixteenth-century reader makes marginal notes on Luke 2 in his copy of a separately published edition of Erasmus's new Latin translation of the New Testament; Erasmus, Novum Testamentum ad Graecam Veritatem Recognitum (Basel: Froben, 1521). *Courtesy of University Libraries, University of Minnesota, Minneapolis.*

Scholarship was never an end in itself for Erasmus, only a means to a badly needed reform of Christian doctrine. If people lived as they did—slaughtering one another in senseless wars—it was because they had been taught that religion was only a matter of ritual practices, like not eating meat on Fridays or confessing one's sins to a priest once a year. This false "religion of ceremonies" rested on a misreading of the Gospels. For example, when John the Baptist prepares the way for Jesus's coming by urging listeners to "do penance" (Luke 3:8), the term used in the Latin Vulgate was referred by medieval interpreters to the penance one was assigned by the priest in the sacrament of confession. Erasmus pointed out, correctly, that the original Greek word means "have a change of heart," and thus does not refer to any ecclesiastical ritual. Similarly, when the apostle Simon confessed Jesus to be "the Christ, the Son of the living God," Jesus gave him a new name, calling him "Peter," that is, the "rock" on which he would build his church (Matt. 16:16–19). Medieval commentators took the text to mean that Jesus was making Peter the first pope (fig. 3.5). But Erasmus followed those Fathers who took the "rock" on which the church was founded to be Peter's faith in Jesus, not Peter himself.

Erasmus did not believe such distortions were accidental. He claimed that members of religious orders, especially the mendicant friars, "twisted" scripture deliberately in order to promote religious practices that feathered their own nests, like the custom of having oneself buried in a Franciscan habit. The grip that these "mendicant tyrants" had on the minds of the common people could be broken only by the power contained in the native meaning of scripture. Theologians must set aside Aristotle's logic and study scripture in the original languages. Preachers must set aside their talk of ceremonies and teach people about the love that Christians are to bear one another. And lay people must find their own ways of prayer, based on reading scripture, and forget about imitating the monks. Despite vociferous objections from scholastic theologians, who found it unseemly that mere "grammarians" like Erasmus meddled in sacred theology, this message found an audience among laymen and wealthy clerics who could read Erasmus's Latin and conscientious young men preparing for the priesthood (fig. 3.6). University lectureships in Greek and Hebrew were endowed at Louvain (1517) and Paris (1519), for study of the Old Testament as well as the New. Graduates trained in the new theology were beginning to occupy endowed preacherships in important churches. By about 1520, Erasmus's program for a reform of doctrine was taking shape as an alternative to the prevailing vision of Christian life. By this time, however, it was not the only alternative.

4 | Doctrine

Martin Luther, to 1521

Few individuals have shaped history as Martin Luther did. The way he overcame his personal religious anguish became the model for a new understanding of Christian life. His keen mind and passionate spirit, breaking through the conventions of academic theological discourse, won over men who had sat down to read the works of this notorious heretic in order to refute him. His courageous challenge of papal authority gave him immense prestige among those who called themselves "evangelicals" or followers of the gospel (*evangelium*). His word sufficed to guide many into one channel rather than another, forming in the end a new church. But Luther's greatest importance to history lies in the fact that his protest against Rome touched off a many-sided explosion that no man could control. This chapter will consider Luther's early life and thought down to 1521. Chapter 5 will take up the extraordinary and often conflicting proliferation of responses to Luther's message during the years 1520–1526.

Luther speaks in his writings of a breakthrough moment, when he felt himself delivered from the dread of God's punishment by a new insight into the meaning of scripture. Assuming that Luther had this experience before his life of public controversy began (1517), some scholars have combed surviving notes of the early lectures he gave at Wittenberg, looking for evidence of his new understanding of scripture. Others point to the fact that Luther's fullest description of his breakthrough dates it from the time of his second course of lectures on the Psalms (1518–1519). Perhaps the most sensible view is that Luther's theology cannot be reduced to a single point; rather, it is made up of several strands, some of which appear in the early lectures, others not before 1518. Thus the climax of his inner struggle came

47

in the midst of furious battle with his enemies. In this case, religious doctrine took form not in a quiet compartment unto itself, but right in the middle of that nexus of conflicts we call history.

Luther was born in 1483, the son of a Saxon miner. Hans Luther, Martin's father, rose from laborer to partner in one of the small operations typical of Saxony's mining boom in this era. It was a measure of the family's rising status that Martin was the first Luther to receive a bachelor of arts degree, from the University of Erfurt. He followed the traditional scholastic curriculum, dominated at Erfurt by the "modern way," though he also had friends among Erfurt's upstart humanist scholars. Martin was a strong student, and he doubtless made Hans Luther proud when he enrolled in the law faculty in 1505. But en route back to Erfurt from a visit home, passing through a frightening summer storm, he impulsively vowed to St. Ann, the patron saint of miners, that he would become a monk if she delivered him from peril. His father had misgivings and friends were surprised, but Luther persisted. He entered the Erfurt cloister of the reformed Augustinian friars, a congregation distinguished for its learned members. Johann Staupitz (d. 1525), the father-superior in Erfurt, soon would be called away by the elector of Saxony to help found a new university in Wittenberg (1502). Staupitz was the first holder of the theology chair reserved for his order; Luther would be the second.

The traditional monastic routine emphasized self-scrutiny. Friars regularly confessed their sins to a father confessor, and there was a weekly "chapter of faults" at which each recounted his failings publicly. But Brother Martin was unusually scrupulous. In his *Table Talk* he recounts that when he sang in choir the Psalm verse "In Thy righteousness deliver me" he recoiled inwardly, measuring his own sinful heart against the righteousness of God. He could not confess his sins often enough or long enough: "Once I confessed for six hours." Even when his confessor absolved him from the guilt of his sins he was not content, for the formula of absolution required the penitent to be sorry for his sins: How could one be sure of feeling what theologians called contrition (sorrow for sin because one had offended God), not just attrition (sorrow for sin because one feared the pains of hell)? Work was a standard remedy for monks unduly preoccupied by their sins. Luther apparently began the study of theology at Erfurt, shortly after his ordination as a priest (1507). The next year Staupitz, his superior, bade him transfer to Wittenberg to earn his doctorate. When Brother Martin proffered a list of fifteen reasons why he was unworthy to be a theologian, Staupitz commanded him under his monastic vow of obedience to go.

At first, Wittenberg intensified Luther's anxiety. Since one of his theology professors had been a student of the late Gabriel Biel, the monk who could never be sure of being properly sorry for his sins was confronted with the calm assurance of a late-great theologian that one need only "do what is in you" in order to be saved. Staupitz, a noted student of St. Augustine, came to the rescue by admonishing his protégé not to give heed to "recent" theologians, that is, the scholastics. True wisdom was to be gleaned from the Church Fathers, above all St. Augustine. Luther's lectures on St. Paul's Epistle to the Romans (1515–1516) show how carefully he studied Augustine, especially his writings against Pelagius, presenting the human will as captive to sin unless freed by God's grace. The prevailing scholastic view was that man with the help of divine grace could perform actions that were inherently righteous in the sight of God. Augustine too believed that God's grace made man righteous. But Luther taught that God in his mercy merely imputes righteousness to those who confess that they remain steeped in sin, utterly incapable of living up to the commandments. Augustine maintained that those who are saved by God are predestined for salvation from all eternity, and this Luther accepted. But knowing the duplicity of his own heart, he could not believe that God had chosen such a sinner as himself for eternal glory. Hence he adopted from other sources the view that the true Christian is one who resigns himself to the prospect of damnation in hell and still praises the justice of God. In fact, he could not resign himself to an eternal punishment, and the awful spells in which he was numbed by a dread of God's justice only grew worse.

Luther had been named superior of the reformed Augustinian friars in Wittenberg in 1512. In this capacity he developed what would later be important contacts at the court of Elector Frederick the Wise (d. 1525). As preacher at the elector's castle church (since 1514), he was also gaining a sense of how difficult it was for ordinary folk to accept the hard truths of Christian life as taught by St. Augustine and St. Paul. Within the theology faculty he built an Augustinian "school," as may be seen from the "theses" or propositions that were posted and then publicly defended by doctoral candidates he had trained. He also began winning over faculty colleagues, such as Andreas Bodenstein von Karlstadt (d. 1541), who abandoned his allegiance to the "way" of Aquinas once Luther persuaded him to read Augustine.

This busy but quiet life was disrupted by a small incident that became the hinge of something huge. In Rome, Pope Leo X (r. 1513–1521) was rebuilding the great basilica of St. Peter. He proclaimed indulgences for all who contributed to the project and recited certain prayers. This was a familiar practice, for popes claimed to have disposal over a spiritual "treasury of the church" consisting of the merits of all the saints through the ages, so that by his fiat these merits could be applied to the remission of

Figure 4.1. Sale of indulgences. Anonymous caricature of the sale of indulgences (by Dominican Friar Johann Tetzel) to which Luther's *Ninety-five Theses* responded. The last couplet of the text reads, "As soon as the gulden in the basin rings, another soul to heaven springs." *Stiftung Luther-Gedenkstätten in Sachsen-Anhalt, Wittenberg.*

punishment in purgatory. Frederick the Wise, mindful of widespread complaints that Germany was "the pope's cow," had barred the pulpits of his land to the preaching of any indulgence that involved sending contributions to Rome. But the indulgence was preached in a neighboring territory by a Dominican friar, who advertised his wares with printed circulars (fig. 4.1).

To Luther, the popularity of this indulgence among his parishioners showed how easily people were misled by quick and easy paths to salvation. Some even got the idea that the certificates of indulgence they obtained involved a remission of their sins, not just of time in purgatory. So, on 31 October 1517, he made public his *Ninety-five Theses*, written in academic Latin, challenging the whole practice of indulgences. Among other things, he asserted that the true treasure of the church is the gospel, not the merits of the saints, and that the pope had no power to release souls from purgatory. Moving on to related subjects, he also maintained that whoever receives absolution from a priest in the sacrament of confession must have firm faith that his sins are forgiven.

Quite unexpectedly, the *Ninety-five Theses* were circulated all over Germany, even translated into the vernacular, and Luther became an overnight celebrity. German humanists who resented what they saw as papal domination of their country seized on the fact that a German monk was challenging Rome. Printers sensed there would be a market for anything of Dr. Luther's they could get their hands on. In Rome and elsewhere, Dominican theologians came to the aid of their indulgence-preaching confrere by heaping abuse on the "heretic" of Wittenberg. Luther responded in kind, and then some—invective was one of his real talents. He also published an *Assertion of the Ninety-five Theses*, defending everything he had said, point by point.

Meanwhile, Luther continued his work as a professor of theology. In his second course of lectures on the Psalms (1518–1519), he wrestled once more with the question of how sinful man might escape God's judgment, and this time he found some new answers. First, to those whom God has chosen for salvation, He imputes a righteousness that is "passive," not active, given by God, not accomplished by man. The sinner does nothing for his own salvation, not even (as Luther had said in earlier lectures) accusing himself of sin before God. Sorrow for sin, faith in God—in short, everything that conduces to salvation—is from God alone. Second, to have faith means the sinner has firm confidence that God has forgiven him his own sins. For Luther there is a vital distinction between believing in one's mind that Christ by his life and death has redeemed humankind from sin and believing in one's heart that Christ is one's own redeemer, sinner though one knows oneself to be. The latter, not the former, is what St. Paul means when he says (Rom., 1:17) "the just shall live by faith."

This doctrine of "salvation by faith" was henceforth for Luther the "key of scripture," opening up the mystery of how sinful man might be saved. Though he would still be plagued all his life by doubt and anxiety, Luther never forgot the deliverance he felt when this key of scripture was given to him, possibly in the early months of 1518. He could now see the torment of earlier years as a necessary preparation: Had he not been driven to despair of his ability to do anything worthy in the sight of God, he could never have experienced the joy of Christ's wondrous and gratuitous mercy.

This new understanding of Christian faith was soon tested in a confrontation with Pope Leo X's emissary to Germany, Cardinal Tommaso de Vio (d. 1534), known from the town of his birth as Cajetan. Initially, the papal court did not take seriously the ruckus caused by an obscure professor at a fledgling German university. But Rome did have important business in Germany. For centuries, the papacy had sought to rally Latin Christendom against the military might of Islamdom, first in an ultimately futile campaign for possession of the Holy Land during the era of the Crusades (1096–1293), then in a struggle to stem the steady advance of the Ottoman Turkish Empire. Since the Ottoman sultan had recently (1517) subdued the Mamluks, a rival Muslim dynasty based in Egypt, there was every likelihood of further Turkish attacks against Christian Europe. Hence, in the summer of 1518, Pope Leo sent Cajetan, a seasoned diplomat, to address the princes and the envoys of Germany's cities assembled for a diet in Augsburg. Cajetan carried proposals to mobilize a Christian army with German support, but he could not overcome deep skepticism of papal motives in Germany, where people could remember previous occasions when money was collected but no crusade was launched.

Cajetan was also instructed to lay down the law to the troublesome professor from Wittenberg, summoned to Augsburg for the meeting (12–14 October 1518). Cajetan, a respected theologian, had evidently decided that all questions raised in the *Ninety-five Theses* could be treated as still open to dispute, except for two points. Speaking as a defender of papal authority, he demanded that Luther recant his assertion that popes had no power to declare that souls were released from the pains of purgatory. Luther replied that he could not do so, unless taught from scripture that his opinion was false. Speaking for the theological tradition (including Augustine), which held that no man could ever be certain of his standing before God, Cajetan demanded that Luther recant his assertion that anyone absolved by a priest must believe he is free of sin. This too Luther refused; to him, Cajetan was contradicting the plain meaning of St. Paul's words, "the just shall live by faith." He appealed from the pope's emissary to the pope himself, or to a council of the church. Word spread that he had defied Cajetan. Luther returned to Wittenberg, meeting admiring crowds en route.

Johann Eck (d. 1543), a theology professor at the university of Ingolstadt and a celebrated debater, thought he could bring Luther to heel. He challenged Karlstadt (Luther's Wittenberg colleague) to a debate, confident that Luther too would take up the gauntlet. The debate was held in Leipzig, under the auspices of the duke of Saxony, whose lands had been ravaged within living memory by Hussite armies from nearby Bohemia. In debate with Luther (4–13 July 1519), Eck played to his audience, pointing to similarities between Luther's writings and those of Jan Hus, the Bohemian heretic condemned and burned by the Council of Constance (1414). Since he evidently discounted the authority of Constance, did Luther still wish to appeal to a council of the church, as he had done in Augsburg? This attack placed Luther at a crossroads. He would have much company among theologians if he merely questioned papal authority, but none at all if he rejected the common belief that ecumenical councils cannot err in matters of faith. Having asked for a few days' time to examine Hus's writings, Luther returned with an unequivocal answer: Hus had been unjustly condemned, Constance had erred, and councils of the church were not infallible. By implication, the only source of religious authority was scripture itself—*sola scriptura.*

Events now moved rapidly toward schism in Latin Christendom. In Wittenberg, studying the papal decrees constantly cited against him, Luther found little he could respect. In letters to close friends, he wondered if the papacy had fallen under the grip of Satan. The New Testament Book of Revelation prophesies a day when many of the faithful will be deceived by Christ's great adversary, described in one text as the seven-headed beast, in another as the Whore of Babylon (Rev. 13:1–10, 17:1–7). Reform-minded visionaries of the medieval era predicted that the Antichrist would some day occupy the emperor's throne or even the seat of St. Peter in Rome. In private, Luther now believed the day had come: papal Rome was the Whore of Babylon (figs. 4.2, 4.3).

Figures 4.2 and 4.3. The papacy as Antichrist. While Christ Himself refuses the crown offered by the man to the right of St. Peter, a greedy pope "fishes" money from secular rulers: engravings by Lucas Cranach the Elder (1472–1553). Passional Christi und Antichristi (Wittenberg, 1521), as reproduced in Harmann Grisar, S.J., and Franz Heege, S.J., Luthers Kampfbilder (4 vols., Freiburg: Herder, 1921–1923). *Michigan State University Libraries.*

In public, he set forth his understanding of the gospel in three influential treatises published in 1520. *The Freedom of a Christian* explains his doctrine of salvation by faith, starting from the sharp distinction he found in the Epistles of St. Paul between the false righteousness of works and the true righteousness of faith. Only those who despair in the righteousness of their own deeds can grasp what faith in Christ means and how it makes Christians free from the anxiety that oppresses all who place any trust whatsoever in their own righteousness. In effect, Luther's own spiritual journey had become the model of Christian life. *An Address to the Christian Nobility of the German Nation* called on the secular leaders of German society to take a hand in reforming the church, since no help was to be expected from the pope or his bishops.

The Babylonian Captivity of the Church tears down the church's authority point by point. The pope claims to be the final interpreter of scripture, but scripture's message—the promise of forgiveness in Christ—is clear and needs no interpreter. The church claims to govern the lives of Christians by canon law, but coercive authority belongs only to the secular rulers to whom God has given it, not to those designated to preach the Word. The church teaches that God's grace must be mediated by an ordained priesthood, but this claim too is false. For Luther there are indeed unique rituals or sacraments of the church through which believers have access to divine grace. But for him the efficacy of the sacraments depends solely on Christ's promises in the Gospels, not on a power to make holy received by priests in ordination.

Furthermore, for Luther there were not seven sacraments, as in Catholic doctrine, but only two, baptism and the Lord's Supper—and the latter was distorted by false teaching. With his disciples at the Last Supper, Jesus had said of the bread He blessed, "This is my body," and of the wine, "This is my blood . . . Do this in memory of me" (Luke 22:19–20). Luther believed, as Catholics did, that these words meant the body and blood of Christ were truly present in the consecrated bread and wine. But he rejected the Catholic doctrine of transubstantiation, according to which the substance (an Aristotelian term) of the bread and wine is transformed into that of the body and blood of Christ. The words of Jesus must speak for themselves, unencumbered by human efforts to explain God's ways.

Meanwhile, the papal court moved toward a formal condemnation. Johann Eck volunteered his help in combing Luther's writings for propositions worthy of censure as heretical (he claimed to have found 4,000). *Exsurge, Domine* ("Rise up, O Lord"), a papal bull demanding that Luther recant forty-one specific assertions, was issued on 15 June 1520. Luther greeted the news with derision. When a copy of the bull finally reached Wittenberg some months later, he celebrated with a bonfire (10 December) fed by the papal bull and a copy of the canon law. A further bull (3 January 1521) excommunicating Luther for refusing to recant was anticlimactic. Luther shed his hesitation to speak publicly about the papacy: the see of Peter had become a cesspool of iniquity, the Antichrist.

The voice of Emperor Charles V was yet to be heard. At the death of Maximilian I of Habsburg (r. 1493–1519), two great princes had vied for the succession, King Francis I of France (r. 1515–1547) and Maximilian's grandson Charles of Habsburg (b. 1500), hereditary ruler of the Low Countries and, in Iberia, king of Castile and Aragon. Charles won the contest by offering larger bribes to the electoral princes (including the elector of Saxony) by whose vote the emperor was chosen. Patriotic German humanists rejoiced: as archdukes of Austria, the Habsburgs were hereditary German princes. Many hoped the new Habsburg emperor would defend the empire against papal domination as well as French aggression. But Charles himself had no sympathy for Luther's rebellion against the papacy. Raised in the belief that he as emperor would be the divinely appointed leader of the Christian world, he resolutely opposed any division within Christendom, especially at a moment when Islamdom, led by the Ottoman sultan, seemed more dangerous than ever.

One of Charles's first acts as emperor was to request that the princes and urban deputies assembled for the Diet of Worms condemn Luther. Since the diet would not act without hearing what the Saxon monk had to say, Luther was summoned to Worms. He told the emperor (17–18 April 1521) he could not in conscience recant his opinions unless taught from scripture. Many at Worms were deeply impressed. The pope's representative at Worms exaggerated only slightly when he reported that "nine-tenths of the people here cry 'hurrah for Luther', the other tenth cry 'death to the pope'." But once Luther had departed, under safe-conduct, Charles induced a majority of the diet to issue the Edict of Worms, placing Luther outside the protection of the law (whoever harmed him would not be punished) and prohibiting the dissemination of his teachings.

The emperor now returned to his Spanish kingdoms, threatened by impending war with France, leaving behind as his deputy for imperial affairs his younger brother, Archduke Ferdinand of Austria (1503–1564). As for Luther, he was fortunate in that his prince, Elector Frederick the Wise, did not believe he had received a fair hearing. Under Frederick's protection, and living in disguise as a nobleman at the Wartburg, one of the elector's castles, Luther disappeared from view for the better part of a year (April 1521–March 1522). When he emerged from seclusion, it would be a different world.

5 | Doctrine

The German and Swiss Reformation, 1520–1526

At the Wartburg, Luther completed a translation of the New Testament from Greek into German, published in 1522, and began learning Hebrew for the Old Testament. (His epoch-making translation of the full German Bible would be published in 1526.) In Wittenberg during these months, his designated spokesman was Philip Melanchthon (1497–1560), a brilliant young professor of Greek who had switched to theology at Luther's suggestion. But Karlstadt took the lead by pushing ahead with reform on several fronts—he introduced a new German-language liturgy and persuaded the city council to remove images from the churches. To make it clear there was no longer any real distinction between clergy and laity, Karlstadt took a wife, breaking with the church's rule of clerical celibacy; he also began dressing as a layman.

Meanwhile, three men had taken refuge in Wittenberg after being expelled from nearby Zwickau for professing religious ideas the city council deemed too radical, including the abolition of infant baptism (see below). The so-called Zwickau prophets claimed direct inspiration from God. Melanchthon and others hesitated—Could these men be right? The city dissolved in furious controversy among ardent, image-smashing supporters of Karlstadt, angry defenders of the now-abolished Latin mass, and followers of the three prophets. Alarmed, Luther came out of hiding and laid down the law from his accustomed pulpit (March 1522): The "prophets" must leave town; the Latin mass must be restored until such time as people could be weaned away from it (Luther introduced his own German liturgy four years later). The university faculty prohibited Karlstadt from publishing anything. Dr. Luther could still control the flow of events in Wittenberg. The rest of Germany and Switzerland was a different matter.

✝

In far-off Zurich, Huldrych Zwingli (1484–1531) launched the most important alternative to Luther's understanding of the evangelical message. As a student at the Universities of Vienna and Basel, Zwingli became a part of the humanist movement, as is evident from his study of Erasmus. He displayed a typically humanist patriotism while serving as a pastor in the town of Glarus, writing poems in praise of the noble Swiss Confederation. He was also chaplain to the men of his town who, as was their custom, marched across the Alps (1512, 1515) to fight under the papal banner as mercenary soldiers in Italy's wars (fig. 5.1). For his services, Zwingli received an annual papal pension. He used the extra income to purchase works in "ancient theology," including Erasmus's Greek New Testament of 1516 and a grammar for learning ancient Greek.

In the Italian campaign of 1515, French gold enticed the men of some Swiss cantons to change sides at the last moment, attacking their erstwhile allies, including fellow Swiss; this maneuver turned the tide of battle, but left bitter memories in Switzerland. Zwingli, familiar with Erasmus's critique of contemporary warfare, began speaking out against the current vogue for mercenary contracts with the king of France, whose agents were signing up Swiss cantons one after another. The town council of Glarus, eager for French pensions, dismissed Zwingli from his pastorate, forcing him to take a parish in a smaller town. But Zwingli's stance won admirers in the important city of Zurich, a holdout against the French alliance, where he became endowed preacher of the "great church" in January 1519 (fig. 5.2). It was the custom to preach each Sunday on the scripture texts assigned for the mass of that day. But Zwingli, mindful of the differences among New Testament authors to which humanist scholars had called attention, broke with precedent by announcing a series of sermons on the Gospel of Matthew, from beginning to end.

He also attacked the cult of the saints (fig. 5.3), indulgences, and other long-established practices. He preached justification by faith, a doctrine he claimed to have learned directly from scripture rather than from Luther. Zwingli's emphasis was in any case slightly different, because of his belief that God's grace made it possible for the righteous to live according to God's commandments. How Christians lived was for him a touchstone of doctrinal truth. For example, he now believed it was wrong for Christians to fight as mercenaries in any war, not just for the French. It was a victory for Zwingli (January 1522) when the city council banned all inhabitants of the canton from signing up as mercenaries, despite opposition from the countryside, where men supplemented their income by soldiering. Knowing he had the support of the council, Zwingli arranged

Figure 5.1. Swiss mercenaries crossing the Alps. One of Zwingli's accomplishments was to stop (in the canton of Zurich) the practice by which Swiss men earned their bread fighting in foreign wars: from Diebold Schilling, Amtlicher Luzerner Chronik, as reproduced in Walter Muschg, E. A. Gessler, Die Schweizer Bilderchoniken des 15en/16en Jahrhunderts (Zurich: Atlantis, 1941), no. 135. *Courtesy of University Libraries, University of Minnesota, Minneapolis.*

Figure 5.2. View of Zurich, ca. 1500. The Grossmünster ("great church") where Zwingli would become People's Preacher in 1519, may be seen clearly in Franz Leu, the Elder, "View of Zürich," ca. 1500. *Swiss National Museum, Zurich, AG-7.1.*

a disputation (January 1523) in which he defended *sola scriptura* against Catholic opponents, and attacked clerical celibacy, monasticism, and belief in purgatory.

The council declared Zwingli the winner on the main issue, *sola scriptura,* but it took two years to overcome resistance to the abolition of Catholic worship throughout the city and the canton. Guided by Zwingli, the council sanctioned a new German liturgy (April 1525) and mandated removal from the churches of all images—crucifixes, statues, paintings, and stained glass windows. Zwingli believed the Christian people, like the Hebrews of Old Testament times, had a covenant with God and were thus bound to honor His commandments to the Jews of old, including the prohibition of graven images. Prior to 1525 there had already been outbreaks of spontaneous iconoclasm, as people convinced of a new faith laid violent hands on the "idols" by which they had so long been deceived (fig. 5.4). Like all educated men of the era, Zwingli abhorred riots, and he counted on the city council to ensure that the remaining "idols" would be removed from the churches in an orderly fashion. Orderly on not, Luther viewed this whole development with misgiving. He believed images encouraged piety

Figure 5.3. Image of a patron saint. Albrecht Dürer (1471–1528), "St. Sebald," from Valentin Scherer, Dürer. Des Meisters Gemälde und Kupferstiche (Berlin/Leipzig: Deutsche Verlagsinstitut, 1926); the church model Sebald holds is recognizable as the Seballdskirche (St. Sebald's church) in the artist's native Nuremberg. *Courtesy of University Libraries, University of Minnesota, Minneapolis.*

and should be kept. He also found that those who were zealous to cleanse the churches of images (like Karlstadt in Wittenberg a few years earlier) seemed to think they were performing a righteous deed in the sight of God—thus reintroducing the old idea of justification by works.

Differences between Wittenberg and Zurich became acute when Zwingli espoused a new understanding of the Lord's Supper. In 1524 a visitor from the Low Countries showed him a treatise arguing that the words of Jesus at the Last Supper had been grossly distorted by the church. "This is my

Figure 5.4. Iconoclasm in the German lands. "Lament of the Poor Persecuted Idols and Temple Images," ca. 1530, attributed to Erhard Schön (Germanisches Nationalmuseum, Nuremberg). Images are being removed in orderly fashion, as Zwingli would have wanted. In the upper right corner, a defender of images claims to see a mote in his neighbor's eye, but cannot see the beam in his own (cf. Matt. 7:3). *Germanisches Nationalmuseum.*

body" should be taken figuratively, not literally, as had been believed for so many centuries. In 1525 Zwingli presented this view in a treatise of his own. The true body of Christ, he maintained, was not a piece of bread, but the assembly of the faithful gathered to commemorate the Last Supper. Luther reacted much as his Catholic adversaries did: this was blasphemy, plain and simple. How could anyone who so capriciously dismissed the plain meaning of scripture be counted as a Christian? And how could sinners trust in the promises of Christ if His very words in the Gospels were not to be believed? The pamphlet war between Wittenberg and Zurich that now began lasted into the following century.

One thing Luther and Zwingli had in common was that German and Swiss-German humanists were of incalculable importance in spreading their doctrines. These men, mostly a bit younger, had been moving into influential positions as endowed preachers, secretaries to town councils, and councillors to princes. They cheered the two Reformers on as they attacked the established scholastic theology in the name of a new or rather "ancient theology" based on scripture and the Fathers. As patriotic students of the German past, they also blamed the papacy for waging war against the great emperors of the medieval centuries, and thus weakening the empire. During Emperor Maximilian I's occasional conflicts with the papacy, humanists in imperial service promoted the common view that Germany was being exploited by papal greed.

Northern humanists also connected papal Rome with a special kind of Italian snobbery. Italian humanists, styling themselves heirs to the glories of ancient Rome, heaped scorn on "barbarian" lands north of the Alps that had no history worth remembering. Young scholars eager for study in Italy, the font of humanist learning, often found that "barbarians" speaking correct classical Latin with a northern accent were treated with the curiosity one might bestow on a talking ape. Hence, German and Swiss-German humanists combed old manuscripts for evidence of forgotten heroes whose great deeds would give the lie to Italian arrogance. One whose name came to light was Arminius, a war chieftain who kept Rome out of northern Germany by annihilating three legions that crossed the Rhine in 9 A.D. When Luther came on the scene, humanists acclaimed him as the new Arminius, the man destined to free the German nation from Roman tyranny in its modern and clerical guise.

Many believed, in the words of a humanist friar who heard Luther preach at Augsburg (October 1518), that Luther was saying what Erasmus said, only more boldly. Zwingli's career illustrates the possibility of a seamless progression from "ancient theology" to Reformation doctrine. Yet there was no necessary connection between the humanist agenda—sound biblical scholarship as the basis for a reform of Christian life—and the doctrine of salvation by faith. This became clear in Erasmus's debate with Luther.

After publication of the first edition of his Greek New Testament (1516), Erasmus (fig. 5.5) settled at the University of Louvain, near Brussels, where the endowment by a wealthy friend of chairs in Latin, Greek, and Hebrew laid an institutional foundation for the new theology. But the growing controversy over Luther made Louvain more and more difficult, as conservative theologians, already suspicious of the mere "grammarian" they had admitted to their faculty, now blamed Erasmus's novel approach to scripture for all of Luther's heresies. Moreover, Emperor Charles V expected that the most famous scholar of his Low Countries provinces must surely take up his pen against Luther, sooner or later. Erasmus himself had feared from the start that Luther's vehement "spirit" portended schism in Christendom, a prospect he deeply abhorred. Yet he also admired Luther as an expositor of the Gospel, and he saw "mendicant tyrants" reigning supreme in the church if Luther, their great foe, were laid low. Thus, he could neither support Luther nor attack him. Late in 1521 he moved to Basel, where

Figure 5.5. The older Erasmus. Hans Holbein the Younger (1497–1543), "Erasmus of Rotterdam." *The Metropolitan Museum of Art, Robert Lehman Collection, 1975 (1975.1.138), photograph. All rights reserved. Metropolitan Museum of Art.*

his publisher was, lest he be confronted with a request from Charles V to write against Luther.

In Basel, part of the Swiss Confederation, evangelical zealots assailed Erasmus as a hypocrite for continuing to profess loyalty to the pope, after he himself had so sharply attacked superstitious practices of the church. On the other hand, it also became clear he would lose credibility among those in the church who defended him—including officials at the papal court—if he remained silent. He therefore decided to write against Luther, but chose an issue he felt would not give support to the errors of the "mendicant tyrants." Erasmus's *Consideration of Free Choice* (September 1524) assumed the stance of one willing to weigh the evidence pro and con: Did man have free will in matters pertaining to salvation?

Erasmus thought scholastically trained theologians (Luther included) had a tendency to dogmatize, to see their own opinions as binding on all Christians. He preferred to be "skeptical" of dogmatic assertions, save for doctrines supported either by the clear teaching of scripture or by the "consensus" of the church over the centuries. Far from meeting this test, Luther's complete denial of free will was not defended by any respected theologian. But as a concession to Luther's insistence on *sola scriptura*, Erasmus limited his discussion to evidence from scripture. There were, he admitted, passages in the Epistles that seem to support Luther's interpretation of St. Paul's teaching on predestination, especially Romans 9:9–23. But as theologians taught, the fact that God foreknows every choice human beings make does not mean that God causes us to make one choice rather than another. Moreover, Erasmus argues, the many scriptural passages that summon believers to walk in the way of the Lord leave no doubt that man must have some freedom to respond to God's grace.

Luther's *Bondage of the Will*, published a year later, attacked Erasmus as an "atheist" for his skepticism about dogmatic assertions. Where Paul speaks plainly about divine predestination and human impotence, Luther argued, Erasmus stops up his ears, unwilling to hear a truth that human vanity cannot bear. Scripture is indeed full of commandments, not because man will ever be capable of achieving perfect love or the other virtues commanded by God, but because sinners must be taught to despair in their own powers before they can learn to place their trust in Christ. Luther ridiculed the idea that God's foreknowledge does not exclude human freedom. It is, he insisted, God's foreknowledge that causes human beings to make one choice rather than another: "This bombshell knocks free will flat." This debate, perhaps the most important of the Reformation era, showed that Luther and Erasmus were not after all pursuing the same goals, as many who admired both men had thought. On the whole, younger humanists continued in Luther's wake (or Zwingli's). Men of Erasmus's generation now placed their hopes, as he did, in a reform of the Catholic Church from within.

Much as Erasmus, Zwingli, and Luther differed from one another, they all believed ordinary folk should be guided in matters of faith by learned men like themselves. No one appreciated the fact that the advent of the printing press allowed men and women of little formal education to join in public discussion of any and all questions. From 1521 to 1525, even as the number of books published in Latin for scholars and churchmen declined in the German-speaking lands, there was an explosion of books published in German for those who could read only in their native tongue. Printers in Strasbourg, an important book market, turned out nearly ninety books in German per year during these years, as opposed to the twenty or so books per year published during the previous decade. This was largely because Luther and other reformers made a conscious decision to appeal to the lay public by writing in the vernacular or having Latin works translated. In Strasbourg, over half the German-language books in the peak years dealt with the Reformation controversy, and Catholic writers attacking Luther were significantly outgunned by their adversaries. Works by Luther accounted for 49 percent of religious books in the vernacular, evangelical preachers in Strasbourg for another 11 percent. Yet 22 percent of the vernacular books on religion were penned by lay authors, mostly in support of Luther's cause, but from their own perspective. Women too dared to make use of the printing press. Katherine Zell, wife of a former priest and Protestant preacher, published as a pamphlet a letter of consolation she had written for the women of a small Habsburg town, whose husbands had chosen exile rather than submission to the Catholicism prescribed by their Catholic ruler.

On the major doctrinal issues, some lay writers grasped exactly what Luther meant by the freedom of a Christian, for they too found in his doctrine of salvation by faith a deliverance from the dread of God's punishment. As a group, however, they attached greater importance to his doctrine of *sola scriptura*, the issue most often discussed in books and pamphlets by lay authors. Lay men and women took great comfort in the idea that God's Word was just as accessible to them, through vernacular translations of scripture, as it was to clerics who flaunted their Latin learning. They also tended to find Zwingli's interpretation of salvation by faith more congenial than Luther's. Man is saved by grace rather than by his own works, but the gift of grace is given that Christians might live righteously. Luther's insistence that even the sinner who has been saved does nothing at all for his own salvation was not easy to grasp, certainly not for hard-working men and women reared in the good-works Catholicism of the late Middle Ages.

The Anabaptist current of the broad evangelical movement provided the greatest scope for a distinctively lay theology. Rejection of infant baptism can be seen as a final stage in the tearing down of the Catholic sacramental system and with it the authority of the priesthood that administered the sacraments. Luther had rejected five of the traditional seven sacraments, retaining only baptism and the Lord's Supper. Zwingli demystified the Lord's Supper by proposing that the bread and wine remained bread and wine, nothing more. In Catholic belief, the guilt of sin was cleansed through baptism; the ancient practice of baptizing infants was explained by reference to the doctrine of original sin, inherited by all, for the guilt of original sin was by itself believed sufficient to bar a person from admission to God's presence in heaven. Once baptism came to be understood as a profession of faith by adults, not a ritual by which infants too may receive forgiveness, nothing was left of the Catholic idea that God has entrusted to the priesthood certain signs or actions that are efficacious in the communication of His grace.

The attack on infant baptism originated among Saxon evangelicals who felt Luther himself was moving too slowly, including Karlstadt, and Thomas Müntzer, a preacher whose radical ideas got him expelled from Zwickau shortly before the three "prophets" (his disciples), who then went to Wittenberg. The theory of adult baptism was first put into practice among a circle of Zurich evangelicals who felt Zwingli was moving too slowly. Meeting privately for prayer and scripture reading, they laid great stress on literal interpretation of the New Testament as a guide for Christian life. For example, true Christians must refuse to take oaths, whether in a law court or elsewhere, because Jesus instructed his disciples not to swear (Matt. 6:34–35). The first adult baptism took place among this group, in a village outside Zurich (January 1525). Their leader was Konrad Grebel (1498–1526), scion of a leading Zurich family. This clean break with over a thousand years of religious tradition sparked intense religious excitement as the men of Grebel's circle fanned out, preaching their version of the gospel. Huge crowds gathered in the open air, witnessing what many saw as a spiritual rebirth in the Holy Spirit, with men and women, lifted out of their ordinary selves, speaking in tongues, as is recorded in the Acts of the Apostles (Acts 2:4).

Those who agreed on rejecting infant baptism often disagreed on many other points. Müntzer believed the righteous were entitled to take up arms against their oppressors, but for Grebel and his followers, true Christians must eschew violence, following Jesus's command in the gospel: "Resist not evil" (Matt. 6:38–39). Further differences may reflect the fact that subsequent Anabaptist leaders (unlike the university-trained Grebel) often had the assurance of the self-taught, having learned theology from their own study of scripture in the vernacular. For example, Melchior Hoffman (1495–1543), a furrier by trade, believed the Holy Spirit had given him the power to discern a hidden or spiritual meaning that was superior to the literal meaning of scripture. Anabaptists debated among themselves whether they should practice community of goods, as described in the Acts of the Apostles (Acts 2:44), but Jacob Hutter (1500–1536), a hatter, made community of goods the test of a true following of Jesus.

None of these differences mattered to civil authorities, Catholic or evangelical, for they saw all Anabaptists as dangerous radicals bent on undermining public order. Without infant baptism, what was the shared foundation for a Christian society? Without the taking of oaths, and the belief that perjurers would answer to God, who could be trusted to keep his word? The spread of Anabaptism evoked ferocious persecution, of which Grebel himself would have been an early victim had he not escaped from a Zurich prison, only to die of the plague.

In south and central Germany Anabaptism never claimed more than a miniscule fraction of the population. But the religious ideas of the "common man" found a broader expression in the Peasants' War that broke out across much of southern and central Germany from 1524 to 1526, by far the greatest peasant rebellion of medieval or early modern European history. The circumstances that drove so many peasants to fury against their noble and monastery landlords will be discussed in Part IV. Some radical evangelical preachers, notably Thomas Müntzer, preached rebellion from their pulpits; others aided in drafting the states of grievances used by peasant assemblies to justify their actions. But the ideas seem to have come mainly from the peasants themselves. The connection with Reformation doctrine lies in the fact that in a traditional society ordinary folk can accept as legitimate a social order in which they are badly treated, so long as they see it as part of a world willed by God, rather like the unforgiving order of nature. A great rebellion thus needs a rationale, a reason for believing God has not in fact willed the world to be so. This the peasants of Germany found in the teaching of the Reformers, especially Zwingli. Unlike Luther, Zwingli saw scripture as a "law" in the sense that it provided true Christians with a guide to righteous living.

The *Twelve Articles* (1525) published by leaders of the peasant movement takes this view one step farther. The law of scripture—godly law—is a guide not just for personal conduct, but also for social relations within a Christian society. Was it godly to discriminate among men and women redeemed in the blood of Christ so that some were held as serfs by others who claimed to be their lords and masters? Surely not. For many peasants, the "freedom of a Christian" meant that no Christian man or woman must be kept in bondage. Luther, initially sympathetic to peasant grievances, reacted sharply to what he saw as a perversion of the gospel. In two pamphlets he urged princes to cut down in good conscience all who showed their contempt for divine law by rebelling against the authorities God had set over them. In fact, princes and noble lords needed no encouragement. Despite victories here and there under peasant commanders trained as mercenary soldiers, rebel armies were crushed one after another.

In the long perspective of religious history, the ferment of the years 1520–1526 was uncommonly creative. Most forms of Protestant Christianity now active in the world have roots in this brief period. But for many who lived through the turmoil in Germany and Switzerland, it seemed as if the world were coming apart at the seams. What was left of all that people had been taught to revere? The pope was unmasked as the Antichrist, the consecrated host as a mere piece of bread, and miracle-working statues as "idols" to be smashed to bits. Scripture, learned men now said, was guide enough for Christian folk. But these same learned men—Luther, Zwingli, Erasmus—were at one another's throats, figuratively at least, about what scripture had to say. The "common man" had rendered his interpretation of scripture with powder and shot. Was there to be a time of naked repression, as princes drowned in blood the remnants of peasant resistance? Or was the social order again to be shaken to its foundations by another great uprising? Where amid all the chaos was the gospel? Or was the gospel itself somehow responsible for the chaos? These questions, shaped by the events of several years, demanded a response. Hammering out answers would take several decades.

6 | Doctrine

The German and Swiss Reformation, 1526–1555

The Holy Roman Empire was not a unitary state, but rather a loose federation of territories ruled by princes and of free cities. The diet was the only forum in which the major imperial princes met regularly with representatives of the major free cities. Because of the many prince-bishops, the Catholic party had a majority in the diet and was determined to maintain the Edict of Worms (1521), which prohibited the dissemination of Luther's doctrines, even if it could not now be enforced. But evangelical princes and magistrates were under pressure from townsfolk to dismantle altogether what remained of the old religion. In these circumstances, it seemed unlikely the diet could play in Germany's religious conflict the peacemaking role it had so often played in the political conflicts of earlier centuries.

The turmoil of the Peasants' War changed everything. Many Catholic princes were now persuaded that a religious order imposed by heretical governments was better than the chaos that seemed to loom on the horizon. The Habsburg dynasty, the anchor of Catholicism in Germany, also had reasons for compromise. Archduke Ferdinand wanted evangelical princes to help defend Austria against a possible Ottoman invasion, but their cooperation had a price. His brother the emperor was at this time less willing to countenance negotiation with heretics, but all his resources were engaged in conflicts outside of Germany (see chapter 8). Hence, both sides were able to agree to the Recess (closing statement) of the Diet of Speyer (1526): Until an ecumenical council of the church should be convened to settle disputed issues, princes and imperial cities were free to regulate religious matters according to the dictates of conscience. In effect, the Edict of Worms was suspended.

This compromise allowed the diet to become a forum for further discussion of religious differences. Meanwhile, local governments proceeded with the implementation of evangelical reform, even as radical preachers proposed visions of reform that no government could accept. This chapter, organized chronologically, follows each of three different tracks: the reforms implemented by evangelical governments; deliberations at the diet; and the continuing spread of radical religious ideas, despite everything the diet and the territorial governments could do to stop it.

The Recess of Speyer provided legal cover for governments eager to build a new religious order. The landgrave of Hesse, Philip the Magnanimous (1504–1567), was the first to seize the opportunity. Philip had a church ordinance drawn up for presentation to the parliament or estates of his territory. Like similar ordinances soon to be adopted elsewhere, it prescribed worship in the vernacular language, preaching based on the doctrine of salvation by faith, reception by the laity of the wine as well as the bread in the Lord's Supper, a married clergy, and catechism classes to instruct the young. These were the founding principles of a new, distinctly evangelical church. The Hessian ordinance was accepted by the estates (October 1526) but was never implemented because it was in effect vetoed in Wittenberg. Luther had no fixed ideas on how an evangelical church should be governed, but he objected to the provision that each congregation in Hesse would be free to choose its own preacher. Events in Electoral Saxony had convinced him that congregational autonomy was not a good idea.

Luther's protector, Elector Frederick (d. 1525), was traditional in his beliefs and respected the authority of the Catholic hierarchy in Saxony. But for many of his subjects that authority had now ceased to exist. Thus the Saxon clergy had little or no supervision. Radicals like Karlstadt and Müntzer were free to gain acceptance from local congregations and preach whatever doctrines they wished—rejection of infant baptism or even rebellion against the prince. But Frederick's nephew and successor, Elector John (r. 1525–1532), was an ardent evangelical. Luther now had direct access to the ruler; indeed, because of long friendship with Georg Spalatin, a humanist councillor, he now had virtually an alter ego at the prince's side. The elector expressed to Luther his concern about the lack of discipline for rural pastors. Luther in turn wanted assurances that Saxon nobles would not be allowed to grab for themselves all the properties of the monasteries that were now to be dissolved—something had to be kept back to support the ministers of the Word.

One first had to take stock of things. For this purpose Wittenberg theologians reinvented the practice of visitation, whereby a bishop toured the parishes of his diocese at regular intervals. In canon law, visiting bishops had the right to dismiss unworthy pastors. But there were (as yet) no bishops in Germany who supported the new doctrines. Hence, Luther proposed that the prince be seen as a "stopgap bishop," so that visitors acting in his name had power to deal with pastors found to be wild-eyed radicals or stubborn "papists." Preliminary visitation of a few areas in 1526 was followed by systematic visitation of the whole territory between 1527 and 1529, with Luther himself acting for a time as a visitor.

The problems the visitors uncovered were sobering. It was now clear that the present clergy would have to be replaced as soon as possible by a new body of clergy trained in evangelical theology at a university theology faculty and paid at a level that would compensate educated men for spending their days among peasants. This goal would take decades to achieve. By making a beginning, Saxony served as a model for other evangelical princes and town councils.

In the canton of Zurich, a much smaller territory, supervision of the clergy was relatively easy. Rural pastors, many with little education, were kept in line by a council requirement that they read their Sunday sermons from sermon books prepared by clergy in the city. Urban pastors had to participate in weekly "prophecies," or discussions of scripture, organized and led by Zwingli himself. To educate a new evangelical pastorate, Zwingli persuaded the city council to set aside for creation of a theological school the income from tithes that peasants were still required to pay.

The problem Zwingli could not control stemmed from the fact that Zurich was but one among thirteen Swiss cantons. The two other cantons based on sizable cities, Bern and Basel, embraced the Reformation soon after Zurich, as did two smaller cantons. But seven others remained fiercely loyal to Catholicism, including the founding members of the Swiss Confederation (1291), the so-called forest cantons of the Alpine meadows. Since each canton had one vote in the Confederation Diet, the Catholic party confidently arranged a disputation (1526) in which their spokesman, Johann Eck, was adjudged the winner over an evangelical preacher from Basel.

What sparked real bitterness on both sides was the treatment of lands that had been conquered by the confederation, each ruled as a subject territory, each year by a different canton. Under evangelical rule, evangelical preachers were installed even if parishioners did not want them. Under Catholic rule, the new preachers were forced out even if people wanted them, and in a few cases they were tried and executed for the crime of heresy. This changing of religious truth with every change of administration was not sustainable, especially not in a country with Switzerland's military traditions. Evangelical cantons formed a Christian Civic Union (1527); Catholic cantons responded with a Christian Union (1529).

Under Zwingli's leadership, Zurich believed that war was a godly means to advance the evangelical cause, but Bern demurred, and in 1529 arranged a peace between the two sides. When tensions mounted again, Bern proposed economic warfare in lieu of an outright assault. The evangelical cantons controlled the Swiss lowlands, between Germany and the Alps. The pastoral economy of their Catholic adversaries, concentrated in the Alpine valleys, depended on imports of grain from the German side, since access was more difficult via the steeper slopes of the Italian Alps. In May 1531, Bern, Zurich, and their allies blocked roads leading into the mountains, intending to compel Alpine "idolaters" to submit. Instead, the men of the forest cantons mobilized for war. Bern now proposed abandoning the blockade but Zurich refused. At Kappel, near Zurich (11 October 1531), a large Catholic force overwhelmed the men of Zurich. Huldrych Zwingli, a chaplain once more, lay among the dead (fig. 6.1).

This defeat had consequences. All of Switzerland now agreed to a treaty prescribing that no canton would interfere in another's religious affairs. In Zurich, mourning hundreds of its young men, many put the blame on the fact that Zurich's relations with other cantons had been guided by the religious zeal of Zwingli and his party. Zwingli believed the "Christian magistrates" of his city would govern the church wisely. They appointed the preachers (like himself) and approved the order of worship. Only the interpretation of scripture was, in his view, reserved to the competence of

Figure 6.1. The Battle of Kappel, 1531. The larger army of the Catholic cantons is at the right, Zurich's force at the left: from the Chronicle of Johannes Stumpf (1548). *Zentralbibliothek Zurich.*

the clergy. But one reason Zwingli had such confidence in the magistrates was that he himself, in the words of a Catholic critic, "acted like a burgomaster." For example, he seems to have participated in meetings of an informal inner circle of magistrates known as the secret council. This was to change. In 1532 the council decreed that neither the preachers nor the secret council would be allowed to interfere in Zurich's external affairs.

Heinrich Bullinger (1504–1575), the humanist scholar who succeeded Zwingli as leader of Zurich's clergy, understood that a line had been drawn (fig. 6.2). It was the preacher's duty to tell magistrates how the teaching of scripture might bear on contemporary issues, but magistrates were not obliged to listen. Bullinger could accept this arrangement because he believed, as had Zwingli, that the magistrates had a God-given mandate to govern the religious life of Christian society, except as regards the interpretation of scripture. This explicit acceptance of state control of the church was a hallmark of the Zwinglian branch of the evangelical movement.

Meanwhile, confessional alliances were also forming in Germany, where many feared a much wider religious war. Catholic princes, including the powerful dukes of Bavaria, sometimes consulted together, but with little practical result. Common action to stem the advance of heresy would have required cooperation with Habsburg Austria, against which Bavaria (Austria's neighbor) had unsettled grievances. In 1528 one of Philip of Hesse's councillors made public what he claimed was a secret pact among Catholic princes (in fact, a forgery of his own devising) to attack their evangelical confreres. Alarmed, Philip of Hesse and Elector John of Saxony mobilized their armies, standing down only when it was clear no attack was forthcoming.

Amid growing suspicion on both sides, the Catholic party in the diet pushed through at the 1529 Diet of Speyer a Recess nullifying the 1526 Recess and reinstating the Edict of Worms, with added clauses prohibiting the dissemination of other new doctrines besides Luther's. Six evangelical princes, together with the representatives of fourteen free cities, signed a protest against this action: they could not submit to the will of the majority in a matter of conscience. This was a milestone, the first time leaders of the evangelical movement were sufficiently conscious of their common interests to act as a body. The Protestant Reformation takes its name from the "protestants" of Speyer.

Full unity among evangelicals was impeded by discord between Wittenberg and Zurich. Elector John of Saxony insisted that parties to any political alliance must accept the articles of belief recently drawn up by

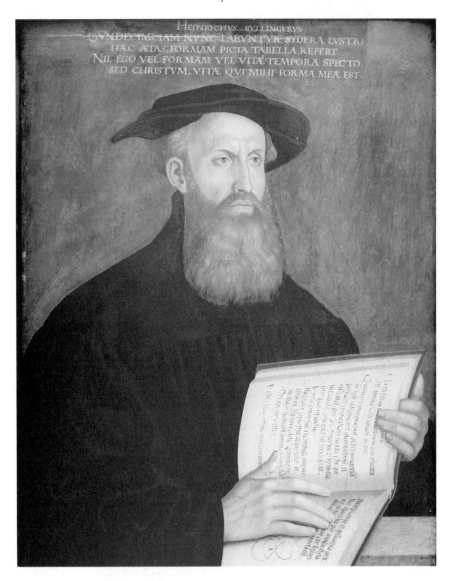

Figure 6.2. Heinrich Bullinger (1504–1575). An anonymous portrait of Zwingli's successor in Zurich (1531–1575). *Zentralbibliothek Zurich.*

Wittenberg theologians. Philip of Hesse, hoping for a broader theological consensus to allow inclusion of Swiss and south German cities that supported Zwingli, invited Luther and Zwingli to meet in his city of Marburg (October 1529), along with many other evangelical theologians. The climactic moment of the Marburg Colloquy came when Luther met privately with Zwingli and one other Swiss preacher. Taking a piece of chalk, Luther wrote on the table the Latin for "This is my body," insisting on the literal meaning of Jesus's words at the Last Supper. Zwingli offered a modification of his purely symbolic interpretation, but to no avail. Wittenberg and Zurich would henceforth go their separate ways, politically as well as doctrinally.

Charles V now announced his intention to come to Germany (his first visit since 1521) for the diet to be held in Augsburg in the summer of 1530. Protestants had feared the emperor would insist on the terms decreed by the recent Diet of Speyer. Instead, he called for consultations concerning the resolution of Germany's religious conflict. Charles wanted religious unity in Germany, not necessarily by force. One of his Spanish advisors, Alfonso de Valdes, was promoting an idea first proposed by Erasmus, namely that the doctrinal disputes might be settled if reasonable men from both sides could be brought together under the auspices of a great prince. Erasmus had suggested that concessions would have to be made to legitimate complaints against clerical privilege, for example, by allowing lay people to receive the wine as well as the bread in the Lord's Supper and allowing priests to marry.

Erasmus rightly guessed that Philip Melanchthon (fig. 6.3) might be willing to enter into such a discussion on behalf of the evangelical party. Melanchthon had taken the lead in framing a statement of Lutheran belief for presentation at the diet (June 1530). Without diluting Luther's teachings, Melanchthon's Augsburg Confession answered the emperor's goodwill gesture by stressing points of agreement with Catholics, notably in the belief that Christ's body and blood are truly present in the eucharist. At Augsburg, many Catholic observers were impressed by the confession's moderate tone. Melanchthon in turn was impressed by the flexibility he found in private conversations with Valdes and with Cardinal Lorenzo Campeggi, the representative of Pope Clement VII (r. 1523–1534). They discussed, for example, a plan whereby Lutherans might recognize the papacy as wielding an authority that had evolved historically, but not (as in Catholic belief) as wielding an authority originally granted by Christ to St. Peter.

But no agreement was forthcoming. The Catholic majority in the diet resumed its agenda from the previous year. Enforcement of the imperial legislation prohibiting the spread of evangelical doctrine was now entrusted to the Imperial High Court, made up of judges appointed exclusively by Catholic princes. Fearing the worst, Elector John of Saxony and Philip of Hesse met (December 1530) in the small town of Schmalkalden to conclude

VIVENTIS·POTVIT·DVRERIVS·ORA·PHILIPPI
MENTEM·NON·POTVIT·PINGERE·DOCTA
MANVS

Figure 6.3. Philip Melanchthon. Albrecht Dürer, "Philip Melanchthon," 1526, from Valentin Scherer, Albrecht Dürer. Des Meisters Gemaelde und Kupferstiche (Berlin/Leipzig: Insel, 1926), p. 172. *Courtesy of University Libraries, University of Minnesota, Minneapolis.*

a defensive alliance with several other Protestant princes. Luther at first objected to the idea of an agreement directed against the emperor; in his view, scripture (notably Rom. 13:1–2) did not permit Christians to rebel against the rulers God had set over them. Others persuaded him, however, that princes of the empire were not mere individual believers, but rulers in their own right, whose duty it was to prevent the emperor from behaving in tyrannical fashion. Thus was born the Schmalkaldic League, led by Saxony and Hesse and limited to signatories of the 1530 Augsburg Confession. Other territories joined as they converted to the Lutheran Reformation. Strasbourg's Martin Bucer arranged an agreement, known as the Wittenberg Concord, whereby Strasbourg and other cities in south Germany, which were Zwinglian in theology, accepted Luther's doctrine of the Lord's Supper as the price of admission to the Schmalkaldic League.

Catholic princes were sobered by this development; they were not willing to go to war to stop the spread of heresy. Also, some of those involved in the discussions at Augsburg took away the impression that agreement might yet be possible. Hence, the next diet (Regensburg, 1532) issued a Recess suspending religious proceedings before the Imperial High Court and declaring that if no ecumenical council were convened in the interval, the following diet, slated for 1534, would attempt to craft a religious compromise on its own authority.

This was alarming news in Rome. Pope Clement VII refused to convene the ecumenical council that many were calling for—he feared a council, invoking fifteenth-century conciliar doctrine, might challenge the authority of the papacy. But he was even more opposed to seeing an imperial diet usurp the role of a council by claiming to decide matters of doctrine. The pope urged Charles and Ferdinand not to convene the diet slated for 1534. As it happened, Charles was again distracted by affairs outside Germany. There would not be another diet until he returned in 1540.

In the interim, both the Lutheran and the Zwinglian versions of the evangelical movement continued winning new adherents. So too did doctrines that may be called "radical" in two senses of the term. First, most proponents of these doctrines consciously rejected an assumption Luther and Zwingli had taken over from the Catholic past, namely that all baptized Christians, saints and sinners alike, were members of the church as well as subjects of their territorial government. In this view, church and state, the dual aspects of a single Christian commonwealth, were obliged to support each other in multiple ways. By contrast, radical preachers held that the church embraced only those dedicated to the following of Christ; the brutal power of the state was established by God not for true Christians, but only to curb the evil ways of sinners. Second, radical preachers also rejected one or more of the elements of orthodox Christian belief that Luther and Zwingli retained, such as the doctrine of the Trinity, the need for a visible church, or infant baptism. Luther and Zwingli (like their Catholic foes) expected Christian rulers to suppress all who preached against such fundamental doctrines. But radical reformers saw in the hostility of the state a proof of their claim to be the true Christians who in this wicked world must needs be persecuted.

The doctrine of the Trinity—that Father, Son, and Holy Spirit are three distinct Persons in one God—had been professed by all Christians since the Arian controversy of the fourth century. But Michael Servetus, a Spanish physician, published his *On the Errors of the Trinity* in Basel in 1531. Drawing on sources from an impressive array of religious and intellectual traditions, Servetus argued that the New Testament named the one and only God using different terms, including "Father," "Son," and "Holy Spirit," just as the Old Testament had different names for the one and only Lord. The doctrine of the Trinity was thus a great falsehood, demeaning to the unity of God. Catholics and Protestants were equally shocked. But theologians who wrote books refuting Servetus unintentionally disseminated his doctrines by summarizing them, and when Servetus himself was burned at the stake in Geneva (1553), martyrdom gave his teaching added prestige, especially among Italian religious refugees, including Lelio Sozzini (d. 1562) and his nephew Fausto Sozzini (d. 1602). In lands to the east and north of Switzerland, these men became apostles for the gospel known as Anti-Trinitarian, Arian, or Socinian—a forerunner of modern Unitarianism.

Kaspar von Schwenkfeld (1489–1561; fig. 6.4), a noble courtier in the duchy of Legnica (part of Bohemia), led the way in questioning the need for a visible church. Having experienced what he believed was a revelation from God convincing him of the truth of Luther's teaching, Schwenkfeld became the leader of an influential Lutheran party at the ducal court. Distressed by the quarrel over the Lord's Supper, he experienced a second divine visitation that persuaded him that Zwingli's symbolic interpretation was correct. From 1526 Schwenkfeld refused to partake in a ritual that caused so much hatred among Christians and urged his followers to do likewise. Schwenkfeld also objected to the fact that churches, like states, employed coercion in matters of belief—true Christians know that belief comes from the Holy Spirit, not from force. Hence, Schwenkfeld became an early advocate of religious toleration. Local Lutherans joined with Archduke Ferdinand of Austria, now king of Bohemia, to expel Schwenkfeld from his homeland (1529). He spent the rest of his years in south Germany, traveling and living among friends he had won over to his spiritual interpretation of the gospel.

The radical religious movement that had the greatest numerical appeal was a form of Anabaptism tracing its origins to a lay preacher from the Baltic coast, Melchior Hoffman (1495–1543). Having espoused first Lutheran and then Zwinglian ideas, Hoffman was expelled from several northern territories for claiming the God-given ability to discern a "spiritual" or hidden meaning of scripture that was superior to the literal meaning. Arriving in Strasbourg (1529), he accepted the Anabaptist view of baptism and also fell in with a circle whose members believed they were

Figure 6.4. Kaspar von Schwenkfeld (1489–1561). Engraved portrait, "Caspar Schwenkfeld von Ossing in his 56th Year, 1566." The Schwenkfeldian Church, founded by his disciples, survives in Pennsylvania. © *Copyright The Trustees of the British Museum.*

prophets inspired by God. Hoffman now began preaching a spiritual interpretation of scripture that confirmed the prophecies of his new comrades. The Final Days foretold in the Book of Revelation (19:1–11, 20:1–10) were drawing near: Very soon, Christ would come again to establish on earth his kingdom, the Heavenly Jerusalem. Expelled from Strasbourg, Hoffman took his message to Emden in East Friesland, where he was able to baptize over 300 adults before being expelled yet again. As Hoffman returned to Strasbourg, some of his converts crossed from East Friesland into the Habsburg Netherlands, where their message found fertile ground. Owing to a war that blocked import of grain from the Baltic, bread prices in the Netherlands were at historic highs. Hungry folk flocked to hear the "Melchiorite" message of imminent deliverance, especially in the populous province of Holland. Meanwhile, seeing his Strasbourg followers arrested in droves, Hoffman suspended the practice of adult baptism. By now, however, Melchior was no longer in control of the Melchiorite movement.

Jan Matthijs, a Holland Melchiorite, resumed adult baptism in 1533. In contrast to Hoffman's belief that true Christians must suffer persecution meekly, as Christ himself did, Matthijs announced that the time had come for God's elect to take up the sword against their oppressors. With Jan Bockelszoon, another Hollander, Matthijs traveled to nearby Münster in Westphalia, a Low German–speaking city that had recently ejected its prince-bishop and adopted the Lutheran Reformation. He quickly won over the city's chief evangelical preacher and his followers. Back in the Netherlands, the faithful received an urgent message: God's Kingdom was to be erected in Münster; true Christians must sell their possessions and be in Münster before the Last Days were to begin (March 1534). Thousands streamed toward Münster from the Low Countries (fig. 6.5), just as unbelievers— Catholics and Lutherans—were being forced out. Lutheran princes in Westphalia joined Münster's prince-bishop in besieging the city. When Jan Matthijs fell in battle (April 1534), Jan Bockelszoon succeeded him and had himself proclaimed king of the Heavenly Jerusalem. Pointing to examples of polygamy among Old Testament patriarchs, King Jan decreed that God's elect were no longer bound by monogamy—he set the example by taking sixteen wives. When Münster fell to its besiegers, Bockelszoon and his chief supporters were punished with exemplary cruelty (June 1535).

The debacle at Münster marked a turning point for the Anabaptist movement. A persecution that was already fierce became ferocious. Even in the few places where Anabaptists had been tolerated, civil authorities now suspected that seemingly peaceful folk secretly harbored violent Münsterite fantasies. In Moravia, part of the kingdom of Bohemia, followers of Jacob Hutter (1500–1536) had established themselves as a peasant community practicing the common ownership of goods. Their landlords— Hussite noblemen and an open-minded prince-abbess—had no problems with these hardworking tenants. After Münster, however, Archduke Ferdinand, the king of Bohemia, saw to it that the "Hutterites" were expelled. They were not able to return to Moravia for several years.

Among Anabaptists in the Low Countries, reactions to Münster led to a stronger form of organization. When the city fell, some Münsterites took up an outlaw existence, robbing churches to support themselves. Menno Simons (1496–1561), a priest in Friesland (fig. 6.6), came to the fore among Anabaptists who denounced the excesses of Matthijs and Bockelszoon, traceable to false doctrine. Scripture must be interpreted literally, Menno insisted, not according to the imaginings of self-styled prophets. Discipline was another problem: loose living among those who claimed to be the true followers of Christ was a terrible scandal. Menno and his supporters introduced the ban, a form of excommunication in which public sinners were to be shunned by all believers. The principled

Figure 6.5. The trek to the Anabaptist kingdom of Münster, 1534. Engraving of "Anabaptists Selling Their Jewels for the Trek to Münster," from Lambertus Hortensius, Het Boeck . . . van den Oproer der Weder-Dooperen. *Mennonite Historical Library, Goshen College, Goshen, Indiana.*

pacifism of the Mennonites calmed the fears of authorities in some areas; in others, their discipline gave them the strength to withstand continuing persecution.

✛

What Menno Simons achieved for Anabaptism, John Calvin (1509–1564) was to achieve for a major segment of the broader evangelical movement

Figure 6.6. Menno Simons (1496–1561). Engraved portrait of Menno Simons, bound with Christoffel van Sichem, Beschryvinge ende Afbeelindinge der Voornemste Hooft Ketteren (Amsterdam, 1608). *Bridwell Library, Southern Methodist University.*

(fig. 6.7). Calvin's father was a lay official in the service of the bishop of Noyon (northern France). After a bachelor's degree at the University of Paris he enrolled in the theology faculty, preparing for a career in the priesthood, as his family wished. But Calvin senior quarreled with the bishop, and John switched to the faculty of law at Orléans. This faculty was known for its humanist approach to legal scholarship, and the taste he acquired for pagan and Christian antiquity made Calvin shift direction once more. Returning to Paris to study ancient languages, he fell in with a group of humanist students and professors who were eager for religious reform. When a leader of this circle gave a public address endorsing the doctrine of salvation by faith (November 1533), the inquisitor of the diocese of Paris demanded action by royal officials. For the speaker and his associates, including Calvin, France was no longer safe.

As a refugee in Basel, Calvin embarked on a period of study resulting in his *Institutes of the Christian Religion* (1536), the single most important doctrinal work of the Protestant Reformation, especially in its final and most complete edition (1555). Though Luther and others had initially proclaimed that scripture required no interpretation, it was now evident that

PROMPTE   ET   SINCERE ·

IOHANNES · CALVINVS ·
· ANNO ·ÆTATIS ·53·
· B. ·

Figure 6.7. John Calvin (1509–1564) at the age of 53. René Boivin, "John Calvin at the Age of 53," 1562. *Bibliothèque Publique et Universitaire de Genève, Geneva.*

devout readers of the bible needed a guide, and this the *Institutes* provided. Like Luther, Calvin taught that God's commandments serve a "pedagogical" purpose, for sinners must first be taught to despair in their own ability to fulfill the commandments. Like Zwingli, he taught that for those to whom God grants saving faith, the commandments serve also as a guide to holiness. Indeed, the grace of forgiveness is given so that God may be glorified in the lives of his saints. Like Zwingli again, Calvin believed that religious images of any kind were an abomination in the sight of God: churches must be cleansed of all "idols," whether sculpted, painted, or molded in stained glass. Finally, Calvin too rejected Luther's belief that the body and blood of Christ are truly present in the Lord's Supper, though he did not endorse Zwingli's view that the bread and wine were mere symbols. Instead, he contended, one receives in the sacrament the "virtue" or power of Christ's flesh, even though the Lord's body itself is not in any way present. Because of these areas of agreement, Calvin and Zwingli are often grouped together as the founders of a "Reformed" Protestantism that was the major alternative to the Lutheran Reformation in continental Europe. But there were also differences, as became evident when Calvin accepted a post as preacher in Geneva (1536) (fig. 6.8).

Geneva's choice for the Reformation was connected with its struggle for independence from its two Catholic overlords, the duke of Savoy and the prince-bishop of Geneva. Geneva was able to defy both princes because it had found a backer in neighboring Bern, largest and most powerful of the Swiss cantons. Bern sought to cement the alliance by having Geneva adopt a French-language version of its evangelical worship service. The eagerness of Geneva's city council to comply placed Calvin at a crossroads, comparable to that faced by Luther at the Leipzig debate. Had he obeyed Geneva's Christian magistrates, no one in the Zwinglian tradition of re-

Figure 6.8. A View of Geneva in the Seventeenth Century. From Matthaeus Merian, Martin Zeiller, Topographia Germaniae (17 vols. facsimile reprint of second edition [Frankfurt, 1655], Kassel: Bärenreiter, 1959–1967), vol. 4, Topographiae Heluetiae, following p. 68. *Courtesy of University Libraries, University of Minnesota, Minneapolis.*

form would have had any words of blame. But the fact that a civil government proposed to decide questions of worship offended his sense of what scripture taught about the church. Rather than accept the new order of worship, Calvin, together with his colleague Guillaume Farel, chose exile in Strasbourg (1538).

Calvin's convictions about the autonomy of the church were greatly strengthened in Strasbourg (1538–1541), where he served as pastor for a congregation of Protestant refugees from France. Martin Bucer, Strasbourg's leading evangelical preacher, had a tale of woe to tell. Like other Swiss and south German reformers, Bucer expected the proclamation of the true gospel to bring a change in the way people lived. In fact, Strasbourgers went about their sinful ways much as before: The Reformation was incomplete, and Bucer thought he knew why. The problem was that Strasbourg's magistrates governed the church, just as in Bullinger's Zurich. If preachers demanded stronger action against religious radicals (like Melchior Hoffman), the magistrates cited the need to avoid coercion in matters of belief. If preachers wanted some prominent person excommunicated from the church as a public sinner, the magistrates preferred not to add one more feud to the many they already had to contend with. When Bucer published a treatise proposing that the church rather than the civil government take over the supervision of morals—"we must decide once and for all if we mean to be Christians"—the magistrates pointedly ignored it. Casting about for some way to free the church from control by the magistrates, Bucer toyed with the idea of a limited recognition of the religious authority of Strasbourg's prince-bishop, which had ceased to exist in the city with the triumph of the Reformation in 1529.

Calvin had a better idea. His study of the New Testament convinced him that the primitive church had a clearly articulated governing structure, which needed only to be re-created. In the Acts of the Apostles, Christian communities are headed by (ἐπισκοποί = overseers) or by (*presbuteroi* = elders). In subsequent centuries, bishops (a word derived from the first of these Greek terms) had come to be recognized as sole rulers of their religious communities, with full authority over those called elders or, somewhat later, priests. Calvin believed that this historical development falsified the collegial relationship between "overseers" and "presbyters" in the New Testament. Each local church should be governed by a minister of the Word (the overseer) together with a board of lay elders, joined in what Calvin called (using a canon law term) a consistory. A church government so constituted, based on the teaching of scripture, could reclaim the authority that civil magistrates had wrongfully usurped. When he was again given the opportunity to lead Geneva's church (see below), Calvin would know how to proceed.

+

In 1540 Charles V summoned a diet in order to resume negotiations between the religious parties. During his absence from Germany several princes had sponsored "colloquies" between the two sides. In the process, important theologians had developed genuine interest in reaching agreement, notably Martin Bucer, Strasbourg's leading preacher, and Johann Gropper, a Catholic scholar from Cologne who promoted the study of Augustine as a possible common ground. When the Diet of Hagenau convened (June 1540), Protestant estates insisted on starting from the 1530 Augsburg Confession. Many Catholic princes urged the emperor to reject this demand. But in Charles's council the "soft hand" faction that favored negotiation had won out over the "hard hand" faction that favored war in order to end Germany's politically dangerous religious division. Thus Charles accepted the Augsburg Confession as the basis for discussion at the forthcoming Diet of Worms (November 1540–January 1541). Meanwhile, a committee of Protestant theologians, including Bucer and Calvin as well as Melanchthon, agreed on the text of a Revised Augsburg Confession that was more acceptable to south German evangelicals.

Some progress was made at Worms. But Charles's advisers wanted to move things along more quickly. Prior to the next diet, to be held in Regensburg, Gropper and Bucer were secretly commissioned to draft articles of agreement on each of the main points of doctrine. The Regensburg Colloquy (April–July 1541) featured three theologians on each side, including the Protestant Bucer and the Catholic Gropper. When the conferees met, Charles's spokesman placed before them as the new basis for their discussion the "book" by Bucer and Gropper, without telling the others whence it had come. Between meetings the Catholic conferees consulted with Cardinal Gasparo Contarini, whom Pope Paul III (r. 1534–1549) had sent as his representative. The choice of Contarini boded well for compromise, since this respected lay theologian and diplomat was also known to be sympathetic to Luther's theology of grace.

The six conferees found themselves in accord on one issue after another. When several days of hard bargaining led to an agreement on salvation by faith, Regensburg's church bells rang out in celebration of this apparent victory for religious peace. But subsequent discussion stalled over language describing the authority of the church and reached a dead end on the Lord's Supper. Catholic conferees reluctantly dropped the term "transubstantiation," as Protestants demanded, but Contarini reinserted it in the text. Charles summoned Contarini to ask why it was so important to insist on a single word. In reply, Contarini called to mind the Arian controversy of the fourth century, when a single word that many Christians rejected was deemed necessary by others to assert the full divinity of Christ. The emperor needed peace in Germany, but politics was not the final reality.

No one realized it at the time, but with the failure of the Regensburg Colloquy, the moment for theological compromise had come and gone. Following the article to which the six conferees agreed in 1541, there would not be another joint Lutheran-Catholic statement on salvation by faith until 1998. As the chance for reconciliation faded, so too did the reputations of those who had promoted the idea of compromise. In 1535, a year before his death, the aging Erasmus had declined a cardinal's hat offered by Pope Paul III. Twenty-four years later, in 1559, all of Erasmus's works were placed on the *Index of Forbidden Books* promulgated by Pope Paul IV (r. 1555–1559). Melanchthon too came under attack (see below). On either side of the confessional divide, thinkers (often humanists) seeking to reach out to men of goodwill in the other camp faced increasing suspicion among their coreligionists.

Conversely, those who all along took a dim view of theological compromise gained in credibility. German Catholics were strengthened in the belief that only an ecumenical council could provide a remedy for the church's ills. The obstacle to a council now lay not in Rome, as previously, but in Paris. Charles needed, for the sake of unity in Germany, the reform of abuses in the church that only a council could mandate. Precisely for this reason, the king of France made it clear that no French bishops would be permitted to attend a council—and without their participation, a council would be seen as a mere imperial enterprise, not a truly ecumenical assembly. This problem Charles dealt with by force of arms. In the treaty concluded following a two-year war begun by France (1542–1544), the king of France undertook not to obstruct a future council.

Pope Paul III then summoned the bishops of the Latin Christian world to a council in Trent, an imperial city on the Italian side of the Alps. The doctrinal decisions of the first session of the Council of Trent (1545–1547) will be discussed in chapter 7. The point to be made here is that those who argued for adopting language that Protestants might conceivably accept were in the minority. On key issues, the council's majority preferred language that sharply distinguished between the false teachings of the Reformers and what was henceforth to be orthodox Catholic doctrine. For the bishops and their theologian-advisers, it was a time not for compromise, but for mobilizing the minds and hearts of the faithful for a protracted struggle on behalf of Catholic truth.

Within Charles's council, the failure at Regensburg meant that the Schmalkaldic League would probably have to be dealt with as the "hard hand" councillors had envisioned. German affairs had to wait their turn on the emperor's agenda—war with France engaged his full attention from 1542 to 1544. But in the treaty ending this war Charles also compelled the king of France to abandon his alliances with Germany's Protestant princes; one could not make war against the Schmalkaldic League without assurances that France would not interfere. When Charles returned to the empire in 1545, he spoke of resuming the theological discussions broken off at Regensburg. This time, however, his soothing words were meant to calm the fears of the leaders of the league, Philip of Hesse and Elector John's son John Frederick of Saxony (r. 1532–1547), and to conceal his preparations for war—including a secret treaty with John Frederick's Lutheran cousin, Duke Moritz of Saxony.

Following Charles's defeat of Hesse and Electoral Saxony in the First Schmalkaldic War (1547), he imposed, at the Diet of Augsburg (May 1548), an "Interim" religious settlement intended to prevail until matters were settled by the ecumenical council. The Augsburg Interim contained some concessions to evangelical sensibilities: Preachers would be free to profess the key doctrine of salvation by faith, clergy would still be allowed to marry, and lay people would still receive the wine as well as the bread in the Lord's Supper. In all other respects, the Interim mandated full restoration of Catholic worship, including the Latin mass and the seven sacraments. These provisions evoked sullen acquiescence in Lutheran territories that had submitted to the emperor and redoubled the determination to resist among those that had not. As fighting sputtered on, it began to seem that Charles's victory was not irreversible. A new coalition between France and a revived league (Second Schmalkaldic War, 1552–1555) shattered Charles's hopes for restoring religious unity to Germany.

The ensuing Peace of Augsburg (1555) guaranteed freedom of religious choice in the empire, but only for ruling princes and the governments of free cities. "Where there is one lord," the treaty declared, "let there be one religion." Subjects who disagreed with the religious policy of their rulers were promised the right to sell their property and move elsewhere, nothing more. Moreover, the choices were limited to Roman Catholicism and the religion of the Augsburg Confession. These two faiths were recognized in imperial law, but "sects" like Anabaptism, Zwinglianism, or Calvinism (see below) had no rights whatever.

The Augsburg Interim caused deep division among Germany's Lutherans. Prior to Luther's death (1546), there had been occasional complaints that Philip Melanchthon accepted some aspects of the doctrine of free will and of John Calvin's interpretation of the Lord's Supper. Melanchthon had in fact evolved his own views on both of these points, but his close personal collaboration with Luther kept such disputes in the background so long as Luther lived. The Interim put a spotlight on Melanchthon. His and Luther's University of Wittenberg was part of Electoral Saxony, hitherto ruled by Charles's defeated enemy, John Frederick. But Duke Moritz now claimed Electoral Saxony as his reward for assisting in the emperor's victory—John Frederick was left with the lesser title of duke and a smaller territory. Moritz did not seek to impose the unpopular Augsburg Interim on his new lands. Instead, he had his Catholic councillors and the Wittenberg theologians, including Melanchthon, work out (1549) a version of the Interim more consistent with evangelical theology. Melanchthon thus gave his name to a partial restoration of Catholic ceremonies. He did so because he believed that outer forms of worship were "indifferent things" that could be accepted if essential doctrine was not compromised.

This policy was bitterly attacked by Matthias Flacius Illyricus (1520–1575), a professor of Hebrew at Wittenberg. Flacius argued that "indifferent things" imposed by a secular government became violations of Christian freedom. He fled Wittenberg for Magdeburg, a city that had renounced the rule of its prince-archbishop some time previously and was now the center of armed Lutheran resistance to Charles V and his Interim. With Magdeburg's preachers, Flacius and others who now claimed to represent the "Gnesio-" or "Genuine-Lutheran" party took it on themselves to expose the errors of the all-too-compromising Melanchthon and his "Philippist" disciples. If Melanchthon held (following Luther) that Christians must obey their rulers as far as possible, Magdeburgers argued it was the Christian duty of their city council and other "lesser magistrates" to resist the tyranny of the emperor. Genuine Lutherans also attacked Wittenberg theologians for not issuing a blanket condemnation of John Calvin's teaching on the Lord's Supper. Many of these controversies were eventually settled in a credal statement adopted by a majority of Lutheran territories, the Formula of Concord (1580). In the intervening years, however, just as Germany's Lutheran territories gained full recognition in imperial law (1555), their theologians were at daggers drawn. Further expansion of Lutheranism was curtailed by this discord, if not halted altogether.

Just in these years the Calvinist movement, based in Geneva, was reaching the height of its influence. Geneva's city council had asked Calvin to return in 1541. He quickly gained the council's approval for a confession of the evangelical faith and for a church ordinance embodying his distinctive ideas on ecclesiastical polity, or church government. Geneva's church was to be ruled by a minister of the Word (appointed by the council) acting with lay elders elected by citizens, along with deacons to serve the needs of the poor. Minister and elders together formed the consistory, to which the supervision of morals was entrusted. Questions of doctrine were to be settled not by the consistory, but at periodic synods including ministers and elders from each of the towns in a given territory. As the church was being organized along these lines, city officials went door to door with copies of the new confession of faith. Persons above the age of fifteen were given a choice between swearing to these articles of belief or leaving the city. Calvin's Geneva was not to be a haven for the godless.

There was, however, a sticking point. Like other Swiss and south German Reformers, including Zwingli, Calvin believed that the test of true doctrine was how church members lived. To have public sinners numbered among those receiving the Lord's Supper was a great scandal, to be warded off by the excommunication of errant believers. Calvin's self-governing church polity, unlike a city council, could be expected to uphold God's law regardless of the person of the offender. But not everyone in Geneva accepted this view of church authority, and the 1541 church ordinance was vague about whether the city council could or could not overrule consistory decisions on excommunication. Calvin had many supporters among prominent families, but other Genevans, having cast off the authority of the papal clergy, had no taste for a new kind of clerical power and made no secret of their feelings. One man, for example, was cited before the consistory for naming his dog "Calvin." For many years the outcome was uncertain, as city council elections yielded majorities for or against Calvin's vision of the place of the church in Geneva. The breakthrough came when Calvin's foes, having lost badly in the elections of 1555, attempted a coup d'etat with help from Bern. They were defeated in a street battle.

The new council solidified the church's position by undertaking not to interfere in decisions regarding excommunication and by changing citizenship rules to allow religious refugees to gain voting rights more quickly. Geneva now became a magnet for men and women who suffered or feared persecution for their Protestant beliefs in France, Italy, the Low Countries, and parts of Germany. The Word of God was proclaimed in many areas, but only Geneva had a church polity capable of making God's Word efficacious in the life of the commonwealth. Gauging how people actually behaved is notoriously difficult for historians, but it seems the refugees were right in thinking that godly discipline was becoming a visible reality in Geneva: Children learned their catechism, men were less likely to indulge in casual swearing, and magistrates were less likely to line their own pockets.

When the council established an academy (1559) for the training of pastors, many of the first graduates were refugees who made the dangerous trip back whence they had come, eager to plant in their home countries the seeds of godly commonwealths like Geneva. Calvin's study, and later that of his successor, Theodore Beza (1516–1605), became a command post for communications from the new mission territories. Thus, just in the years when papal Rome was regaining its lost authority in the Catholic Church, Calvin's Geneva was becoming a Protestant Rome.

In addition to the aura of godly discipline that drew refugees from far and wide, Calvinism was also distinctive in certain aspects of its theology. In the early editions of his *Institutes* Calvin did not highlight predestination, but he did insist that there was no such thing as chance. Everything that happened in the world happened by God's will: If one blade of grass greened while another did not, if one nursing mother had milk for her infant but another did not, it was because God had willed it so. During the course of controversies with Protestant as well as Catholic opponents, this emphasis on God's will crystallized in a specific formulation of the doctrine of predestination. In 1550 Calvin debated before the city council of Geneva an ex-friar who maintained that while God does indeed predestine for salvation all who are saved, He offers his grace to all men; those who are damned are damned through their own fault, not because God decrees it so. Calvin responded that it made no sense to say that God decrees the salvation of those who are saved but not the damnation of those who are damned. God offers his grace only to those whom He chooses, and if man has no free will to participate in his own salvation, neither has he the free will to turn aside from God's decree. God displays his infinite mercy by saving those sinners He chooses to save and his infinite justice by condemning to hell those sinners He chooses to condemn. Neither Bullinger in Zurich nor Luther's heirs in Wittenberg accepted Calvin's unusual doctrine of "double predestination." Two years after Calvin's death, Beza and other leaders of the Genevan church signed off on Bullinger's Second Helvetic Confession (1566), a statement of faith expressing what the Swiss Reformed churches held in common, not including double predestination. Nonetheless, this awesome understanding of God's power was for Calvin's followers a great source of spiritual comfort. The person who trusted that he or she was predestined for salvation by such a God had, in an ultimate sense, nothing to fear.

By comparison with Lutheranism in particular, Calvinism was also much more emphatic in its rejection of Catholic tradition, root and branch. Luther's conception of the Lord's Supper was close enough to the Catholic view to permit discussion at Regensburg, even if there was no agreement. Calvin believed that the Catholic mass "swarmed with idolatry" from top to bottom. Luther's acceptance of religious images permitted Lutherans and Catholics in some north German villages and small towns to use the same church, even if they were careful to use it at different times. Calvin, like Zwingli, insisted that the churches be cleansed of "idols" of every sort, as may be seen from the whitewashed walls and clear-glass windows of churches where Calvinism triumphed. Nowhere is it recorded for the sixteenth century that Calvinists and Catholics used the same house of worship. In the absence of firm disciplinary structures, Lutherans often found it prudent to attend Sunday mass in countries with a vigilant Catholic government. Calvinists who did the same had to face the consistory; in effect, they had to choose between the fires of persecution and the fires of hell. Meanwhile, the Counter-Reformation church was forming a generation of Catholics who took an equally uncomplimentary view of Protestantism and of Calvinism in particular. The next chapter portrays the two movements that battled most fiercely for the allegiance of Christian Europeans during the century between 1550 and 1650: militant Calvinism and militant Catholicism.

7 | Doctrine

The European Reformations

CATHOLICISM

Both as a movement for internal reform and as a campaign against Protestantism, the Catholic Reformation (or Counter-Reformation) was blended from locally differing proportions of four basic elements: the spiritual energy of new religious orders emerging in Spain and Italy; a slow restoration of the moral authority of the priesthood, starting with legislation by the Council of Trent; rulers who legitimized their authority by criminalizing Protestant dissent and backing Catholic reform; and popular loyalty to the old religion. These four strands of the story overlap chronologically, but it will be simpler to treat them one by one.

In 1476 two Spanish kingdoms were brought together in the marriage of Queen Isabella of Castile (r. 1473–1504) and King Ferdinand of Aragon (r. 1468–1516). Spain was, in the early sixteenth century, a land of religious ferment like Germany, but in a different way. From Roman times Iberia had had a large Jewish population. Since the conquest of most of the peninsula by invaders from Morocco (711), it had as well a large Muslim population. By the thirteenth century, Christian kingdoms based originally in the far north—Castile and Aragon—had extended their dominions to the far south, a process known in Spanish history as the *reconquista*. Under Christian kings relations among the three religious communities were sometimes relaxed, sometimes tense. In the fourteenth century, in the wake of the Black Death, attacks on the Jewish quarters of many towns by Christian mobs had an unexpected sequel: a large portion of Spain's Jews, led by their rabbis, presented themselves for baptism. Both church and

95

crown welcomed these "New Christians" into the fold, in part by encouraging intermarriage with "Old Christians." Yet Castile's Old Christian majority remained suspicious. In fact, the religious loyalties of the New Christians remain an intriguing puzzle. Some secretly kept faith with the Jewish rites of their ancestors, others came to the fore as leaders of new currents of spirituality among Spanish Catholics. To ferret out those among the New Christians whose loyalty to their old religion made them heretics in the eyes of church and state, Queen Isabella created a special royal tribunal staffed by clerics: the Spanish Inquisition (1478). Over the next two decades, several thousand people were burned at the stake, and many others were punished in lesser ways (fig. 7.1). From about 1500, the Inquisition turned its attention to the *Alumbrados* (Illumined), men and women who sought a more personal union with God through mystical prayer. Seekers of God studied one or more of the popular printed manuals of meditation, consulted men or women known for their holiness (the women were called *beatas*), and sometimes quarreled with one another about the efficacy of different methods of prayer. To the Inquisition's way of thinking, the *Alumbrados'* focus on inner spiritual experience implied a dangerous disregard for the sacraments of the church. The fact that many leaders of the movement were of New Christian parentage seemed all the more reason for suspicion.

Ignatius of Loyola (1491–1556; fig. 7.2), a Basque nobleman, had his leg broken by a cannonball in his first military engagement (1521). For want of the chivalric tales he was familiar with, during a long convalescence he read and reread a traditional compilation of saints' lives. By the time he was able to walk again, Ignatius found himself daydreaming not about great feats of valor, but about preaching to infidels in the Holy Land. This conversion of the imagination was the door to a new life. Ignatius sold his property and gave the money to the poor, went on pilgrimage to Jerusalem, and returned to a wandering life in his native Spain, seeking spiritual counsel from holy men and *beatas*.

The Spiritual Exercises, a record of Ignatius's own spiritual quest, eventually became a manual of initiation and daily prayer for his followers. Ignatius adopted a particular form of meditative prayer. Starting from an incident in Jesus's life as recorded in the Gospels, one was to fix the scene as vividly as possible in one's imagination and dwell on Jesus's words and actions. In later years, Ignatius guided each new member of his company through the full thirty-day sequence of meditations outlined in the *Exercises*. The objective was to build as it were a mental armory against temptation, so that at crucial moments scenes from the life of Christ would come to mind as if unbidden. It is not known if Ignatius had even heard of Martin Luther when he first wrote the *Exercises*. But those who learned from

Figure 7.1. The Spanish Inquisition. In the terminology of the Inquisition, the burning of heretics was an "act of faith" (*auto da fe*): Pedro Bereguette (1450–1504), "St. Dominic Presiding at an Auto-da-Fe." *Alinari/Art Resource, NY.*

Figure 7.2. St. Ignatius Loyola. Jacopino del Conte, Posthumous Portrait of Ignatius of Loyola, 1556. *Curia Generalizia of the Society of Jesus, Rome.*

the *Exercises* to use the powers of the mind in shaping their thoughts to the service of Christ would have little patience for Luther's assertion that the human will is incapable of any action pleasing to God.

Ignatius needed a university education to make himself heard in the world, but after being twice detained by the Inquisition, suspicious of anyone who behaved like an *Alumbrado*, he opted for study beyond Spain's borders. As a mature man he took his place among teenagers at the arts faculty in Paris. Bachelor's degree in hand, he and a small group of followers planned to sail from Venice to the Holy Land. Prevented from embarking because of war, the company instead offered their services to the pope in Rome. In 1540 Pope Paul III recognized the Society of Jesus as a religious order. As the first elected father-general (1540–1556), Ignatius charted the new society's future. Jesuit overseas missions began in 1542 when, heeding a request from the king of Portugal, Ignatius sent Francis Xavier, one of his Paris companions, as a missionary to Portugal's new possessions in India. In 1548 Ignatius prescribed a humanist curriculum for the first Jesuit secondary school, at Messina in Sicily. Jesuit schools quickly became the preferred means, even in some Protestant territories, for young men of prominent families to acquire the polish of a classical education. Ignatius also provided a form of governance unprecedented among religious orders. Local superiors were appointed by the father-general, not elected by their confreres; general meetings of the order convened not annually, as was customary, but only as the father-general and his advisers deemed necessary. Ignatius envisioned his men as troops to be sent quickly wherever the church needed help. Increasingly, they were to be enlisted in the battle against Protestantism.

If the tight, top-down structure of the Jesuit order resembled the ambitions of strong monarchs in the early modern era, the Oratories of Divine Love made up a loose-knit federation reminiscent of Italy's tradition of autonomous city-states. In the Italian towns, confraternities devoted to charitable work were larger and better funded than elsewhere, and controlled by the laity, not the clergy. Several of the new religious orders in Italy began as variants on the confraternity. What the Oratories of Divine Love had in common was the example of Caterina Fieschi Adorna (1447–1510), later venerated as St. Catherine of Genoa. A daughter of Genoa's premier families, Catherine chose to live as a celibate lay woman, devoting herself to prayer and to the poor of her native city. She attracted disciples, often wealthy bankers like her kinfolk, and it was they who founded the first Oratory (Genoa, 1497), which in turn founded Italy's first hospital for the incurably ill. Oratories soon appeared in other Italian cities. The Roman Oratory was a training ground for men who carried a zeal for reform into higher echelons of the church. Four of its members (including one who later became pope) founded a new order for priests, the Theatines (1524), aimed at fostering common prayer and devotion to the unfortunate, especially the incurably ill. A fifth, Gasparo Contarini (d. 1542), was the pope's representative at the Regensburg Colloquy.

In 1525, a Franciscan friar in a small central-Italian town, Matteo da Bascio, resolved to devote himself to prayer and preaching, based on a literal observance of the rule of St. Francis. The pointed hood (*capuccio*) he chose to wear gave its name to the Capuchins, recognized by the pope in 1528 as a separate branch of the Franciscan movement. The Capuchins were to be, with the Jesuits, the great preachers and literary protagonists of the Counter-Reformation. In 1535 Angela Merici and twenty-eight young women of her native Brescia founded the Company of St. Ursula. They took vows of virginity, as nuns did, but each was to live with her family, dress in lay garb, and devote herself to the Christian education of girls. Church authorities, ever suspicious of religious women not living in convents, eventually forced the Ursulines to adopt a cloistered life, but they continued their work of operating schools for girls. Girls had few opportunities for formal education, and one of the traditional "spiritual works of mercy" (as distinct from "corporal works of mercy," like feeding the hungry) was to instruct the ignorant. The work of the Ursulines exemplifies a Catholic Reformation understanding of "good works" that was very different from Luther's.

The Council of Trent (fig. 7.3) convened in three sessions (1545–1547, 1551–1552, and 1561–1563), interrupted twice by war and once by the reign of the autocratic Pope Paul IV (r. 1555–1559), who refused to reconvene it. At its first session the council took up doctrinal issues raised by the Reformers, none of which had ever previously been the subject of any dogmatic pronouncement by the church as a whole. First on the agenda was justification (salvation). Girolamo Seripando (d. 1563), father-general of the Augustinian friars, proposed wording similar to what Protestant and Catholic conferees had accepted at Regensburg (1541). Diego Lainez (d. 1565), one of Ignatius Loyola's early companions, proposed instead a vigorous statement of traditional Catholic beliefs concerning free will. Though it shows traces of Seripando's language, the council's decree on justification flatly asserts what Luther and Calvin had flatly denied: the human will is free to accept or reject God's grace. The next question concerned scripture and tradition. Catholic theologians were agreed that the traditions of the church were authoritative, but what did this mean in relation to scripture? The minority view, which some Protestants might have accepted, was that "tradition" was simply the way in which the church had always understood scripture. The view that prevailed was that unwritten traditions in the keeping of the church are a distinct source of divine revelation, having an authority equal to that of scripture. These doctrinal definitions ensured that it would henceforth be clear (up to a point) which opinions were Catholic and which were not.

Reform of the clergy came to the table at the council's third session (1561–1563). Bishops were supposed to be shepherds of the faithful, but they were commonly appointed at the behest of the ruler, for political rea-

Figure 7.3. The Council of Trent. Sixteenth-century engraving of the Council of Trent. © *Copyright The Trustees of the British Museum.*

sons, and as members of a king's council or a papal bureau in Rome, many seldom actually saw the dioceses of which they were titular heads. The council was unable to reach agreement on the precise nature of a bishop's obligation to reside in his diocese, and it did not even attempt to set aside the various agreements, formal and informal, by which popes had recognized local rulers as having a voice in the selection of bishops. What it did was strengthen the authority of bishops vis-à-vis the regular as well as the secular clergy. Bishops were given more say in the appointment of pastors by noble "patrons" of parish churches, as well as the right to "visit" monasteries and other religious establishments that had previously gained exemption from episcopal control.

The priesthood needed reform as much as the episcopate. Canon law provided that only men of a certain age be ordained, following an examination of their theological competence by the ordaining bishop. Both provisions were widely ignored, the first in favor of younger sons of prominent families being groomed for important positions, the second in favor of men of humble background who hoped only to scrape out a meager existence as parish vicars or chantry priests. The council forcefully reasserted the law:

only men of twenty-five or older were to be ordained, and only with a university-level education including training in theology. To make this possible, the council mandated that each bishop find the resources (this was not easy) to endow a "seminary" for the training of diocesan priests.

Most in need of reform was the papacy itself, as late medieval reform treatises often pointed out. The Roman Curia was both a collection of networks based on nepotism and a vast bureaucracy whose members had a natural interest in perpetuating the functions that kept them gainfully employed. One of their more lucrative functions was the granting of dispensations that exempted recipients from given provisions of canon law, such as the rule prohibiting "pluralism," that is, the holding of ecclesiastical positions in two or more locations at once. The Council of Trent issued new regulations that, over time, had some effect in curbing clerical double-dipping, but it played little role in reorganizing the Curia (this was to be done somewhat later by the popes themselves).

The council's real significance for the papacy lay in the fact that this great engine of Catholic reform was called into being by the popes, who also guided the council's deliberations through emissaries who always presided at formal sessions. Bolstered by Rome's new standing, papal *nuncios* fanned out to advance the Catholic cause. Armed with the *Index of Forbidden Books* promulgated by Pope Paul IV in 1559, permitting ready identification of allegedly dangerous authors, they pressed bishops and secular rulers to join in the repression of heretical books and other expressions of false doctrine. The church had its own procedures for trying persons accused of heresy, but the effective suppression of dissent required active cooperation from the secular courts (see below). Papal emissaries also pushed for the appointment of zealous clergymen to important positions in the local church. They urged princes to accept the Tridentine decrees for their territories, countering as best they could the influence of those whose interests would be adversely affected by their implementation—noble patrons of parish churches and monasteries that objected to having some of their property taken to endow the new seminaries. By these means, the papacy assumed leadership of the movement for Catholic reform and of the battle against Protestantism, gaining by about 1600 a moral prestige in the Catholic world such as it had not enjoyed for centuries.

Catholic rulers typically responded to the Reformation by attempting to suppress it. The religious justification for this policy was that since princes were seen as ruling "by the grace of God," they had a responsibility to see that God was worshiped properly. The legal justification was that medieval law codes often defined heresy as "treason against God," meaning that it was a crime punishable by death, as was treason against the ruler. At least since the thirteenth century, rulers had cooperated with the church in putting convicted heretics to death. Each diocese had an official known as the inquisitor, in whose court accused heretics could be tried and convicted, but not sentenced to death. Convicted heretics were handed over to "the secular arm," which alone had the power of capital punishment.

Queen Isabella's Spanish Inquisition was a state court established to suppress heresy. In some provinces of the Low Countries, Charles V relied on a territorial inquisition based on the Spanish model; in others, he relied on provincial courts that were more willing to prosecute people for crimes of belief than were the town courts. The dukes of Bavaria followed the latter course, issuing laws that criminalized behavior recognizable as "Lutheran" and were enforceable in the secular courts. In France, too, the crown was content to leave the enforcement of heresy laws in the hands of the chief law courts, known as *Parlements*.

This church-state collaboration in Catholic Europe claimed an estimated 3,000 Protestant martyrs in the years between 1520 and 1600. Where dissenters were few in numbers and poorly organized, like Lutherans in the Netherlands in the 1520s, or Protestants of any kind in Spain, the application of brute force was effective. Where they were strong in numbers and well organized, like Calvinists in France or in the populous province of Flanders, persecution made martyrs, and the blood of martyrs was, as in early Christian times, the seed of new conversions. In these circumstances repression did not work.

Another strategy was to improve the training and discipline of the Catholic clergy. Charles V carefully checked the religious and educational qualifications of those he proposed for high positions in the church, but this was in Castile, which had an unusual tradition of royal involvement with church reform, tracing back to Queen Isabella. In other Catholic lands, bishops continued to be appointed first and foremost for their family connections. Change came only with a generation of Jesuit-educated princes willing to override opposition to reform of the clergy. Archduke Charles of Inner Austria (r. 1564–1590) and Archduke Albert of the Spanish Netherlands (r. 1595–1621) accepted the Council of Trent's decrees as a basis for regulating the often contentious issue of lay patronage of ecclesiastical appointments. In Bavaria Duke William V (r. 1579–1598) functioned as the effective ruler of the church. In France, where the civil wars had ended with a formal grant of toleration for the kingdom's Huguenot minority (1598), the Parlement of Paris refused to recognize the Tridentine decrees as part of French law. But the crown began exercising more care in the appointment of bishops, while members of parlement joined the crown in promoting the new religious orders. By the early seventeenth century, many areas had zealous bishops who were indefatigable in "visiting" their dioceses. The ranks of the parish clergy were being filled with a new kind of priest, making new demands on populations that were often loyal to Catholicism, if seldom enthusiastic for reform.

"Innovation" was not a friendly word for sixteenth-century Europe's rural majority. Novelties came not from the peasants themselves (at least not in ways they were conscious of), but from the landlord's countinghouse or from lawyers at the prince's court, who, like city-bred preachers, appealed to books illiterate folk could not read. The old ways were the ways country dwellers could control (who else knew the local customs?) or could at least bear because of their familiarity. By and large, the old ways meant the old religion, with its familiar rites and gestures. The alliance between the grievances of Germany's peasants and Reformation doctrine had proven to be temporary, and in France Reformation doctrine had very little appeal to the peasantry, save in a few areas. To be sure, where peasants had a generation or two to get used to Lutheranism, they strongly resisted efforts by princes to make them change their minds again. But in the outward forms by which illiterate people measured religious propriety, Lutheranism was not so different from Catholicism, save for the use of the vernacular. In territories where Lutheranism was imposed from above, like Norway and Finland, the fact that a largely Catholic peasantry offered little active resistance seems related to efforts by authorities to change as little as possible in the outward ceremonies of religion.

Reformed Protestantism had a different trajectory. Zwinglian as well as Calvinist doctrine required that worship be thoroughly "cleansed" of all the artifacts and all the gestures of the Catholic cult, and this was often accomplished by violent outbursts of iconoclasm, with or without the encouragement of Reformed preachers. To provocations of this kind, Catholic people in Switzerland and France (though not the Low Countries) responded with violence of their own. Sympathizers of the Reformation were chased out of Switzerland's forest cantons well before the conflict between Catholic and Protestant cantons had crystallized into open warfare. Since Switzerland's cantons enjoyed an unusual degree of local autonomy, not being subject to any kind of control by a princely court, it is perhaps not surprising if individual cantons made their collective decisions about the Reformation, for or against, quickly and with force. France was a different story.

Beginning in the 1520s and 1530s, France was crisscrossed by itinerant Catholic preachers, prophesying that men and women now living would yet see the Last Day, the hour of God's final victory over Satan and all the forces of evil. Apocalyptic rhetoric of this sort was a common theme of medieval preaching, concentrated in certain periods and regions in a way that can sometimes but not always be linked to social and economic crises. French preachers of these decades seem to have been influenced in part by widespread astrological prognostications to the effect that a rare alignment of the planets portended some momentous change on earth. Whatever its source, this wave of doomsday preaching prepared people on both sides of France's eventual religious divide to believe that combating the devilish evils they saw before them ("heresy" for some, "idolatry" for others) was of transcendent significance.

The centralizing claims of France's monarchy made the struggle that was to come more intense than it might otherwise have been. For the king and his officials, all aspects of French life, including religion, properly came under the scrutiny of royal courts, of which the Parlement of Paris was the most important (fig. 7.4). The antiheresy legislation of Kings

Figure 7.4. The arrest of Councillor Anne du Bourg in the Parlement of Paris. Councillor du Bourg was arrested for heresy (later tried and burned) when he spoke in favor of the Reformation before the Parlement of Paris and in the presence of King Henry II (upper right): from Alfred Franklin, Les Grandes Scènes Historiques du XVIe Siècle, Reproduction Fac-Simile du Recueil de J. Tortorel et J. Perrissin (Paris, 1886). *University of California at San Diego Library.*

Horribilia ſcelera ab Huguenotis
in Gallijs perpetrata.

Figure 7.5. A Catholic view of Protestant violence in France. "Horrible Crimes
Perpetrated by the Huguenots," from Richard Verstegen, Teatrum Crudelitatum.
Courtesy of Thomas Fisher Rare Book Library, University of Toronto.

Francis I (r. 1515–1547) and Henry II (r. 1547–1559), even if occasionally
relaxed, created a mechanism of judicial repression that was ineffective in
stamping out dissent, but odious to friends and kinfolk of its victims. The
anger that built up, fueled by the fiery rhetoric of Reformed preachers,
found a ready target in the visible symbols of "idolatrous" Catholic worship (fig. 7.5).

French Catholics, egged on by their preachers, responded by targeting
the "heretics" themselves (fig. 7.6). By 1560 France was gripped in a deep-
ening spiral of reciprocal violence. For example, in Paris, passersby, hearing the distinctive tones of Protestant plainsong from a merchant's house,
quickly became a Catholic mob that stormed the house and murdered its
occupants. At Christmas Eve mass in a Paris church, two young Huguenots

Figure 7.6. A Protestant view of Catholic violence in France. "Massacre at Cahors, 19 November 1561," from Alfred Franklin, Les Grandes Scènes Historiques due XVIe Siècle, Reproduction Fac-Simile du Recueil de J. Tortorel et J. Perrissin [1586] (Paris: Fisachbacher, 1881). *University of California at San Diego Library.*

(as French Protestants were called) rushed up to the altar at the moment of the elevation, stabbed the priest, and trampled on the host; they were killed immediately by the congregation. When quarrels among the great families of the realm were added to this volatile mixture, France fell into a long cycle of civil and religious wars (1562–1598).

The fanatical zeal with which Catholics in France defended their faith was a striking example of a more diffuse phenomenon. So long as Protestant preaching had not had a generation or more to take root, Catholic authorities could count on a certain residual loyalty to traditional beliefs. But it was a loyalty that ordinary men and women gave on their own terms. The religious temper of ardently Catholic Paris made it difficult for France's monarchs to make the concessions to the Huguenot party that peace in the realm required. Reform-minded Catholic pastors were to find their flocks unwilling to accept modification of traditional observances. As far as country people were concerned, innovation was still innovation, even if propounded in the name of the old religion.

CALVINISM

Certain features of the Calvinist movement in Geneva reflected the character of Geneva itself. As a self-governing commune, whose citizens formed one body, Geneva had no tolerance for religious dissension; citizens were given a choice between acceptance of the new Calvinist confession or exile. Though dependent on Bern's aid against enemies like the duke of Savoy, Geneva was a self-standing republic, with no need for any kind of church authority at a higher level than that of the city. Hence, it was the large and complex canton of Bern, not Geneva, that developed Reformed synods, with pastors and lay elders elected by local churches deliberating on matters of doctrine. With the collaboration of men who had come to Geneva as exiles and returned as missionaries to their native lands, Calvin guided the building of similarly structured Reformed churches in places as far away as Poland. But the Calvinism of larger and more complex territories also assumed characteristics suitable to each local context. The varieties of Calvinism may be illustrated by looking at churches in France, the Low Countries, Scotland, the Rhineland Palatinate in Germany, and, in the Kingdom of Hungary, Transylvania.

In France, reform of the church was promoted by a circle of preachers and scholars around Jacques Lefèvre d'Étaples (1460–1536), a scholastic professor of Aristotle's logic who ended his learned career as a humanist biblical scholar. One of the preachers was Guillaume Farel (1489–1565), later to be Calvin's collaborator in Geneva. Enthused for Luther's works, Farel went to Basel, where he made contact with Zwingli and his ideas. Bern installed him as the first Protestant preacher in the French-speaking city of Neuchâtel (1530), a Bernese dependency, which then began printing Protestant works for distribution in France, including vernacular Bibles. Farel's intemperate zeal was evident in the broadsides denouncing "the horrible, gross and insupportable popish mass" (1534), printed in Neuchâtel and posted all over France, including on the door of the royal bedchamber.

During the 1540s Geneva replaced Neuchâtel as the command post for diffusion of Protestant works into France, and Calvin's personal influence began to be felt in many of the places where Reformed movements coalesced. In the city of Nîmes, to the south, a strong Protestant movement formed around the staff of the humanist secondary school, whose rector (from 1542) had met Calvin in Strasbourg. In the Rhone valley city of Lyon, France's mercantile capital, local Protestants became numerous enough to appoint a regular pastor (1546), one of Calvin's correspondents. Near the southwestern port city of La Rochelle, a Benedictine abbot of noble birth, another correspondent, converted all his monks to the new faith in 1553.

From about 1555, Calvinism expanded rapidly. Nobles accepted the new faith in large numbers, often at the behest of their female kindred. A spectacular example at the highest level of French society was Jeanne d'Albret (d. 1572), Queen of Navarre, who made a public announcement of her conversion in 1560. Her husband, Antoine de Bourbon, was less steadfast in his loyalty to the new creed than she was, but he had the great advantage of being first in rank among the princes of the royal blood, who were closest to the throne after King Henry II and his sons.

At the local level, the visible presence of armed noblemen allowed Huguenots to worship in public, often in the open air, without fear of disturbance by the king's officers. Meanwhile, in a number of cities in the south and southwest, merchants, magistrates, and even some royal officials joined hands with the artisans who were often the earliest recruits to the Protestant cause. Many congregations could now support more than one preacher; presbyters were elected and consistories met, after the Genevan model, to discipline the wayward. Strong in numbers as well as social prestige, Huguenot congregations demanded (but did not get) churches for their own use. Their preachers joined with nearby colleagues to form "colloquies," or regular meetings of regional clergy, to ensure uniformity of doctrine and to provide pastors for new congregations.

The capstone of this organizational edifice was achieved in 1559, when deputies elected by the colloquies met secretly in Paris for a national synod, which adopted, with slight modifications, a confession of faith drawn up by Calvin. Not all French Protestants accepted Calvin's views on church governance. A treatise published in 1562 argued that decisions regarding the appointment of preachers should be made by each congregation, not by a "colloquy" or synod. But the congregationalist idea, though not forgotten, was condemned by two national synods of the French church. By 1561, leaders of the Huguenots counted some 2,000 congregations that were "organized" in the Genevan manner, with pastor, elders, and consistory. This suggests that some 10 percent of France's roughly twenty million people were Protestant.

Many in France clamored that true Christians would be justified in striking out against their tyrannical oppressors. But despite the continuing persecution, Calvin insisted, time and again, that the gospel must never be compromised by any use of force. The 1559 edition of his *Institutes* urged "magistrates" to prevent rulers of their realms from acting as tyrants—Calvin may have been thinking of France's princes of the blood and of Antoine de Bourbon in particular. This became more than a theoretical question when King Henry II, a lover of jousting, was killed by an errant lance (1559), leaving the throne to a weak boy whose council of regency was dominated by Duke Francis of Guise, a determined foe of the Reformation. Huguenot nobles led by the prince of Condé, Bourbon's younger brother, plotted to seize the person of the king and install Bourbon as head of a new council of regency. When the plot was uncovered (1560) suspicious eyes turned toward Geneva. Calvin kept aloof, but it seems his second-in-command and eventual successor, Theodore Beza (1516–1605), had signaled approval of the attempted coup. Calvin's attempt to limit the right of resistance to potentates of the realm, though intellectually defensible, was not readily comprehensible to zealous Huguenots who had seen coreligionists burned at the stake by order of the king's courts.

Whether Calvin wished it so or not, French Calvinism was becoming a revolutionary movement. When a party of Protestant worshipers was massacred by the duke of Guise (1562), Condé called Huguenot nobles to arms, and Huguenot factions seized control of twenty cities, including Nîmes, Lyon, and La Rochelle. This first of France's religious wars began auspiciously for the Huguenot rebels, but by the time the last war was concluded (1598) they gladly accepted a recognition of their rights limited to the few parts of the kingdom they still controlled. Calvin's caution about mixing violence and religion had been vindicated. The Protestant movement in France never again reached its numerical strength of 1561, just before the religious wars began.

Charles V's attempt to create in the Low Countries a special state tribunal modeled on the Spanish Inquisition evoked a firestorm of opposition, as provincial parliaments demanded respect for their customary legal privileges, never mind the claim that such privileges were suspended in cases of "treason against God." Nonetheless, the new territorial inquisition was able to snuff out a nascent Lutheran movement by targeting the highly visible preachers and scholars who were its natural leaders. In Lutheranism's stead more radical forms of dissent emerged, especially among men and women of humbler background who were almost invisible to the authorities. Anabaptists and "Sacramentarians" were put to death, but there was no wholesale rounding up of suspects until the Melchiorite scare of the 1530s, when town governments—usually loath to prosecute citizens for crimes of belief—took a real interest in enforcing heresy laws. By about 1540, magistrates in some towns began to realize that new-style Mennonite congregations posed no danger to public order. During the 1540s there were relatively few martyrs.

Just at this time, however, Calvinism appeared in the French-speaking provinces closest to France and started making its way to Netherlandish-speaking provinces farther north, like Flanders and Brabant. With Geneva-style consistories monitoring their behavior, Calvinists found it difficult to compromise with idolatry by attending Sunday mass now and then to avoid drawing attention. Together with local Anabaptists, they were targets for the territorial inquisition in Flanders, led by Peter Titelmans, a zealous Louvain theologian. The courage of the martyrs won sympathy, especially among skilled workers in the centers of Flanders's "new textile" industry. Sixteenth-century Europeans enjoyed watching public executions of criminals, and in Spain this was true of the burning of heretics as well. But townsfolk in the Low Countries, Catholic as well as Protestant, had a clear distaste for seeing people hung or burned at the stake because of their beliefs. In the province of Holland, a crowd gathered in Rotterdam for the execution of Anabaptists rioted, freeing the condemned persons and chasing the magistrates into the relative safety of the town hall (1558). In the new textile towns of Flanders, starting in 1562, Calvinists were broken out of jail by sizable parties of men.

Facing these disorders was Margaret of Parma, regent in the Low Countries for King Philip II of Spain (fig. 7.7), who had succeeded his father Charles V in 1556. Philip made things more difficult for Margaret when he decreed (with papal cooperation) the creation of new bishoprics for his Low Countries lands (1561). There would now be fifteen bishoprics instead of three, the better to supervise reform of the clergy as well as the campaign against heresy. But noble families feared diminution of their control over high positions in the church, powerful abbots were loath to release monastic properties to endow the new bishoprics, and magistrates flatly refused to allow heresy-hunting bishops within their town gates. The great nobles who sat in Margaret's council of state gave voice to widespread dissatisfaction in the country. Led by William of Nassau, the Prince of Orange (1533–1584), the council demanded and got (1564) the dismissal of Philip's key adviser, whom they blamed for the new bishoprics plan. Sensing that further change was possible, the council sent two of their number to Spain to ask the king to suspend the heresy laws. Philip's reply (1565) came as a rude shock: heretics were to have no mercy whatever.

Margaret's government now seemed to lose its grip. Four hundred noblemen presented a petition for relaxation of the heresy laws. That one of Margaret's advisers derisively called them "beggars" only gave the movement of protest a popular name. Thousands of people flocked to rural settings for the illegal "hedge sermons" of Calvinist preachers. In August

Figure 7.7. King Philip II of Spain. Ruled 1556–1598. Pompeo Leoni (ca. 1533–1608), Bust of Philip II. *Kunsthistorisches Museum, Vienna.*

1566 zealous Calvinists returned from exile in England to organize a systematic tearing down of "idols" in Flanders's new textile district (fig. 7.8). Led by preachers who sometimes paid image-breakers by the hour, the wave of iconoclasm spread through much of the country. Did this smashing of the symbols of the old religion represent the will of the people? And would the guildsmen who made up the town militias stand to arms to prevent it? No one knew. In most towns, magistrates did little to ward off the destruction they knew was coming.

But public order was not so fragile as it seemed. Nobles and magistrates sent Margaret their expressions of support, and when the dust had settled it seemed the number of convinced Calvinists was fairly small. Margaret sought to calm the waters by allowing towns to set aside one of their

Figure 7.8. Iconoclasm in the Netherlands, 1566. Engraving of "Iconoclasm in the Netherlands," 1566, from Michael Eytzinger, *Novus de Leone Belgico eiusque Topographiae et Historiae Descriptione* (Cologne, 1588). *British Library, London.*

churches for "the new religion," an arrangement that seemed in some areas to work. Meanwhile, however, Philip II had already made his decision, based on the panic-stricken reports he initially received from Brussels. A trusted commander, the duke of Alba, marched north from Italy at the head of ten thousand Spanish and Italian troops (1567). Once in Brussels, Alba disregarded notions of due process deeply ingrained among Netherlanders, ordering all key decisions made by a three-man group, known to Spaniards as the Council of Troubles, and to Netherlanders as the council of blood. This council issued death sentences at a rate that dwarfs all persecutions of the Reformation period, though the number of actual victims was much smaller. Hearing that Alba was coming, leaders of the Calvinist movement had fled into exile, some to England, others to the city of Emden in East Friesland, a neighbor of the Netherlands province of Friesland. While in exile, Netherlands Calvinists adopted rules for church governance, based on French models: each town congregation would have a consistory, including lay elders; pastors of nearby congregations would form a *classis* (like the Huguenot colloquy) for supervision of doctrine and preaching; and for the resolution of important matters, each *classis* would elect delegates to a synod.

William of Orange carried on an armed struggle, but without the resources to match Alba's ten thousand men. His forces defeated wherever
they had taken the field, Orange retired to Germany (1568). The only remaining center of active resistance was in England's channel ports, where
Calvinist exiles, following an old Netherlands pattern, continued their rebellion by taking to the sea as pirates. The Sea Beggars disrupted the maritime commerce of the Netherlands but could not prevent Alba from reducing the country to obedience. In Alba's judgment the only thing lacking
was a source of revenue that would allow his troops to remain in the
Netherlands without being a drain on Spain's treasury. He thought he had
the consent he needed from the provincial parliaments, but he did not understand their slow deliberative procedures. When his officials went out
in the early months of 1572 to collect the tenth-penny tax, a new levy based
on Spanish precedents, they met a wall of hostility—it seems no money at
all was actually collected. This form of "Spanish tyranny" the people of the
Low Countries would not stomach.

The Sea Beggars seized an opportunity. Drawing their fleet up before the
small port of Brill (April 1572), they promised protection from the Spaniards
and respect for the Catholic religion of the inhabitants (fig. 7.9). Once in control they cleansed the churches of "idols" and installed Calvinist preachers—but they did keep the Spaniards out. As other cities in the seafaring
provinces of Holland and Zeeland submitted to the Beggars, townsfolk
seem to have accepted an implicit bargain: no Spaniards, but no public
Catholic worship either. The exiles now returned, often to become magistrates of their native towns, and William of Orange guided the revolt from
a headquarters in Holland. He too had become a Calvinist, recognizing that
committed Calvinists were the natural leaders of the war against Spain. But
Orange also made it clear that all Christians ought to be free to worship in
public as they chose: to him, the revolt against Spain was about defending
the traditional "liberties" or privileges of the Netherlands provinces, not
about religion. Calvinist leaders were adamant about not permitting any
public expression of Catholic idolatry. But their worshipers made up only a
small fraction of the population, and forcing everyone to conform to Calvinism would alienate those who opposed the king of Spain but not his religion.
Moreover, Mennonites, now freed from fear of the king's heresy laws, competed with Calvinists for the allegiance of evangelical Christians. With their
strict community discipline, Mennonites would rightly scoff at the moral
pretensions of a Protestant church that claimed to incorporate the whole
community, the indifferent as well as the devout.

Hence, Netherlands Calvinists renounced the idea of inclusiveness.
Theirs was to be what they called "the public church" of rebel territory. No
other form of Christian worship was permitted in public; Catholic worship

Figure 7.9. The capture of Brill by the Sea Beggars, April 1572. Disembarking from their ships, the rebel army draws up in formation and marches toward the main gate of Brill ("Briele"). *British Library, London.*

was banned in private as well. But no citizen would be constrained to join the public church—in fact, admission to formal membership was carefully controlled, in the interests of good discipline. The underlying question—whether the war against Spain was being fought for freedom from tyranny or for true religion—would be sorted out during the long decades of revolt (1572–1648).

Scotland's history was shaped by conflicts with its larger and more powerful neighbor to the south. In the late medieval wars between England and France, France and the royal house of Stuart formed what Scots called "the auld alliance." But the battle of Flodden (1513), a disastrous defeat at the hands of the English, together with a combination of English bribes and border raids, led some of Scotland's great nobles to rethink the French connection. King James V kept Scotland in France's orbit, choosing as his bride Mary of Guise, daughter of one of France's premier families. But James perished in a raid against England (1542), leaving his throne to an infant daughter, Mary Stuart, or Mary Queen of Scots. Pro-English and pro-French factions now vied for control of the kingdom.

This conflict had a religious coloration, since King Henry VIII and his Parliament had severed England's ties with Rome in 1536. Scots Protestants, concentrated in the coastal towns, counted on England for support; also, pro-English Scots saw Protestantism as a way of ending French influence. George Wishart, Scotland's leading Protestant preacher, had a Zwinglian theology acquired on his travels to Germany and Switzerland and connections with pro-English lesser nobles. Meanwhile, David Beaton, archbishop of St. Andrews and a pillar of the pro-French party, worked at bringing reform to a poorly educated and ill-disciplined Catholic clergy. In 1546 Beaton had Wishart tried and executed for heresy. A band of pro-English nobles then murdered the archbishop and occupied his castle. John Knox (1513–1572; fig. 7.10), a former priest and member of Wishart's circle, gained attention with a fiery sermon to the conspirators in St. Andrews castle, denouncing the papacy as the Antichrist. Royal forces captured the castle, and Knox got two years as a galley-slave, but his career as a reformer had barely begun. He preached in England until Mary Tudor's accession to the English throne brought a restoration of Catholicism (1553–1558) and

Figure 7.10. John Knox (1514–1572). Portrait of John Knox engraved by Hondius.
© *Copyright The Trustees of the British Museum.*

thereafter to a congregation of English and Scots refugees in Calvin's Geneva.

Mary of Guise assumed control of the regency council for her daughter in 1554. Mary Stuart had been betrothed as a young girl to Francis, eldest son of France's King Henry II, and their marriage, celebrated in 1558, seemed to bind Scotland to France. But Scots were growing resentful of the visible signs of French control, like French garrisons in key castles, and the accession to England's throne of the Protestant Elizabeth I, also in 1558, opened new possibilities. Returning from the continent, Knox fanned an incipient rebellion by preaching a provocative sermon (May 1559) urging alliance with England against France and the papacy. Unlike Calvin, who limited the right of rebellion to those holding positions of responsibility, Knox believed private individuals had the right to strike down a tyrant ruler. In fact, Scotland's rebellion was firmly guided by the lesser nobility and bolstered by troops sent from England. When Mary of Guise died (June 1560), France withdrew its troops. The Scots parliament, with an unusual number of lesser nobles in attendance, abolished papal authority, forbade the mass, and adopted a Calvinist confession of faith. Even though it seems the majority of Scotland's population was Catholic for some years thereafter, parliament's decision was not to be reversed.

Mary Stuart, now a widow, returned to her kingdom in 1561. She insisted on Catholic worship in her own chapel but had no power to restore Catholicism in her realm, and she also had other interests. Following a series of plots animated by her claims to the English throne, Mary fled to England (1568), where, after one more plot, she was executed by order of Elizabeth (1587). The question that remained was how the new Scots church was to be governed. Initially, decisions on church appointments were made by a council of leading Protestant nobles. This authority was soon transferred to a general assembly in which clergy also voted, though they were outnumbered by lay representatives of the towns and the nobility. A Geneva model, favored by some, would have decisions made by assemblies in which clergy had the dominant voice. But there were also bishops who accepted the Reformation and continued governing their churches, despite the change in theology; some leading Scots, looking to conformity with England, argued for an episcopal form of church government. The debate among these options would continue until Scotland again rose in rebellion in the 1630s, this time against an English king and his bishops.

The Wittelsbach ruler of the Rhineland Palatinate was one of the seven electoral princes of the Holy Roman Empire. Elector Louis V (d. 1544), a close ally of Charles V, kept aloof from the Reformation that was steadily gaining ground in his corner of south Germany. Louis's brother and successor, Elector Frederick II (d. 1556), set his course by the political weathervane: he introduced a Lutheran church order in 1546; rescinded it in 1548, after Charles V's victory in the First Schmalkaldic War; and restored it again in 1553, when the tide had turned against the emperor. Frederick's nephew Ottheinrich (r. 1556–1559) gave Protestantism a firm footing by recruiting leading Protestant scholars for the university of Heidelberg and reorganizing his privy council along confessional lines. He also created a church council to govern religious affairs. The only question was which kind of Protestantism the Palatinate was embracing.

Elector Frederick III (r. 1559–1576), from a junior branch of the Wittelsbach family, had been converted to Lutheranism by his wife. Offended by a bitter dispute over the Lord's Supper between Lutheran and Calvinist theology professors brought in by Ottheinrich, he dismissed both of the chief antagonists. Convinced by his study of the issue that the Calvinist interpretation was correct, he took the bold step of announcing his intention to introduce Calvinism in his lands. Calvinism had no legitimate standing in the empire according to the 1555 Peace of Augsburg, a fact made clear at a 1561 meeting that was intended to demonstrate unity among Germany's Protestant princes but showed instead the deep division between the Lutheran majority and a small Calvinist party led by Frederick III. But persistence by a capable ruler of such an important territory brought tacit recognition of Calvinism in the empire. The *Heidelberg Catechism* (1563), drafted by two theology professors Frederick had appointed, was to be widely used and admired in other Calvinist churches.

The next step was to ensure good discipline, to prevent God's church from being sullied by the presence of ungodly members. The church council's proposal (1564) to leave discipline in the hands of civil officials touched off an important family dispute between the two main branches of Reformed Protestantism. Geneva and Zurich had reached agreement on the Lord's Supper in 1549, and since then theologians of both camps formed a common front against Lutheran and Catholic attacks by minimizing their remaining differences. But Calvin stood for control of church affairs by the church itself, while Zwingli's heirs believed discipline was the prerogative of godly magistrates. Thomas Erastus (1524–1583), a medical professor at Heidelberg, prepared a statement of the Zwinglian view, arguing that the jurisdiction civil authorities exercised over offenses against God (like blasphemy) properly extended to excommunicating public sinners from the church. Theodore Beza, Calvin's successor in Geneva, asserted that only officers of the church, not civil magistrates, were called upon to make judgments based on divine law. The Palatinate's 1570 church ordinance threaded a path between both views: boards of lay elders were created, as the Calvinists wished, but only civil officials had the authority to excommunicate sinners or even scold them in public.

Frederick III knew that his eldest son and heir, a devout Lutheran, would change course once more. In fact, Elector Louis VI (r. 1576–1583) brought in Lutheran professors for the university, Lutheran pastors for the churches, and Lutheran jurists for his administrative councils. But Frederick III in his later years gained immense prestige in the Calvinist world by sending troops to the aid of embattled coreligionists in France and the Netherlands, commanded by his younger sons, John Casimir and Christopher. As regent of the Palatinate (1583–1592) for his nephew, the son of Louis VI, John Casimir was able to bring back the Calvinist professors and administrators his older brother had sent packing. This time the Calvinist imprint took hold. By the time of Elector Frederick V (r. 1610–1623), Louis VI's grandson, a thoroughly Calvinist Palatinate was ready for a leadership role in a grand alliance of European Protestant powers.

Nestled in an upland triangle framed by the Carpathian mountains, Transylvania formed the southeasternmost extension of Latin Christendom. Beyond the mountains lay Orthodox Christendom, Rumanian-speaking Wallachia to the east, and Bulgaria to the south. Transylvania's peasantry was largely Rumanian-speaking and Orthodox as well, but, as in most of Europe, peasants had no voice in the politics of the principality. As part of a Kingdom of Hungary much larger than the modern nation of the same name, Transylvania was governed in the king's name by a Palatine, chosen from among the great noble families. As in the rest of Hungary, Magyar- or Hungarian-speaking nobles were dominant. Since Hungary's medieval rulers had called in German burghers to build towns, especially from Saxony, the Saxons were second in importance. Third were the Szekler, Magyar-speaking commoners who enjoyed privileges in return for military service. From 1437 these three groups were recognized as "nations" having voting rights in Transylvania's provincial diet.

Medieval Hungary was shattered by the battle of Mohács (1526), at which the Ottoman army, commanded by Sultan Suleyman the Lawgiver (r. 1520–1566), annihilated a smaller Christian force, leaving Hungary's young and childless king among the dead. For the next 160 years the central Hungarian plain, eventually including the twin cities of Buda and Pest, was an Ottoman province. Ferdinand of Habsburg, Charles V's brother, claimed the Kingdom of Hungary by right of a marriage treaty between the two dynasties, but was able to control only the northern and western portions of the kingdom, roughly equivalent to modern Slovakia. East of

Ottoman Hungary, Transylvania, along with six counties in the Hungarian plain, rallied to the Palatine, Janos Szapolyai. His claim to the kingship was backed by the Ottomans, who did not want Charles's brother ruling in Transylvania, and by many Magyar nobles, who did not want a German-speaking prince. Szapolyai and his successors (elected by the diet) paid tribute to the sultan, acknowledging Ottoman overlordship.

The Reformation made rapid strides all through Hungary, especially after the battle of Mohács, seen by many as God's judgment on the wickedness of Christians. In Transylvania, Saxon towns gravitated to the teachings of Luther, while Magyar nobles embraced Reformed doctrines emanating from "Helvetia," the ancient name for Switzerland. Although Transylvania had a succession of Catholic princes during the sixteenth century, the diet strongly favored letting towns and nobles make their own religious decisions. In 1564 the diet gave legal recognition to a Lutheran Church for the Saxon towns, and a Reformed Church for the Magyars. The latter came to be known as the "Church of the Helvetic Confession," after a 1566 confession of faith authored by Heinrich Bullinger of Zurich, but written in such a way as to gain the adhesion of all the other Protestant cantons, including Geneva. In its organization the Transylvanian church owed more to Zurich than to Geneva, for there were regional "superintendents" who functioned rather as bishops had done, and no lay elders to establish an autonomous regime of ecclesiastical discipline. But the unity of this church was soon ruptured. Particularly in Transylvania's eastern counties, where the Szekler were numerous, preachers of Anti-Trinitarian doctrines found a hearing. Hence in 1568 the diet extended recognition to Anti-Trinitarians as well as Catholics, so that Transylvania now had four "received religions." The rule was that the majority in each parish should decide its form of worship, while providing alternative spaces of worship for parishioners displaced by their decision.

In this land of equally recognized churches, the Church of the Helvetic Confession was more equal than others, because of its close ties to the dominant Magyar aristocracy. By 1600, of the roughly five thousand parishes in the medieval kingdom of Hungary, about three-fourths were Protestant, and the majority of these were Reformed. The Habsburg dynasty was now more actively promoting Catholicism in the Austrian lands and in Royal Hungary (for Habsburg Austria, see chapter 9), but, in reaction to Catholic and Habsburg pressure, Transylvania's diet chose a series of Reformed rulers, starting in 1605. The most capable of these Calvinist princes, Gabór Bethlen (r. 1613–1628), established in 1622 an academy for the training of preachers in Gyulaféhervár (Alba Julia). In support of the Palatinate's Elector Frederick V, he too would take up arms against the Habsburgs (see chapter 10).

✛

These five Calvinist movements differed from one another as well as from the Genevan church. French Calvinists created the first national church organization, Dutch Calvinists embraced for various reasons a more selective idea of church membership, and Scottish Calvinists departed even more than their French and Dutch confreres did from Calvin's caution about mixing the gospel with political rebellion. The experience of the Palatinate shows that Calvinism, a revolutionary movement in the three other countries, could also accommodate itself to princely rule. Transylvania shows that Zurich's influence could sometimes be as important as Geneva's. What these five churches had in common was an allegiance to the Reformed tradition and its thoroughgoing repudiation of the religious past.

Just as Catholicism in its Counter-Reformation form found nothing of any value in Protestantism, Reformed Protestantism found nothing of any value in Catholicism. The warfare between adherents of these competing doctrines that broke out along many fronts may thus seem to have been inevitable. In fact it was not. Street fighting (as in France) between groups that despise each other's beliefs makes a riot, not a war. The next four chapters will show that the religious wars fought by Europeans of this era must also be understood from the perspective of what contemporaries called reason of state.

III POLITICS

Not all rulers in sixteenth-century Europe were princes. The Republic of Venice, a major trading and naval power, was governed by its large hereditary aristocracy, all of whose adult males had the right to attend meetings of the Senate. Florence, a major banking and cloth-manufacturing center, was a republic until one of its great families, the Medici, succeeded in transforming themselves into hereditary princes. After Switzerland defeated the armies of the Holy Roman Empire (1499, see below), the Swiss cantons too were republics, recognizing no princely authority. Throughout Europe, large and midsize cities thought of themselves as republics, for they governed their internal affairs without much interference from the princes whose military protection they depended on, and whose taxes they paid.

Whether princely or republican, all European regimes of this era had three things in common. First, like governments in other parts of the world, they saw themselves as ruling in the name of God. This meant it was their duty to take measures to ensure that the Lord on high did not withdraw His protection from their land. Late medieval Catholic governments promoted shrines and patron saints especially associated with the territory or its ruling dynasty and closely watched how the clergy conducted its business, to make sure divine worship was performed properly according to church law. Further, since God entrusted the temporal affairs of the realm to its government, rulers had the right to make the temporal wealth of the church serve the common good of the territory. For example, if it seemed money were being drained off to Rome for no good purpose, a ruler like Saxony's Elector Frederick the Wise presumed authority to ban the preaching of papal indulgences within his borders.

Princes preserved the loyalty of great families in part by promising them honorable positions in the church for their younger sons and daughters, as bishops, or as abbots or abbesses of religious houses. Territorial treasuries also had some benefit from revenues that could be extracted from ecclesiastical foundations, despite their claims to immunity from taxation. Since state interests of this kind collided with the papacy's claims to control both the taxation of church wealth and appointments to high positions, governments had to ward off unwanted interference from Rome. Late medieval rulers did this by having friends in the Roman Curia. By about 1450, the college of cardinals had become a kind of central station for Europe's multiple lines of political conflict, as great princes obtained red hats for their own bishops, while lesser ones formed connections among the college's numerous Italian cardinals. Protestant rulers of the Reformation era would solve these problems more simply, by seizing control of church property and claiming the right of appointment for themselves.

Second, the control that every regime had over its own territory represented a fragile truce among potential foes. Town governments had great difficulty containing long-simmering feuds among their great families, and there was also social conflict between the body of great families, who saw themselves as naturally suited to govern, and commoners who did not see their interests being served through rule by the self-styled better sort of people. Kings depended on their nobles to command their armies and staff certain administrative posts, but nobles knew their ancestors had been virtual princes in their family lands and could easily be mobilized to rebellion against the crown, with the backing of their kinsmen who occupied high positions in the church. Towns built and maintained their own defensive walls and had citizen militias to defend the walls against the ruler himself if he infringed on their privileges. These powerful groups—the nobles, the high church officials, and the towns—each had a voice in the representative assemblies or parliaments that were common throughout Latin Christendom. Fortunate was the prince who mobilized the three estates (as they were called) behind his policies, especially since new taxes required the approval of such representative bodies. Unfortunate was the prince against whom the three estates raised a common standard of revolt. In the Reformation era these internal conflicts were overlaid with new religious differences, making new enemies or leading traditional foes to fight one another with real appetite.

Third, every regime had external enemies, usually not very far away. To a monarch nothing was more important than his own honor or esteem; a ruler whose neighbors believed they could injure him with impunity afforded his subjects little protection. Hence, a young prince who did not go to war in the early years of his reign was thought peculiar and might even begin losing the respect of powerful subjects. The prince's councillors, many trained in the law, had no trouble pointing to nearby territories of which their master's ancestors had been wrongfully deprived. Towns of any size had well-defined economic interests putting them at odds with their neighbors; it was not uncommon even for towns subject to the same prince to fight their own miniwars for control of markets or access to the sea. Hence the wisdom of the ancient Roman maxim, "Divide and conquer." To weaken an enemy territory, one offered bribes and suitable promises to powerful men who hated the current regime. Cross-border conflicts were always entangled with internal rivalries in each of the warring states. The complicating factor of sixteenth- and early seventeenth-century warfare was that invading armies of a given religious persuasion also counted on the support of beleaguered coreligionists within the borders of an enemy territory where a rival creed held sway.

This section of the book illustrates the Reformation era entanglement of politics and religion, each influencing the other. Chapter 8, "The Wars of Italy, 1494–1559," reviews the primary nexus of conflicts bequeathed by late medieval rulers to their sixteenth-century successors. This inherited pattern of warfare explains why Charles V, the ardently Catholic emperor, could only devote part of his time and resources to settling accounts with Protestant Germany's Schmalkaldic League. Chapter 9, "Wars of Religion, 1562–1648," focuses on a series of wars fought by the fervently Catholic Habsburgs of later generations. Here one sees the impact of religion on politics, because the Habsburgs' Protestant foes, backed at crucial moments by anti-Habsburg Catholic powers, were able to prevent Europe from coming under the hegemony of a single dynasty. Chapter 10, "The European Reformations," examines the impact of politics on religion through government-sponsored reformations in Scandinavia, the Dutch Republic, Habsburg Austria, and the Commonwealth of Poland-Lithuania. The complex story of England's many rulers and many Reformations requires separate discussion (chapter 11).

8 | Politics

The Wars of Italy, 1494–1559

To understand the network of conflicts that Charles V inherited from his late medieval forebears, it will be helpful to start by glancing at six major players: the Italian states, the Ottoman Empire, Spain, France, the Holy Roman Empire, and the Low Countries.

Italy was Europe's teacher in many respects; the art of the Renaissance was but one (fig. 8.1). But it was not unified as a nation until 1870. There were not nearly as many separate states in 1450 as in 1250, since larger territories had gobbled up smaller ones until there were only five major powers: the Duchy of Milan; the Republic of Venice; Florence; the Kingdom of Naples, which from 1453 also included Sicily; and the Papal States. These five signed a treaty (1454) implicitly recognizing a balance of power: further aggrandizement by any one would be resisted by the others. But during the forty years of relative peace that ensued, wealthy Italy invited the envious gaze of those Transalpine kingdoms, which Italians liked to call "barbarian." From 1494, Italy became the preferred battleground for contests between Europe's great powers.

Italy's Lombard plain—the valley of the Po River—was thickly dotted with flourishing cities and famous for its highly developed agriculture, tracing back to monasteries that drained marshes and enterprising noble landowners who pioneered in introducing new crops. The Duchy of Milan was Lombardy's most important state. Milan's political evolution was typical for cities in north and central Italy. Burghers formed a self-governing commune during the eleventh century, but the communal government was never strong enough to suppress violent feuding among the great families. By the end of the thirteenth century, burghers accepted rule by a single dominant family as a means of restoring order. The family of city-lords that controlled Milan from 1313 to 1451 conquered or annexed other cities far and wide, until their ambition was checked by Venice (see below). The new

127

Figure 8.1. The Christ of late Renaissance art. Titian (ca. 1488–1576), "The Temptation of Christ" (cf. Matt. 4:4). *The Minneapolis Institute of Arts, the William Hood Dunwoody Fund.*

Sforza dynasty (1454–1498) was more modest in its aims. After 1494, rich and compact Milan would be the favored target of foreign invaders.

By tradition, Venice—built on islands in an Adriatic lagoon—limited her ambitions to the sea. She rose to commercial dominance in the eastern Mediterranean first by supplying the Byzantine empire with badly needed naval power, then by fighting off a century-long challenge from Genoa, Italy's other great maritime power. But Milan's expansion toward the Adriatic during the fifteenth century caused Venetians to realize that the republic's small strip of mainland territory did not provide adequate protection. With their characteristic energy, Venetian statesmen built up the needed infrastructure for land warfare, hired the best mercenary generals, and conquered a large swath of northeastern Italy. Unlike the restive subject towns of other Italian states, like Milan, Venice's mainland cities were ruled with moderation and fortified by the latest military technology. Venice was without doubt Italy's best-governed state and most formidable power, on land as at sea. This made her dangerous to foreign invaders but untrustworthy to all other Italian states.

Florence, proud of its communal traditions, resisted longer than other cities the transition to rule by a single family. In the century following the beginning of Medici rule in 1434, citizen revolts re-created the communal republic from 1494 to 1512 and again from 1527 to 1530. The Medici finally secured their authority through alliance with Habsburg Spain, now Italy's dominant power (see below).

In Naples, the kingdom's fractious nobility was strong enough over the centuries to curtail the independence of quasi-autonomous cities and to prevent the crown from undertaking any unwanted administrative streamlining, while dominating the rural economy in ways that left peasant cultivators few incentives for improvement. Naples was the largest and most populous of Italy's great states, but in time of war no one could predict whether its nobles would rally to the king or to his enemy. The strong governance of Charles V's viceroy, Pedro Alvarez de Toledo (1532–1553), brought the nobility to accept Spanish rule, but did not diminish their control of the countryside and the towns.

The Papal States were unified more in name than in fact. Anarchy reigned following the Avignon papacy and the papal schism (1304–1414), forcing popes to devote their energies to squalid wars against bandit chieftains. Finally, Pope Julius II (r. 1503–1513) donned armor himself and led his troops to some important victories. This violated canon law—no priest was to shed blood in battle, much less Christian blood—but by handing his conquests over to papal officials, not to his own relatives, Julius enabled his successors to have their hands free for other matters.

The Ottoman Empire. The first Ottoman sultans were chieftains of a Turkish band influenced by the Islamic warrior ideal of battling infidels on the frontier. Starting from a base in northwestern Asia Minor, the Ottomans were making conquests in Europe's Balkan Peninsula by the fourteenth century. Their capture of Constantinople and the remnants of the Byzantine Empire (1453) created a unified domain stretching from central Asia Minor deep into the Balkans. Land taxes supported a formidable military machine: Janissaries (footsoldiers), who were taken as boys from Christian villages and raised to be Islamic warriors (fig. 8.2), and the mounted Turkish archers whose rapid wheeling tactics long baffled Christian armies. Ottoman rule also provided the justice that stable government requires; many Christian peasants in the Balkans found the taxes demanded by their new Turkish masters more predictable and hence more tolerable than the arbitrary exactions of their erstwhile Christian lords.

Figure 8.2. Sketch of a Janissary. Sketch of a Janissary by the Venetian artist Giovanni Bellini, who visited Istanbul during the reign of Sultan Mehmed II (1451–1481). © *Copyright of The Trustees of the British Museum.*

The early years of the sixteenth century witnessed a series of triumphs that made Ottoman arms seem invincible. The Asia Minor frontier was extended far to the east when the armies of Iran's new Safavid dynasty were crushed in 1514. Egypt's Mamluk Sultanate collapsed in a single battle (1517), giving the Ottomans control of the North African coast as far west as what is now Tunisia. Great Christian citadels on the island of Rhodes and in Belgrade, capital of what remained of the Orthodox Christian kingdom of Serbia, fell soon thereafter (1521–1522). In 1526 Hungary's army was destroyed and its rash young king killed in battle against a vastly larger Ottoman force at Mohács, south of Budapest. Sultan Suleyman the Lawgiver (r. 1520–1566) was young, vigorous, and intelligent. What would be his next conquest? This was Christian Europe's nightmare.

Spain's two separate kingdoms, Castile and Aragon, were not amalgamated by the marriage of Isabella of Castile and Ferdinand of Aragon (1476). Each kingdom, hitherto torn by its own civil war, welcomed the peace this marriage brought. Hence, the parliaments, or *cortes,* in both realms willingly endorsed most of the new measures proposed by Spain's "Catholic Kings," as Ferdinand and Isabella styled themselves. Isabella (d. 1504) tackled Castile's internal affairs with uncommon energy. She reformed the religious orders by backing the efforts of her confessor to make Castilian houses join the observant branch of their respective congregations. She reformed judicial and financial administration by excluding the great nobles from posts they traditionally occupied and replacing them with university-trained lawyers from burgher or lesser noble families. With the consent of Castile's *cortes,* she also required each village to provide a proportional number of able-bodied men for repressing banditry.

Ferdinand (d. 1516) found a military use for Isabella's recruitment system: Granada, last of the Islamic principalities that had once encompassed most of the Iberian Peninsula, was conquered in 1492. Ferdinand next turned his ambitions to Naples, ruled by a cousin who represented the illegitimate branch of his family. Meanwhile, his military advisers designed and devised training exercises for new infantry units that combined new-style firearms (the arquebus) with tactical methods recommended in Roman military manuals. Spain's fighting men would prove their mettle in Italy, first in Ferdinand's time, then under his grandson, Charles V.

France became a different kind of kingdom in the course of its eventual victory in the Hundred Years' War (1337–1453), a struggle with England that dominated European politics of the era. As with other monarchs in Europe, earlier French kings needed the approval of their estates or representative assemblies to introduce and maintain new forms of taxation. But during the last stages of the war, the Estates General made grants of taxation without attaching the usual three-year time limit. It may be that the assembled deputies simply wanted their king to end the dreary years of war by whatever means necessary, but no reason for this novelty is given in the documents. The provincial estates still had to be consulted on some issues, but France's king henceforth had what no other European prince had—the freedom to levy taxes and even raise the rates at will. King Charles VII (r. 1422–1461) used the opportunity to create so-called companies of ordinance, a permanent or standing army, the first in Europe since the collapse of the Roman Empire; in peacetime units were garrisoned in the towns.

Charles VII's son Louis XI (r. 1461–1483) displayed a new and exalted understanding of royal authority. He was not merely the overlord of his vassals, France's great nobles, he also was their sovereign, a Roman law term denoting the source of all lawful authority. Instead of socializing with his nobles, as was customary, Louis preferred the company of honest burghers, loyal to the crown. The great vassals rose in rebellion under the leadership of Duke Charles the Bold of Burgundy (r. 1467–1477), a prince of the royal blood whose family now controlled most of the Low Countries (see below). But Louis XI used the companies of ordinance to quell the revolt. When the same Charles of Burgundy aimed at building a powerful kingdom along France's eastern border, Louis used royal tax revenues to pay the Swiss pikemen who brought Charles's dreams to a dismal end.

Louis XI's son Charles VIII (r. 1483–1498) inherited the throne as a boy, and as he grew to manhood the court was abuzz with plans for France's greater glory. Seasoned commanders pointed to nearby provinces that might be incorporated within the kingdom without much risk, but the young and inexperienced king had grander ideas: the royal family had recently inherited a claim to the Kingdom of Naples, a thousand miles beyond France's borders. In 1494 Charles VIII marched across the Alps at the head of 30,000 men, including the companies of France's standing army and a large contingent of Swiss and German mercenaries.

Foremost among the rulers of the *Holy Roman Empire*'s approximately 3,000 separate jurisdictions were the princes of the empire, especially the seven princes who had the right to elect the emperor. Four of the electors were lay princes, and three were from the ranks of the prince-bishops. Far more numerous were smaller territories, mostly in south Germany, that had purchased from the emperor grants of immunity freeing them from the authority of one of the princes and submitting them instead to a merely nominal control by the emperor himself. There were eighty free imperial cities, including many once ruled by their prince-bishops; over a thousand free imperial knights reigning over postage-stamp territories; and a few communities of free imperial peasants.

The emperor could not overcome this multiplicity of jurisdictions, because his effective authority was limited to the lands in which he was also the hereditary prince. Emperor Frederick III (r. 1440–1493) rarely set foot outside his Habsburg family's Austrian duchies. To make up for the lack of imperial leadership, late medieval towns and princes had formed regional federations among themselves, but only two of these survived into the sixteenth century: the Hanseatic League, a powerful association of merchant cities in north Germany, and the Swabian League, a union of princes and free cities in southwestern Germany.

The imperial diet, dating from the fourteenth century, provided the only forum for a national discussion of Germany's problems. Imperial princes attended in person or sent representatives, as did the magistrates of south Germany's more important free imperial cities. One issue the diets discussed was the lack of public order. Since there was no national judicial framework for settling quarrels, princes, knights, and towns regularly resorted to arms instead. Merchants crossing the borders of Germany's many territories with their goods were liable to encounter robber barons exacting what they called tolls or bandits who made off with the merchandise altogether.

From about 1450, there was talk of addressing this problem through a diet-sponsored "reformation" of imperial government. The plan involved a court to which Germany's princes and towns would be obliged to take their differences, a small standing army to enforce the court's verdicts, and an empire-wide tax (the first ever) to pay the troops. Frederick III was not enthusiastic about seeing the diet increase its authority in this way. But in his first year as emperor, Frederick's son and successor, Maximilian I (1493–1519), struck a bargain with leaders of the diet: He approved the imperial reform plan, and the diet in return granted him money for a military expedition across the Alps to punish Venice for encroaching on Habsburg land. As it turned out, Maximilian failed to capture the city in Venetian territory he besieged, and imperial reform did not fare much better. The diet duly created an Imperial High Court and approved a Common Penny tax, but the Swiss Confederation refused to pay; the troops sent by the diet to make the Swiss change their minds met an ignominious defeat (1499). This did not bode well for compliance with the tax nor for the prestige of the new court. For Germans of Luther's generation, imperial reform was one more "reformation" that fell short of its promises.

For much of the Middle Ages, the *Low Countries* (Nether-Lands) was a purely geographical expression, denoting the low-lying lands formed by the North Sea deltas of the Rhine, Meuse, and Scheldt Rivers. Some of the principalities to be found here were mainly French speaking, but the most important were three Netherlandish-speaking territories with large urban populations: the county of Flanders, including the great cities of Ghent and Bruges; the duchy of Brabant, with Antwerp (fig. 8.3) and Brussels; and the county of Holland, with numerous smaller cities, such as Amsterdam, that only became important in later centuries. Set in an area where major trade routes converged, the Low Countries harbored northern Europe's greatest wool-manufacturing centers (Ghent and Bruges) and its main banking and mercantile hub (Bruges in the fourteenth century, Antwerp in the fifteenth and sixteenth centuries). Peasant cultivators in this market-oriented region developed new farming techniques that increased grain yields dramatically. It remained for the dukes of Burgundy to create a unifying political framework for these enterprising provinces.

Duke Philip the Bold (d. 1404), the first of his line, ruled the French province of Burgundy as the younger brother of King Charles V (d. 1380). By marrying the daughter and sole heiress of the count of Flanders, he put himself in position to arrange further marriages that ultimately brought

Figure 8.3. Antwerp, world entrepôt. Engraving of Antwerp, Dutch School, 1598, private collection. Note the Spanish fort (built in 1567) and the ocean-going ships on the Scheldt. After 1585, with Dutch rebels controlling the mouth of the river, Antwerp's harbor was less busy than before. *Bridgeman Art Library.*

most of the Low Countries provinces, including Brabant and Holland, under Burgundian rule. His son and grandson played key roles in the long war between England and France, first as allies of England, then in the final stages as an ally of their royal cousin, the king of France. The Burgundian rulers kept a lavish court in Brussels, engaging the talents of some extraordinary regional artists and using their tax revenues to fund magnificent pageants that glorified the chivalric values of the European aristocracy. Young Low Countries noblemen connected with the court were reared in a culture that prized above all things the honor that was gained by having vengeance against one's enemies and also by making war in distant lands against the foes of Christendom.

The grandest of Burgundian dreams were those of Duke Charles the Bold (r. 1467–1477), last of his family in the direct male line. Charles overrode the deep-rooted political separatism of his lands and squeezed their wealth in order to finance plans for a new kingdom in the western borderlands of the Holy Roman Empire, between his Low Countries provinces and Switzerland. Twice defeated by the Swiss, he perished in a foolish assault on the fortified city of Nancy in Lorraine (1477). Louis XI took the opportunity to repossess the duchy of Burgundy, a rich prize.

Mary of Burgundy, Charles the Bold's daughter and heiress, chose as her husband and protector Maximilian of Habsburg, the future Emperor Maximilian I. When Mary died in a fall from her horse a few years later (1482), Maximilian had to weather some very difficult years in dealing with provinces that rejected the centralizing machinery put in place by Charles the Bold and resented being ruled by a foreigner. The Habsburg dynasty survived here only because Maximilian's son and grandson were accepted as "natural" princes, that is, born in the country. Archduke Philip died relatively young (1506), but his wife Juana of Castile (daughter of Ferdinand and Isabella) had given birth to a son in Ghent in 1500. This boy, christened Charles, would in manhood bring together the imperial title of his paternal grandfather, Maximilian of Habsburg; the Spanish lands of his maternal grandparents, Ferdinand and Isabella; and the Burgundian dreams of his great-grandfather and namesake, Charles the Bold.

During the campaigning season of 1494, France's Charles VIII led a magnificent army through Italy toward Naples. A force of 30,000 men had not been seen in the peninsula for centuries, and France's innovative military engineers had in their train siege cannon that cracked open strongly walled fortresses one after another. As Florence's Medici ruler went out to meet in person the king whose passage he dared not oppose, his pro-French subjects rebelled, creating the Second Florentine Republic (1494–1512). In Naples the king's armies melted away, allowing Charles to be crowned as king. But even France's treasury did not permit an army on the march to be paid and fed for months at a time, and Charles had not reckoned on the malarial fevers of the southern kingdom's marshy lands. As his men sickened or deserted, Charles ordered a withdrawal, but it was too late to preserve his prestige. States that had hailed his southward march sniped at his northward retreat, and the troops he left behind could not hold Naples for France. Some at the French court were sobered by this great waste of treasure and blood. But dreams of glory do not die so easily.

Upon the death of the childless Charles VIII, the throne passed to his cousin, the duke of Orléans, who became king as Louis XII (r. 1498–1515). Louis immediately focused on the duchy of Milan, to which his branch of the French royal family nurtured a claim tracing back more than a century. French armies repeated their initial victories of four years earlier, so quickly that Louis entered upon a further campaign, to make good his predecessor's claim to Naples. Ferdinand of Aragon had made Louis an offer he could not refuse: the two monarchs would jointly conquer Naples and divide it between them. But Ferdinand gave his remodeled army orders to attack not the armies of Naples, whose loyalty to their own king was doubtful in any case, but the unsuspecting French. Their success left Spain in control of the kingdom of Naples, while France held Milan.

What historians have dubbed the Wars of Italy (1494–1559) were just beginning. Like the great-power conflicts of more recent times, including the Cold War, the Italian wars drew states great and small into a single vortex of rivalry. Pope Julius II, hoping to end Venetian occupation of what had been a part of the Papal States, made an alliance with France (1508–1509). Emperor Maximilian I, having an eye on certain other lands held by Venice, joined the anti-Venetian coalition, setting aside for the moment his long-standing grievances against France. Hard-pressed, republican Venice survived, but she was forced to disgorge some of her recent conquests in separate treaties with the coalition partners. Julius then recruited Venice and Spain for a campaign against the French in Milan, promoted in Italy as a war to drive out the "barbarians" and in the rest of Europe as a Holy League to free the pope from French domination (1511–1512). England's young Henry VIII (r. 1509–1547), eager for a good war, agreed with Ferdinand of Aragon on a joint invasion of southern France. But Ferdinand had other plans. While French troops in the region were kept busy watching the English encampment, Spanish forces occupied the Spanish portion of the hitherto independent kingdom of Navarre. In Italy, French forces won signal victories in Lombardy but were driven from Milan following defeat by Swiss troops fighting under the papal banner (1513). Meanwhile, Spanish troops had restored Medici rule in Florence (1512) and now controlled the vital port of Genoa as well. Milan itself was not in Spanish hands since Ferdinand's Italian allies insisted on its being restored to the Sforza. Still, Spain was becoming the dominant power in the north of Italy as well as the south.

A new French king meant a new cycle of war. Francis I (r. 1515–1547; fig. 8.4) regained Milan through a brilliant victory at Marignano (1515), in which many of the Swiss units, won over by French gold, changed sides at the last minute. But in Brussels Archduke Charles, soon to be France's great enemy, was just now reaching manhood. Following the death of his maternal grandfather Ferdinand (1516), Charles entrusted the regency of the Low Countries to his aunt, Margaret of Austria (d. 1530), and sailed to Spain, where he was recognized by the separate parliaments of each realm as king of Castile and king of Aragon (1517). The Holy Roman Empire was not a hereditary monarchy. Upon the death of Charles's paternal grandfather, Emperor Maximilian I (1519), Francis I of France announced his candidacy for the imperial throne. Charles, backed by loans from south Germany's great banking families, had to outbid Francis in buying the votes of the seven electoral princes. In Castile and Aragon there were rumbles of

Figure 8.4. King Francis I of France (r. 1515–1547). Jean Clouet (1485/90–1540/41), "Francis I." *Réunion des Musées Nationaux/Art Resource, NY.*

trouble over the free-spending ways of the office-hungry courtiers whom Charles had brought with him from the Low Countries. Leaving his subordinates behind to deal with major revolts in both Spanish kingdoms, Charles sailed to the Low Countries and made his way to the German city of Aachen, near Cologne, for his solemn recognition as Emperor-elect Charles V. His coronation as emperor by the pope would have to wait. Since Charles had decided to reside in Spain, the richest of his realms, he delegated control of Habsburg Austria to his younger brother Ferdinand (r. 1521–1564), who was also to represent him in the affairs of the empire. This was the origin of the later division between the Spanish and the Austrian branches of the house of Habsburg.

Having secured his multiple inheritances, Charles was ready for his contest with Francis I. The Habsburg-Valois rivalry was more than a series of battles over territory. French diplomats saw France itself as beset on three sides by Habsburg might—the Low Countries in the north, the empire in the east, and the Pyrenees mountain frontier with Spain in the south. By maintaining a foothold in Italy, France could break out of this encirclement and also serve the larger interests of Christian Europe by preventing its domination by a single power. From Charles's point of view, the interest of Christian Europe lay in having stronger defenses against Ottoman Turkish expansion; he himself was the natural leader in this great cause, but he was prevented from giving it his full attention because the perfidious French refused to accept Charles's control of lands of which he was the lawful overlord.

Charles was as eager as other young rulers to prove himself in combat, but he could only reach the Italian theater of war by crossing seas controlled by his enemies. North African corsairs patrolled the western Mediterranean and raided coastal settlements in Charles's kingdoms of Naples and Aragon. The chief Christian naval power in the area was Genoa, which had cast off Spanish rule and was now allied with the French. Hence, Charles remained in Spain, depending on the German mercenaries whose passage across the Alps was arranged by his brother Ferdinand. The seasoned Spanish commanders and pro-Habsburg Italian princes who led Charles's forces in Italy served him well. On 24 February 1525, the emperor's birthday, a multinational Habsburg army overwhelmed the French at Pavia, near Milan; 8,000 French were killed, and King Francis I, taken prisoner, was sent off to captivity in Spain. In long and courteous discussions with his royal captive, Charles extracted the fruits of victory. In the Treaty of Madrid (1526) Francis I promised to restore to Charles the duchy of Burgundy, the country of his ancestors.

In fact, in an age of growing regional and national patriotisms, no French king could give away Burgundy and keep his throne—especially after Burgundy's estates refused to accept the treaty that would have severed their province from France. Moreover, Francis's repudiation of a treaty he claimed he had signed under duress met with a sympathetic reaction in many quarters. In Italy, even if Charles again restored Milan to the Sforza, Spanish regulars garrisoned key citadels of the duchy, within easy reach of a number of other states. On the wider European stage, after the defeat and death of Hungary's king at Mohács (1526), Ferdinand of Habsburg, the king's brother-in-law, moved in to claim the kingdom of Bohemia and what he could of the kingdom of Hungary. Hence, Charles and his family now seemed dangerously close to a hegemony that made other powers nervous. Little realizing that France was already conducting secret discussions with the Ottomans for military collaboration against the Habsburgs, Pope Clement VII signed a secret treaty of alliance with Francis I (1526).

In 1527, Genoa's fleet ferried a large French army to Naples; by prearrangement (as Habsburg diplomats rightly suspected), Naples's defense forces had been drawn off elsewhere by the attacks of North African corsairs. Quick French victories in Naples threatened to overturn Habsburg power in Italy altogether. But one of Charles's Neapolitan commanders saved the day by reporting that Andrea Doria, Genoa's leading admiral, was unhappy with his treatment by the French. Suitable overtures brought a change of allegiance. Doria's fleet ferried Spanish troops to Naples, where they began pushing out the French. Doria himself, the era's greatest naval strategist, became one of Charles's key advisers.

Meanwhile, some 10,000 German mercenaries, again sent by Ferdinand, were marching across the Alps. But since Charles's credit with his Genoese bankers was overextended, money to pay the troops was not forthcoming, and, as mercenaries often did if not paid, they jumped the traces. They became not so much an army as an angry, ill-disciplined rabble storming through Italy. Since many of the Germans were Protestants (if not the Spaniards, who had joined them from garrisons in Lombardy), they had no trouble choosing one among the emperor's enemies on whom to wreak their fury: papal Rome. The best that Charles's viceroy of Naples could do was to help Pope Clement VII himself escape from his fortified castle of Sant'Angelo. Rome itself was less fortunate: thousands of civilians were slaughtered, untold women were raped, and many of the city's churches were plundered and desecrated. At first, Charles's advisers and pamphlet writers tried to claim credit for this vindication of the emperor's position as head of the Christian world at the expense of a perfidious pope. Only as the horror of the Sack of Rome (May 1527) became more widely known did they switch to arguing that the emperor himself was not responsible for what had happened.

With the protection afforded by Doria's fleet, Charles was able to bring an army to Italy himself, intending to push across the Alps into France. But France now agreed to a treaty (1529) accepting the status quo in Italy. Since another of Charles's goals was reconciliation with Pope Clement VII, a member of the Medici family, he used his army to besiege Florence, which had again rebelled against the Medici and created a republic (1527–1530). Even before Florence was conquered, he arranged to have himself crowned by the pope as Holy Roman Emperor. The ceremony, preceded by talks between pope and emperor, took place in Bologna (November 1529–April 1530), because Charles was en route to Germany. Pope and emperor agreed that the rage visited on Rome by German mercenaries a few years before was but a token of the evils that might be expected if heresy continued to spread unchecked. Clement demanded that Charles combat heresy by any means necessary, including the force of arms. Charles demanded that Clement combat heresy by convoking a council to reform the Catholic Church, but he suspected (rightly) that Clement was too fearful for his own authority to risk a council. Might Charles have to arrange a religious settlement in Germany on his own authority, as some of his advisers suggested? Or could he trust that France would keep the recently concluded peace treaty, permitting him, if need be, to deal with his heretical subjects by sterner means? In this uncertain frame of mind, Charles crossed the Alps, en route to the Diet of Augsburg.

In Germany Charles faced a host of problems. Most worrisome was the security of the empire's southeastern frontier. At Vienna (1529), a massive siege army led by Sultan Suleyman himself had been held off only because a relief garrison force approved by the imperial diet (Protestants as well as Catholics) arrived in the nick of time. To this Turkish provocation there had to be a Christian and imperial response, the sooner the better. Meanwhile, Ferdinand had been complaining that he had no respect among Germany's princes. His solution—to which Charles assented—was to have the electoral princes elect him as King of the Romans, a title borne by the emperor's designated successor. Not surprisingly, it was the leading Protestant princes— Philip of Hesse and Elector John of Saxony—who objected most loudly to this presumption of a Habsburg family claim to the imperial office. Thus Charles needed Protestant cooperation both to have his brother elevated to a new dignity and to build an army to send against the Ottomans. In these circumstances, the fact that Hesse and Saxony were forming what they claimed was a purely defensive alliance (the Schmalkaldic League), though worrisome, was of lesser concern.

Ferdinand was recognized as King of the Romans, even by Saxony and Hesse. In 1532, as Suleyman led perhaps 100,000 men up the Danube valley toward Vienna, some 80,000 imperial troops boarded a war flotilla on the Danube at Regensburg, headed for Austria's capital. Charles's participation in this campaign was minimal, and he turned his face homeward as soon as the withdrawal of the Turkish army made it decent for him to do so. The emperor wanted Ferdinand to negotiate a truce with the Ottomans, rather than incurring the risk of war along this perilous eastern frontier. Charles had great difficulty deploying his resources as far away as Vienna, but he was not shirking his duty as Christendom's defender; rather, as he wrote to Ferdinand, he would do his crusading at sea.

In response to a Habsburg naval assault on Ottoman Greece, Sultan Suleyman commissioned Khair-ad-din Barbarossa, a former corsair, as admiral of the Ottoman fleet. In 1534, Barbarossa, with seventy galleys, unchallenged by Doria's twenty, raided at will along the coasts of Sicily and Naples, then seized Tunis in North Africa as a base for further operations. With Doria as his strategist, Charles devoted the better part of a year to supervising preparations for a massive onslaught on Barbarossa's new headquarters. Meanwhile, a Schmalkaldic League army paid for by France conquered the southwest German duchy of Württemberg, hitherto a Habsburg-administered territory; this was troublesome, but France—the root of the problem—could be dealt with later. The huge armada that sailed against Tunis (1535) won a great victory, perhaps the greatest of Charles's military career. Prints and tapestries showing the crusading emperor taking counsel with his commanders before Tunis were produced in the Low Countries for wide distribution. This was how Charles wanted to be remembered.

It was now time to deal with France. Charles sailed for Italy, raised an army, and pushed across the Alps into Provence (1536). But the careful defenses arranged by Anne de Montmorency, Constable of France, left the imperial army with no choice but an ignominious retreat. For the next two years fighting on various fronts alternated with negotiations, until another peace was concluded (1538). But even as he finally turned his attention to Germany (1539), the emperor was still preoccupied by Muslim corsairs—especially Barbarossa, whose fleet was now based at Algiers. If the theological negotiations recommended by his "soft hand" advisers could solve Charles's problems in Germany, he would be able to deploy his resources for a second great maritime crusade, this time against Algiers. Hence, while Charles kept an ear closely tuned to the doctrinal discussions at the Diet of Regensburg (1541), he was also dictating long missives to Spain full of instructions on topics like providing biscuit for soldiers on board the war galleys. In the end, this dual-track strategy was another of Charles's failures. The conferees at Regensburg did not agree, and since Charles insisted on staying almost to the end, his travels were one of many circumstances that contributed to postponing the armada's departure to a dangerously late date (17 October). A few days after his men had disembarked near Algiers, galleys were smashed and supplies sunk by a fierce and premature winter storm. The campaign was over before it had begun.

Following upon this great blow to his prestige, the next year (1542) was an evil time for Charles. Barbarossa's galleys, openly welcomed for the first time in France's Mediterranean harbors, imperiled the sea link between Spain and Italy. Mary of Hungary, Charles's sister and regent of the Low Countries, had reliable information that two armies were preparing to invade, one from France, another from a formerly Habsburg Rhineland territory that the duke of Cleves had occupied with French help. Preoccupied by dangers along the Pyrenees front, Charles could only tell his sister to withstand the shock of invasion as best she could. In fact, this capable woman, who ordered her commanders about like a seasoned campaigner, turned back both enemy forces. Meanwhile, the Schmalkaldic League occupied Brunswick, a duchy whose staunchly Catholic ruler was threatening to punish towns that claimed to be independent of his jurisdiction and had introduced the Reformation. The league now discussed extending membership to the same duke of Cleves who had occupied part of the Low Countries with French help. This encroachment by the league on his hereditary lands Charles could not tolerate. When he assembled an army in the Low Countries in 1543, the duke of Cleves was his first target.

Charles quickly overran Cleves, forcing the duke to disgorge the Low Countries province he had conquered and renounce his hopes of joining the Schmalkaldic League. From his base in the Rhineland, the emperor marched into France the next spring. A French army followed him along the opposite bank of the Marne River but did not offer battle; instead France proposed negotiations that resulted in the Treaty of Crespy. France made no cession of territory, and observers wondered why an emperor with an army pointed at Paris had not insisted on more. Money was part of the answer, since Charles had barely enough to pay his mercenary soldiers their "going home" fee. But there were also secret clauses reflecting a new focus by Charles on German affairs. This was the treaty in which Francis I promised to break off his contacts with the Schmalkaldic League and to allow French bishops to attend an ecumenical council convened by the pope.

In Germany, there was friction between the Schmalkaldic League's two leaders, because of Philip's bigamous marriage to a young noblewoman attendant on his lawful wife, who was John Frederick of Saxony's second cousin. Charles's diplomats prepared for war by massaging the interests of other princes. The league counted on tacit support from the Catholic Duke William of Bavaria, known for his long-standing quarrel with the house of Austria. But William was won over by a promise of marriage between his son Albert and Ferdinand's daughter Anna. Duke Moritz of Saxony was a Lutheran, but Charles knew that he coveted the electoral title of his cousin, John Frederick. Secret agreements served the emperor well. When it was clear that war was coming, but before Charles had gathered his forces, the league passed up an opportunity to strike at a still vulnerable emperor for fear of offending the duke of Bavaria by sending an army across his lands. Once hostilities were joined Charles did not have to invade Electoral Saxony—the job was done for him by Duke Moritz, who waited until after his cousin had marched south for what he thought was their common struggle against the emperor. It remained for Charles and his chief commander, the duke of Alba, to pursue and defeat John Frederick's retreating forces near the Saxon town of Mühlberg in April 1547 (fig. 8.5). John Frederick was captured; Philip of Hesse soon surrendered.

Charles was better at winning a victory than at exploiting it wisely. He was right to think that most of the league's member cities and territories would sue for terms once the two leaders were in his custody, but some (like Magdeburg) stubbornly continued to resist. Familiar Catholic ceremonies were duly reintroduced, as prescribed by the Augsburg Interim of 1548, but evoked real hostility. Charles could not comprehend the force of such specifically Protestant religious convictions. Moreover, he overestimated the strength of his position. First, he declared that his son Philip would follow Ferdinand as emperor, not Ferdinand's own son Maximilian, so that the two branches of the Habsburg family would have the imperial title by turns. This deeply offended Ferdinand and Maximilian and also the imperial princes, for whom the popular Maximilian was a fellow German and Philip (who spoke only Spanish) a foreigner. Next, Charles alienated Moritz by deciding that some of his promises to Saxony's new elector did not have to be kept. Some Lutheran princes were trying to revive the Schmalkaldic League as a defensive alliance. Moritz, secretly joining their counsels, proposed a more ambitious plan: with French help, the Augsburg Interim could be overturned. France's Henry II (r. 1547–1559) was interested but sought approval for his plan to seize three imperial cities in the border province of Lorraine—Metz, Toul, and Verdun; when the league's negotiators agreed, a treaty was signed (January 1552).

Charles V, suddenly facing armies converging against him from two directions, fled across the Alps to southern Austria. Ferdinand, now willing to act without his brother's approval, agreed to suspend the Augsburg Interim in return for Moritz's help in an attack he launched against Ottoman strongholds in Hungary. Straining all the resources of a now fragile Castilian treasury, Charles gathered funds to assemble a sizable army in southern Germany by the late summer of 1552. How was this precious force to be employed? Charles could have attacked his Schmalkaldic foes in an attempt to revive the Interim. Alternatively, he might have concentrated on Margrave Albrecht Alcibiades of Bayreuth, a rogue Protestant prince who had been terrorizing his neighbors without much regard to confessional differences. Instead, the emperor added Albrecht Alcibiades and his men to his own forces and marched against the imperial city of Metz, now held by the French. This choice revealed Charles's priorities—he really did see France as the root of Europe's problems—and it was also his last campaign. Charles's siege guns battered a breach in Metz's walls, but the duke

Figure 8.5. Emperor Charles V at Mühlberg. Titian (ca. 1488–1576) came from Venice to Augsburg in 1548 to do two portraits of the emperor, one of which was meant to show him as he might have looked after his victory over the elector of Saxony (April 1547): "Charles V as Victor at Mühlberg," 1548. *Alinari/Art Resource, NY.*

of Guise, commanding Metz's garrison, had already built an earthen rampart behind this weak spot in the city's defenses. Guise's men withstood the imperial charge, and the onset of winter storms did the rest. As his army melted away, a defeated and dispirited emperor retired to Brussels (January 1553).

Charles abdicated his hereditary lands in favor of his son Philip in January of 1556. After further fighting against France's Henry II, including a major victory in northern France (1557), Philip and the French king signed the Treaty of Cateau-Cambrésis (1559): the Habsburg dynasty was confirmed in its possessions, including Milan, while France had nothing to show for sixty-five years of intermittent warfare against Spain and the empire, except for Metz, Toul, and Verdun. Meanwhile, a settlement had already been reached in Germany. Before abdicating, Charles gave Ferdinand full responsibility for negotiating with the Schmalkaldic League. It was clear that Lutheran as well as Catholic princes would be recognized as having the right to determine the religious identity of their territories. The sticking point was how to define the status of the empire's many ecclesiastical principalities, for some had become Protestant and more were likely to follow. Reluctantly, Protestant negotiators accepted the "ecclesiastical reservation" demanded by Ferdinand: except for those who had already made a change of religion, prince-bishops or prince-abbots who became Protestant would automatically lose their position. This issue settled, the Peace of Augsburg was proclaimed in 1555.

In the end, the defeat of Charles V's ambition to reunite a religiously divided Germany reflected his failure to grasp not just the strength of Protestant religious convictions but also the polycentric character of European civilization as it had evolved over the past thousand years. Charles had only the best of motives, or so he thought. He saw Latin Christendom as a body of believers gravely threatened by Ottoman power—why did supposedly Christian powers like France prevent him from devoting his attention to this larger struggle? He was more conscientious about the business of government than most of Europe's crowned heads—who could accuse him of failing in his duties as a Christian prince? He knew better than anyone how precarious his family's hold was on each of its hereditary lands—did anyone imagine he wanted yet more territory for himself? Yet it was part of the normal duties of advisers to appraise new opportunities for the ruler and his dynasty, and it was well known that Charles had eagerly (if ultimately in vain) sought Habsburg expansion in some areas. To many observers the emperor's decision to keep Milan for himself (when the Sforza dynasty died out in 1535) seemed proof of an insatiable appetite for power. The fundamental problem was that post-Roman Europe had never seen a dynasty whose territories bestrode the continent from the

Low Countries to Sicily and from Spain to Hungary—not to mention Spain's overseas possessions. To Christendom as most people understood it, made up of independent territories that could be enemies in one war and allies in the next, the mere existence of such a colossus was deeply threatening. Charles never understood that his enemies opposed him not just because of the lands they suspected him of wanting to grab, but also because of the lands he had lawfully inherited.

9 | Politics

Wars of Religion, 1562–1648

For European statesmen of the sixteenth century, a prince's natural desire to expand his territory was a familiar motive for war. Religion was not. The practice by which major powers kept permanent ambassadors in one another's capitals had been invented by Italian states of the fifteenth century and transferred across the Alps by about 1500. An ambassador's main job was to prevent his home government from being confronted with unpleasant surprises, and there was no better guide for guessing another government's intentions than a calculation of its long-term self-interest. Hence, experienced diplomats were skilled at discerning the real interests—what Florence's Niccolo Machiavelli (d. 1527) called "reason of state"—that lurked behind a rival government's professions of good will. The assessments produced by Venice's patrician envoys, or by Machiavelli himself, are uncommonly shrewd, but also cynical. Having identified a "reason of state" for a policy or action, they treated it as the sole explanation, not allowing for the complexity of human motivation, even among princes and kings.

Hence when princes professed to go to war for the sake of religion, they were believed by loyal subjects but scoffed at by the subjects of their rivals. Each side accepted the sincerity of its professions of religious motive and treated the enemy's as sheer hypocrisy. Thus Habsburg rulers had a keen eye for the secret ambitions of their Protestant foes, while anti-Habsburg states (Catholic as well as Protestant) saw with equal clarity the dynasty's interest in absorbing new territories. The importance of reason of state in these wars was obvious enough to cause sensitive observers to feel disgust at the way great men used religion as an excuse for their quarrels. Yet religion was more than a mere excuse, because it led commanders on both sides to reject settlements that might have been accepted if reason of state were the only consideration. In the end, in Europe's civil wars of religion, militant minorities had to accept their minority status, and militant majorities often

147

had to grant their rivals not just freedom of conscience but limited freedom of worship as well. Thus the wars called "religious" were mainly about politics, but also about religion.

This chapter will consider three series of wars: France's Wars of Religion (1562–1598), the Dutch Revolt (1572–1609), and the Thirty Years' War (1618–1648), fought in Germany but involving armies and subsidies from most European powers. One common thread that links these three very different conflicts is that each involved, at least to some degree, a convergence between Habsburg power and the preservation of Catholicism. In France's religious wars, intervention by Charles V's son Philip II was important, though not decisive, in preventing the victory of a Protestant king. In the Low Countries, Philip and his successors managed to retain for the Habsburg dynasty and the Catholic religion only the southern provinces— the northern provinces became an independent nation, officially professing the "evangelical Reformed religion." During the Thirty Years' War, the descendants of Charles V's brother Ferdinand reasserted Habsburg and Catholic control of their hereditary lands (especially Austria and Bohemia), but a coalition between Catholic France and Europe's Protestant nations thwarted their ambitions to transform the loose federal structure of the Holy Roman Empire into a strong monarchy.

France's religious wars began with the premature death of King Henry II (1559). Sixteen-year-old Francis II died after barely a year, and the queen mother, Catherine de Medici (1519–1589), was not able to gain control of the regency council for nine-year-old Charles IX. This opened the door to a classic power struggle among the three great men of the kingdom: Antoine de Bourbon, the prince of the royal blood who was closest to the throne after Henry II's four sons; Anne de Montmorency, France's hereditary constable and greatest landholder; and Francis, duke of Guise, Henry II's most successful military commander. It was to be expected that the clientele of each of these party chieftains would close ranks behind their leader. What was novel in this case was that factional rivalry took on a religious coloration, owing to the fact that each of the great men had a distinct religious identity. Bourbon and most of his kinfolk were Huguenots. Guise and his brother, the cardinal of Lorraine, were partisans of Tridentine Catholicism. Montmorency, some of whose kin were Huguenots, stood for a Gallican Catholicism that prized independence from Rome.

Since no one side had the strength to defeat the others, successive wars ended in treaties allowing some freedom of worship for Huguenots, always including Huguenot nobles on their estates. In the towns, scores were settled during the wars, but also during periods of peace. In the great city of Lyon, for example, the Huguenot minority seized power just after the first war had begun (1562) and suppressed Catholic worship; when Huguenot troops were withdrawn as the first peace was proclaimed (1563), Catholics regained power and suppressed Protestant worship. But major fortified cities that remained firmly Protestant (like La Rochelle in the southwest) anchored the Huguenots' defensive position even when battlefield results were not encouraging.

After the first war Catherine de Medici sought to build a biconfessional basis of support for the crown by taking her son on a slow circuit of the kingdom (1564–1566). But the benefits of this strategy were partly negated by her meeting in the south of France with her daughter Elisabeth, wife of Spain's Philip II, who was accompanied by the duke of Alba. Huguenots suspected some great Catholic conspiracy was afoot, and these fears re-awakened when Alba marched his 10,000 men along France's borders toward the Low Countries (1567). The Prince of Condé, Bourbon's younger brother, and Gaspard de Coligny, France's hereditary admiral, organized a Huguenot plot to capture the person of young Charles IX and pry him loose from the influence of a council dominated by the Guise family. This ignited a new war, which only brought another inconclusive peace. Still another war began (1568) when the cardinal of Lorraine, encouraged by contacts with Philip II, sought to have Coligny and Condé arrested (fig. 9.1). Soon thereafter Coligny and Condé signed a treaty of mutual support with William of Orange, now a refugee from Spanish rule in the Netherlands. Each side now had its allies outside the kingdom.

By 1572, Charles IX had assumed control of the realm in his own name. Coligny, who had won his trust, argued that a war against Spain—France's natural enemy—might heal the kingdom's internal divisions. With the king's permission, Louis of Nassau, Orange's brother, crossed into the southern Netherlands at the head of a Huguenot force and seized two fortified towns (May 1572). The fact that Alba had to gather his scattered units to retake these towns gave the Sea Beggars a precious few weeks to expand their control of towns in Holland and Zeeland. In France, however, this adventure was to have a dire sequel for the Huguenots. During the month of August, Coligny and leading Huguenots were gathered in Paris for the marriage of Henri of Bourbon, Antoine's son and heir, to the king's sister, Marguerite de Valois. On 22 August 1572, Coligny was the victim of a failed assassination attempt. Historians usually point to Catherine de Medici as the culprit in this plot (she feared the consequences of another war with Spain), though some favor the duke of Guise. What matters is that as tensions mounted in Paris, with four thousand Huguenot troops camped outside the walls, the royal council, with Catherine and Charles

Sainct Iean d'Angely afsiegé par le Roy Charles 9, le 14. Octob. 1569. iufques au 2. Decembre 1569.

Figure 9.1. France's religious wars: A Royalist/Catholic siege. View of the unsuccessful Royalist/Catholic siege of a Huguenot stronghold in southern France, St. Jean d'Angely, December 1569: from A. Franklin, Les Grandes Scènes Historiques (see figure 7.4). *University of California at San Diego Library.*

IX present, determined on a preemptive strike against Coligny and other Huguenot leaders. The result, intended by no one, was the grisly massacre of St. Bartholomew's Day (24 August 1572; fig. 9.2). Thinking they were acting on the king's orders, Catholic Parisians slaughtered some two thousand Huguenots. Similar massacres in other cities claimed three thousand more victims. Reaction among Huguenots was deeply divided. Some, taking this terrible catastrophe as a sign of God's disfavor, presented themselves to the authorities for penitence and readmission to the Catholic Church. Others resumed the struggle with renewed determination and a new theory of resistance: they were fighting not just against the king's evil councillors, but also against a tyrannical monarchy that had forfeited the obedience of its subjects.

On Charles IX's death the throne passed to his brother Henry III (r. 1574–1589), but there was another brother whose ambitions were not satisfied, the duke of Anjou. In 1576 the king faced a Huguenot army strengthened by Anjou and by 20,000 German mercenaries brought from the Palatinate by John Casimir. In the ensuing peace, Huguenots were accorded

Figure 9.2. The St. Bartholomew's Day Massacre (24 August 1572). François Dubois, "The Saint Bartholomew's Day Massacre." *Musée Cantonal des Beaux-Arts, Lausanne, Switzerland.*

freedom of worship and the right to build churches everywhere in the kingdom, save in fiercely Catholic Paris. But this Huguenot victory provoked a Catholic reaction. The 1576 treaty included a clause assigning a Catholic city in the north to a Huguenot commander for safekeeping. Local nobles formed a Catholic League among the populace to resist the transfer of power, and their success in this objective led to the organization of a similar league throughout the kingdom, headed by the duke of Guise. Lest he be politically isolated, King Henry III placed himself at the head of the Catholic League; this caused many partisans to lose interest, and the league may have, for a time, ceased to exist altogether.

But in 1584 the king's younger brother died. Because Henry III sometimes dressed as a woman, and enjoyed partying with young male favorites, he was widely (though incorrectly) assumed to be a homosexual. Hence contemporaries concluded that the throne would soon pass to the Bourbon branch of the royal family, headed by the Huguenot leader, Prince Henry of Bourbon. For France's Catholic majority the implication of a Protestant sovereign was both clear and ominous—this was the era when the religion of a territory could be decided by its prince. The Catholic League was quickly reorganized with a much broader popular base, especially among urban guildsmen, and a two-point program: All treaties granting toleration to heresy were to be overturned, and Henry of Bourbon would never be France's king. In some thirty large cities, the league, supported by local notables as well as by the clergy and the guilds, formed a kind of shadow town government. This process was most visible in Paris (fig. 9.3), where a league committee known as the Sixteen gradually assumed effective control of the city.

Head of the league once more, Guise negotiated a secret treaty with Spain's ambassador to France: Philip promised to recognize the league's candidate for the French throne, an elderly uncle of Henry of Bourbon. Guise promised a hefty subsidy for Philip's war in the Netherlands. Facing the isolation he had always feared, King Henry III oscillated between Bourbon and the league. Meanwhile, the popular duke of Guise was all the more popular after his forces turned back a large Protestant army brought from the Palatinate by John Casimir (1587). The king prohibited Guise from approaching Paris, but Guise ignored the ban. His arrival triggered an uprising (May 1588): Parisians built barricades against a possible attack by royal mercenaries, and the king quietly slipped out of the capital he no longer controlled.

Henry III had his revenge when Guise obeyed a summons to attend upon the king and was cut down by his attendants. League preachers and polemicists, hitherto supportive of royal authority, now acclaimed the right of resistance, the idea that subjects of a tyrant-king had a God-given right to overthrow him, and the sooner the better. Meanwhile, Huguenot polemicists also changed their view, now asserting the duty of all to obey

Figure 9.3. A procession of the Catholic League in Paris. Anonymous, Procession of the Catholic League, departing from the Hôtel de Ville (City Hall) in 1590 or 1593; note that friars bearing arms are prominent in the throng. *Musée Carnavalet, Paris.*

France's lawful king. Henry III had no choice but to join forces with Henry of Bourbon. His assassination by a fanatical Dominican friar (August 1589) left the league facing its real enemy, the man who now called himself King Henry IV. It seemed the new monarch had inherited a crown, but not a kingdom.

In fact, Henry IV had important assets not limited to his Huguenot following. First, the rules of royal succession were seen in France as an unchangeable "fundamental law," and by these rules Henry was undoubtedly the rightful king; this counted for something in a country where legitimacy was a sacred principle. Second, a middle party had been building for some years. The so-called *politiques* ("politicals") were mainly Catholic nobles unwilling to sacrifice the peace and unity of France to the cause of religious purity. Some, led by members of the Montmorency family, had experience in keeping religiously divided parts of the kingdom at peace by observing strict parity in the distribution of offices. This faction rallied behind Henry IV, helping him to gain several victories against league armies commanded by Guise's brother, the duke of Mayenne.

By the late spring of 1590, Henry IV completed the encirclement of the great city of Paris, citadel of the league. Having made no preparations for a siege, the Sixteen turned to Spain's ambassador for help. Philip II ordered his commander, the duke of Parma (see below), to break off the fighting in the Low Countries and march to the rescue of Catholic Paris. Outmaneuvering Henry IV with a feigned attack, Parma brought relief to a starving populace. But Henry IV renewed the siege when Parma withdrew, and the defenders of Paris now faced internal problems. The only plausible alternative to Henry IV's elderly uncle had died, opening the difficult question of who should be king. Meanwhile, the league was beginning to fracture along social lines, as parish clergy and the craft guilds, acting through the Sixteen, demanded the dismissal of high-born royal officials thought to be less than resolute in their opposition to Henry IV. When Mayenne and the Spanish ambassador proposed the election of new monarchs—Mayenne's son and Philip II's daughter, to be married for this purpose—only the Sixteen showed any enthusiasm; the Parlement of Paris, bastion of royal officialdom, declared that any transfer of the crown to a foreign prince or princess would violate French law.

This was the moment (July 1593) when Henry IV abjured Calvinism and professed his Catholic belief in a ceremony at the abbey church of St. Denis, outside Paris, the burial church of France's kings. Rather than forcing his subjects to change their beliefs, the king changed his own. Skepticism among ardent partisans of the league prolonged hostilities, albeit at a lower level of intensity. It took several months to arrange Henry's triumphal entry into Paris (March 1594; fig. 9.4) and three years to subdue scattered resistance among league nobles. The fruit of his victory was the Edict of Nantes (1598), proclaimed by Henry IV and (under pressure from the king) accepted by the *parlements* as part of French law. Huguenots were guaranteed freedom of conscience throughout the kingdom and freedom of worship in all the towns they controlled as of 1597 as well as in noble households; Catholics were guaranteed freedom of worship in Huguenot towns. In a separate royal decree not submitted to the *parlements,* Henry IV pledged royal tax revenues to the support of Huguenot garrisons in roughly half of the two hundred towns the Huguenots controlled. This creation of a Huguenot "state within a state" would cause problems for later monarchs, but it was what had to be done to induce Huguenot nobles to lay down their arms.

The Edict of Nantes did not mean France had become a secular state. In the sixteenth and seventeenth centuries almost no one conceived of the idea that a state could (much less should) be indifferent to the religious practices of its citizens. Henry IV's goal in issuing the edict was the goal of

Figure 9.4. King Henry IV of France (r. 1589–1610). Anonymous equestrian portrait, showing Henry IV across the Seine River from the walls of Paris, just before his triumphal entry into the city in 1594. *Bridgman-Giraudon/Art Resource, NY.*

moderate Catholic *politiques* who supported him: France should be re-united in the Catholic faith, but over time rather than all at once, and not by force of arms.

What the settlement did mean was a revival of royal authority. At different times, both the Huguenots and the Catholic League had embraced ideas of monarchy which emphasized the rights of subjects rather than the prerogatives of the crown. The *parlements* that dragged their feet about accepting the Edict of Nantes were defending another version of the theory of limited or constitutional monarchy. *Politique* writers argued that all these theories of resistance served the factional violence that only a strong king could overcome. France needed what other theorists called "absolute" monarchy. This idea gained credibility from Henry's success in ending the terrible civil wars and also from the memory left by his reign—a time of peace, prosperity, and just government, ending only when good King Henry was assassinated by an unrepentant Catholic fanatic (1610).

From 1572 to 1576 the Dutch Revolt was confined to two small provinces, Holland and Zeeland, which were hard-pressed to match Spain's outlay of treasure and troops. William of Orange, who had been governor of both provinces under Philip II, was continued in office by the States of Holland and Zeeland, now as leader of the Revolt (fig. 9.5). Because the rebels had control of the sea, Philip II had the added expense of supplying his Netherlands army by a long overland route from northern Italy. On land, however, Spain's seasoned troops were not to be stopped—until they broke off their siege of Leiden (October 1574). Despite opposition from local farmers, Orange ordered the dikes cut far to the south; as water from the Maas estuary advanced across the fields toward Leiden, with it, in flat-bottomed boats, came the relief army that forced a Spanish withdrawal.

Then the financial problems Philip had inherited from his father came home to roost. In 1575 Castile's monarch declared a kind of bankruptcy, in which lenders were compelled to accept long-term treasury bonds at low rates of interest in lieu of the repayments they had been promised on high-interest loans. This made new loans hard to get, while soldiers in the Netherlands waited at the end of a long credit pipeline. Spain's fighting men were better disciplined than most, but they were not made of steel. In July 1576, not having seen their regular pay for nearly two years, a number of Spanish units mutinied and brutally sacked a loyalist town near Brussels. When Philip II failed to provide a remedy for this outrage, troops engaged by the States of Brabant placed members of the king's council in Brussels under arrest and Brabant summoned a meeting of the States General. While

Figure 9.5. William of Orange. Adriaen Thomasz Key, "William of Orange in his Later Years." *Rijksmuseum, Amsterdam.*

representatives from the hitherto loyal provinces deliberated in Ghent with deputies from Holland and Zeeland, the mutineers converged on Antwerp, smashed through its defenses, and went on a terrible rampage, leaving 8,000 civilians dead and 1,000 houses burned.

Within days of this "Spanish Fury," loyalist and rebel deputies concluded the Pacification of Ghent (November 1576), an agreement to expel all Spaniards from the country. The pacification recognized the religious status quo, with Calvinism as the sole authorized religion in Holland and Zeeland and Catholicism in the other provinces, but also called for an end to Habsburg antiheresy legislation. This was William of Orange's great moment. The Netherlands was united in resistance to Spanish tyranny, and religious differences were pushed into the background—or so it seemed. Orange was not able to prevent radical Calvinist minorities in great cities like Ghent and Antwerp from seizing control of town governments by force and closing the churches to all but Reformed worship. This recrudescence of intolerance did not bode well for keeping politics to the fore in the national struggle.

Spain's position was retrieved through the efforts of one man, Alessandro Farnese, duke of Parma (1545–1592), who assumed command of Philip's forces in 1578. Farnese skillfully exploited the divisions between radical Calvinists and the Catholic nobility of the French-speaking provinces, who had joined in the general rebellion against Spanish troops but could not countenance the violent suppression of Catholicism in Ghent and other cities. In 1579 rebel provinces in the north formed a union among themselves to conduct the war against Spain. The Union of Utrecht (nucleus of the later Dutch Republic) guaranteed freedom of conscience to all citizens but banned the public practice of any but the "evangelical Reformed religion," and Catholic worship was banned even in private. In response, Parma organized a counter-union among southern provinces, based on Catholicism and reconciliation with the king (Union of Arras, 1579). A brilliant strategist, Parma soon began reconquering the major towns one by one. His greatest triumph came with the capitulation of Antwerp (1585), following a siege that involved blocking the Scheldt River with a bridge of boats. Antwerp's Calvinists were given four years to decide whether to convert to Catholicism or sell their goods and move elsewhere.

Protestant powers, especially England, now feared a Spanish reconquest of all the Low Countries. The Revolt's great leader, Prince William of Orange, had been removed from the scene by a Catholic assassin's bullet (1584), and his son Maurits (1567–1625) was as yet young and untried. And could there be such a thing as a republic on the scale of the Low Countries, without any kind of prince at all? In 1585 the States General concluded a treaty agreeing to accept a governor-general sent by England's Elizabeth I. The queen's choice was Robert Dudley, earl of Leicester (1533–1588), who came with an English force meant to help stem Parma's advance. Leicester was hailed by Calvinist ministers and by religious exiles from the southern Netherlands, who hoped that a new English-dominated government would bring stricter enforcement of the laws against popish idolatry and a Reformed church free from control by the town and provincial governments. Aided by his Dutch friends, Leicester dismissed the duly elected magistrates of Utrecht and replaced them with his own supporters. This high-handed behavior plunged Leicester into what proved to be a losing contest with the "regents," or ruling elite of the towns, especially in the populous and highly urbanized province of Holland.

Just now, the regents' party gained an exceptionally able leader, Johan van Oldenbarnevelt, who would serve as chief legal adviser of the States of Holland from 1586 until 1618 (fig. 9.6). Oldenbarnevelt and the magistrates differed from Leicester and his ardent Calvinist backers on several key points. First, like William of Orange, they saw the goals of the Revolt as more political than religious. To be sure, the Reformed religion was the one and only "public church," and the magistrates punished Catholics in particular if they attempted to conduct religious services in

Figure 9.6. Johan van Oldenbarnevelt. Michiel van Miereveld, "Johan van Oldenbarnevelt," Grand Pensionary of the States of Holland, 1584–1619. *Rijksmuseum, Amsterdam.*

public. But many regents saw no harm in allowing non-Reformed Christians, Catholics included, to worship in house-churches discreetly shielded from public view. To keep overly zealous ministers from causing public disturbances on this or other issues, they kept a watchful eye on Reformed congregations in their towns. Further, since their own power base was in the towns and in the provincial States (parliaments) to which the towns sent deputies, the regents were also adamantly opposed to any kind of strong central government, such as Leicester seemed intent on creating.

Thinking that England's help was prolonging the Revolt, Philip II determined on an ill-fated effort to punish Elizabeth I for her intervention in the Low Countries. All of 1587 was devoted to preparations for a great Armada that sailed from Spain the following year; instead of engaging the enemy, Parma was ordered to keep his troops on the coast of Flanders, ready to embark on Spanish ships as they headed for England. Philip's objective was to land an expeditionary force in southeastern England and conquer territory that could be held in exchange for Elizabeth's withdrawal from the Low Countries. But as the Armada sailed into the English Channel, its tight formation was broken up by the superior gunnery of attacking English vessels. Parma's men never had a chance to embark and scattered elements of the Armada, sailing north into unfamiliar waters around Britain and Ireland, were driven against the rocks by storms. This disaster weakened Spain's prestige immeasurably; unlike his father after the calamity at Algiers (1541), Philip II (d. 1598) in his remaining years never repaired the damage by subsequent victories.

In the rebel provinces, Oldenbarnevelt and the regents' party were now firmly in control. Ardent Calvinists were aggrieved when the States of Holland adopted (1591) a church ordinance giving town governments final authority in the appointment and dismissal of pastors. Proponents of a stronger central government were disappointed that each separate province remained sovereign in determining how to raise its quota for the war budget managed by the States General. This decentralized system, a puzzle to outside observers, worked surprisingly well, especially in the financial sphere, which was one of Oldenbarnevelt's special domains. Soldiers of the rebel provinces, paid in full and more or less on time, rarely broke loose in the savage mutinies that so bedeviled the Spanish government in the Low Countries.

Oldenbarnevelt and the regents had an important partner. Maurits of Nassau (d. 1625) proved an able strategist and an innovator in military tactics. Following Parma's death (1592), he recovered many towns and secured the new state's boundary against provinces loyal to Spain with a line of new-style fortifications that resisted easy assault. As conditions stabilized in the early 1600s, observers could sense rival patriotisms developing on either side of a hardening frontier between north and south. This equilibrium was ratified when Oldenbarnevelt and the representatives of Spain's Philip III (r. 1598–1621) signed a Twelve Years' Truce (1609). At least provisionally, the Dutch Republic and the Spanish Netherlands—forerunners of the modern Netherlands and Belgium—took their places among the nations of Europe.

Philip II could draw on the wealth of highly urbanized provinces as well as a stream of silver from the Americas. The Austrian branch of the Habsburg family was rich only in its titles. Following the battle of Mohács (1526) Ferdinand claimed the crown of Bohemia as well as of Hungary. But Bohemia was ruled less by its monarch than by its parliament or estates, in which the nobles had the greatest influence; since most of the nobles were either Lutheran or Hussite, the new monarch, a German and a Catholic, was treated with suspicion. In Hungary Ferdinand controlled only the west and the north, and his resources there did not support the cost of frontier defenses against the Ottoman Pasha (governor) of Buda. From 1547 on, Ferdinand got Turkish agreement to prolong the truce between the two sides only by paying a humiliating annual tribute.

In his hereditary Austrian lands, including six duchies, Ferdinand presided over a kind of aristocratic confederation. Territorial administrators were appointed by the estates of each duchy, dominated as in Bohemia by the nobles. The nobles, mostly Lutheran, did not allow their ruler much room for pursuing a Catholic agenda. Ferdinand had called members of the new Jesuit order to Vienna (1551) to serve as professors at the university and as preachers at St. Stephen's Cathedral, but he could not prevent Austrian town councils from following the example of the nobles by appointing Lutheran pastors to their churches. Finally, during Ferdinand's reign as Holy Roman Emperor (1556–1564), the balance among Germany's confessional parties tilted toward the Protestant side. Though displaced by Calvinism in the Palatinate and some other territories, Lutheranism was still expanding in ecclesiastical principalities where cathedral chapters that had become Lutheran elected a Lutheran bishop, notwithstanding the so-called ecclesiastical reservation. Ferdinand had insisted on inserting this clause into the 1555 Peace, but he lacked the authority to enforce it. Rather than abandoning altogether the principle that ecclesiastical principalities must remain Catholic, he granted "indults" or exceptions for Lutheran bishops seeking admission to the diet as imperial princes.

Maximilian II (r. 1564–1576) succeeded his father as emperor, while two younger brothers, Charles and Ferdinand, administered Austrian duchies. In inner Austria, Archduke Charles took important steps to roll back the gains of Lutheranism in his lands, but Maximilian as a young man gave every indication of sympathy for Lutheranism. In order to avoid being disinherited, he had to swear an oath in the presence of his father and his brothers never to abandon the Catholic faith. As emperor, Maximilian continued Ferdinand's practice of granting to newly elected Lutheran bishops the recognition they sought as imperial princes.

Maximilian's eldest son, Rudolph II (r. 1576–1611), transferred his capital in 1583 from Vienna to the much larger city of Prague, capital of Bohemia. Rudolph took a somewhat stricter Catholic line—refusing to grant any more exemptions from the ecclesiastical reservation—but politics was not his interest. Instead he devoted himself to his art collection and to the recondite pursuits of the scholars attracted to Prague by his patronage—astronomers (including Johannes Kepler, d. 1630), alchemists, and practitioners of what was called natural magic. Rudolph's indifference to problems in the empire (see below) raised questions about the dynasty's future, all the more so because the emperor never married. His brother Mathias conferred with their cousins about ways of easing the emperor from his throne and managed to have himself elected in Rudolph's place as king of Hungary (1607) and king of Bohemia (1611). As the brothers competed for support that in Bohemia was only to be had by making religious concessions to the estates, both signed the so-called Letter of Majesty (1609), granting full toleration for Hussites, and, by implication, for all other Christian creeds.

Meanwhile, Bavaria and the Palatinate were the focal points for a growing confessional polarization. Bavaria's Duke Albert V (r. 1550–1579), having beaten back a Lutheran movement among his nobles, put the machinery of state behind Tridentine reform. His "spiritual council" took over direct management of church affairs in 1570, bypassing Bavaria's bishops and their foot-dragging cathedral chapters. Dukes William V (r. 1579–1598) and Maximilian (r. 1598–1651) were ready to defend the Catholic cause on a larger stage. In the Palatinate, the championship of Calvinism under Elector Frederick IV (r. 1583–1610) was guided first by John Casimir, the elector's uncle (d. 1592), then by his chief minister, Prince Christian of Anhalt. Anhalt had great plans for the young Elector Frederick V, whose marriage to Elizabeth Stuart, daughter of England's King James I (r. 1603–1625) he arranged in 1613.

Twice during Emperor Rudolph II's long reign Bavaria and the Palatinate almost went to war. In 1582, when Cologne's prince-archbishop publicly married his mistress and converted to Protestantism, the ecclesiastical reservation was upheld by having Duke William V's brother Ernest of Bavaria elected as his successor. John Casimir raised an army to defend the claims of the Protestant prince-archbishop, but withdrew from the field when Lutheran princes, ever distrustful of Calvinists, refused to support him. In 1608 Bavaria's Duke Maximilian, acting on the authorization of the emperor, occupied the Protestant free imperial city of Donauwörth, and supervised its reconversion to Catholicism. Christian of Anhalt organized a union (1609) among leading Calvinist territories as well as a few Lutheran princes and cities, but a lack of broader Lutheran support prevented the union from taking action. Meanwhile, the rivalry between Bavaria and the Palatinate was overshadowed by the interest that powerful states outside the empire took in the disputed succession to a cluster of five Rhineland territories (1606–1614); what threatened to be a European conflagration was prevented only by unforeseen events.

The crisis that did not subside came in Bohemia. The childless Emperor Mathias (r. 1612–1619) planned for the eldest of his cousins, Archduke Ferdinand of Inner Austria, son of Archduke Charles, to succeed him in his various offices, starting with his election as king by the estates of Bohemia (1617). Since Archduke Ferdinand was known for his persecution of Lutherans in Inner Austria, the largely Protestant estates demanded, as an afterthought, that Ferdinand add his signature to the 1609 Letter of Majesty. But Ferdinand named as his governors in Bohemia two deputies whose ardent Catholicism had alienated their Protestant colleagues, and almost immediately there were disputes about the circumstances in which the Letter of Majesty permitted Protestants to build new churches. Tempers flared at a specially called Protestant assembly in Prague (May 1618); those in attendance marched to the royal palace, seized the two governors, and, consciously repeating a revolutionary gesture of their Hussite forebears, dragged them up a marble staircase and threw them out the window.

This "Defenestration of Prague" meant war. The Protestant assembly formed a new government for Bohemia, raised an army, expelled the Jesuits, and confiscated the lands of Catholics loyal to Ferdinand. Among the adventurers who proffered assistance, Christian of Anhalt came to the fore; he saw a chance to have Elector Frederick V chosen as Bohemia's king in place of Ferdinand. Initial fighting in Bohemia went well for the rebels, and in 1619, shortly after Ferdinand was elected Holy Roman Emperor, the states of Bohemia voted to have the Elector Palatine as their king. Frederick was joyously greeted when he arrived, but Hussites and Lutherans were put off when Calvinist ministers acting in the new king's name began removing from the churches the religious images that they too cherished.

Maximilian of Bavaria agreed to raise an army of the empire's Catholic League to join Habsburg forces for an invasion of Bohemia from the south, under the command of Jan Tserclaes, count of Tilly (1559–1632), a seasoned Counter-Reformation warrior from the Low Countries. The Lutheran Elector John George of Saxony (r. 1611–1656) agreed to invade from the north in return for the right to occupy Lusatia, a border province of the Bohemian crown. Finally, Ferdinand's cousin in Madrid, Philip III, agreed to have an army from the Spanish Netherlands invade the Palatinate. All three invasions went as planned. The climax came when Tilly's men caught up with Anhalt's Bohemian army entrenched on the brow of White Mountain, just west of Prague; charging uphill in the fog (8 November 1620), they routed their enemies. Frederick, a king no more, found refuge with Denmark's King Christian IV (r. 1588–1648). Bohemia's towns and provinces hastened to submit to Ferdinand.

Following the battle of White Mountain, Bohemia was thoroughly subjected to Habsburg and Catholic rule. Noble families that supported the rebellion were dispossessed, their lands handed over to a polyglot nobility formed from officers in Tilly's army. Some forty leaders of the revolt were beheaded on the main square of Prague (1621), and Bohemia was declared a hereditary possession of the Habsburgs, no longer an elective monarchy. The Letter of Majesty was revoked; Protestant and Hussite pastors were evicted and replaced by Catholic priests. Seldom has a major kingdom been so completely transformed by the fortunes of a single battle.

This great victory evoked dreams of Habsburg grandeur for Ferdinand and for Spain's new king, Philip IV (r. 1621–1665). Neither Spain's continuing occupation of the Palatinate nor Ferdinand's transfer of the electoral title to Maximilian of Bavaria (1623) were accepted by the diet—both were thus violations of imperial law. But among the imperial princes only King Christian IV of Denmark (a prince of the empire in his capacity as duke of Holstein) seemed willing to do anything more than protest. Supported by Dutch and English subsidies, Christian IV marched into Germany twice but was twice defeated by Tilly (1624, 1626). Meanwhile, Spain's control of the Palatinate helped provide a safe route of passage for men and supplies traveling from northern Italy to the Low Countries. After hostilities in the Low Countries were reopened, Philip's commanders in Italy secured another link in the "Spanish road" by annexing the Valtellina, a strategic Alpine valley connecting the duchy of Milan to the friendly territory of Switzerland's Catholic cantons.

Count Albert of Wallenstein, a Bohemian military adventurer, now contracted to raise an army on Ferdinand's behalf, without any charge to the imperial treasury—his men would support themselves by pillage. Having raised a force of over 100,000, Wallenstein crunched through the Protestant territories of north Germany that had not yet submitted to the emperor. Despite misgivings about the independent position Wallenstein was carving out for himself, Ferdinand recognized his conquests by depriving the Lutheran duke of Mecklenburg of his land and title and awarding both to Wallenstein (1628). Not since Frederick Barbarossa (d. 1191) had any emperor controlled north Germany's Baltic coast as Ferdinand II now did. But the empire's electoral princes, now including Maximilian of Bavaria, denounced the transfer of an imperial principality to the upstart Wallenstein as a flagrant violation of imperial law and informed the emperor that they would not elect his son Ferdinand as King of the Romans unless Wallenstein were dismissed and deprived of his ill-gotten gains.

Instead, Ferdinand chose to exploit Tilly's and Wallenstein's victories by redressing the empire's political balance in favor of Catholicism. The emperor and his advisers (including his Jesuit confessor) had discussed the idea of reversing all the changes of religion that had occurred in the empire's ecclesiastical territories since the 1555 ecclesiastical reservation, regardless of whether or not the changes were sanctioned by "indults" granted by Emperors Ferdinand I and Maximilian II. The imperial diet would never endorse such a revolutionary step, involving the lands of some fourteen bishoprics and fifty important monasteries or convents; the emperor would have to act on his own authority, in effect daring the imperial princes to react. Ferdinand took the risk, promulgating his Edict of Restitution on 6 March 1629. From the imperial princes came letters of protest, nothing more. Backed by Tilly's and Wallenstein's troops, the emperor's agents began implementing the new decree in one territory after another. Though there was resistance in places, as in Magdeburg, which had been Lutheran for a hundred years, this was the high point of the Counter-Reformation in Germany. Since Ferdinand II was in effect governing the empire by decree, rendering the diet superfluous, it was also the high point of Habsburg claims to hegemony in Europe.

In fact, Ferdinand's success was possible only because potential foes chose not to intervene in imperial politics. England and the Dutch were distracted by other concerns. France, the Habsburgs' ancient enemy, was the key player. Cardinal Richelieu (fig. 9.7), prime minister for King Louis XIII (r. 1610–1643), saw the containment of Habsburg power as France's most important priority. But a strong "devout" party in the king's council, backed by popular opinion, wanted France to pursue a "Catholic" foreign policy, which certainly did not include backing the Habsburgs' Protestant foes. Also, royal power in France had been seriously challenged when the Huguenot "state within a state" rose in rebellion (1625). But events in Italy played into Richelieu's hands. When the duke of Mantua died without issue, Spain's Philip IV persuaded Ferdinand II to send troops to occupy the duchy, technically a principality of the empire (1628), rather than allowing it to pass to the French prince who was the duke's

Figure 9.7. Cardinal Richelieu. Philip de Champagne, "Cardinal Richelieu." *National Gallery, London.*

rightful heir. Pope Urban VIII (r. 1623–1644) made no secret of his opposition to this Habsburg land grab in Italy—a circumstance that greatly facilitated Richelieu's contention that an anti-Habsburg policy was not anti-Catholic. Meanwhile, royal troops ended Huguenot resistance by conquering the heavily fortified port city of La Rochelle (1628). Though he did not find it necessary to revoke the Huguenots' civil and religious rights, Cardinal Richelieu rendered them politically harmless by having royal garrisons occupy their former strongholds. Finally, he gained a clear victory against his foes in the royal council (1630); Louis XIII dismissed leaders of the "devout" party and reaffirmed his confidence in Richelieu. Richelieu was now free to look about for a partner willing to challenge Habsburg supremacy in Germany.

Sweden's King Gustavus Adolph (r. 1611–1632), already alarmed by imperial successes along the Baltic coast, was incensed when Wallenstein provided 12,000 troops to his enemy, King Sigismund III Vasa of Poland (r. 1587–1632). After French diplomats arranged a truce in the fighting between Poland and Sweden (1629), Gustavus Adolph landed an army on Germany's Baltic coast, announcing his intention of defending Sweden's interests in the region. Finding that his large force could not gain much by pillaging land already picked clean by Wallenstein's regiments, Gustavus Adolph accepted (January 1631) French subsidies to keep his men on the march. Sensing an opportunity to present himself as the Protestant champion, he hoped to break Tilly's siege of Magdeburg, but north Germany's Lutheran princes, suspicious of the Swedish intruder's intentions, barred the way. Tilly's men stormed Magdeburg (May 1631) and went on a murderous rampage; thousands more perished as fire raced through the city's timber houses. Elector John George of Saxony now joined forces with Gustavus Adolph, and the combined Protestant army caught up with Tilly's force at Breitenfeld, north of Leipzig (September 1631); Tilly's men turned back the Saxons but broke and fled before the firing by ranks of Gustavus Adolph's well-trained Swedish infantry.

Breitenfeld was the first major defeat for Ferdinand II and a cause of joy for Protestant Europe. But Richelieu was alarmed as Gustavus Adolph marched unopposed into the south German lands of the Catholic League, with which France had a separate treaty. To protect French interests along the border with the empire, he compelled the prince-archbishop of Trier to hand over two fortresses on the right bank of the Rhine. While one of his German Protestant allies drove Spanish troops from the Palatinate, the Swedish king ravaged the Main valley and parts of Bavaria before turning back to the north, pursued now by Wallenstein, who had been given a new army. At Lützen, west of Leipzig, Gustavus Adolph was killed, but his men won another victory (November 1632). The king's chancellor, Axel Oxenstierna (d. 1654), organized the empire's Protestant princes into a new federation under Swedish leadership. But the emperor's son Ferdinand and Spain's Philip IV had not given up the fight. A Spanish army en route to the Low Countries made a juncture with Ferdinand's men and routed the Swedes at Nördlingen in south Germany (September 1634). Within a few weeks, all of the south German lands that Gustavus Adolph and his Protestant allies had conquered were regained by the Habsburgs and the Catholic League. Saxony's John George now arranged a treaty with the emperor's son: the Peace of Prague (1635) nullified the Edict of

Restitution, except for ecclesiastical territories reconverted to Catholicism before 1627. As in 1555, Lutheranism and Catholicism would enjoy the protection of imperial law; Calvinism would not. Weary of war, most German princes of both confessions accepted this treaty.

Richelieu could not permit the Habsburgs and their Saxon allies to settle Germany's future. In May 1635 France openly declared war on Spain. While French diplomats arranged another truce with Poland, permitting Sweden to rebuild its forces in north Germany, French commanders occupied most of the imperial province of Alsace and launched campaigns against Mantua and the Valtellina in Italy. For thirteen years more the various combatants marched their armies back and forth across an exhausted Germany. The end result secured France's gains and was somewhat more favorable to the empire's traditional character as a federation of independent states than the Peace of Prague had been. The Treaty of Westphalia (1648) transferred to France all rights claimed by the emperor in the imperial province of Alsace; France also retained the bishoprics of Metz, Toul, and Verdun as well as two key fortresses on the right bank of the Rhine. The Dutch Republic, somewhat expanded beyond the frontiers of the 1609 truce, won permanent recognition from Spain of its status as an independent nation. The imperial constitution was vindicated by restoration of Frederick V's eldest son to his family's Rhenish lands as well as the title of Elector Palatine, but Maximilian of Bavaria was awarded territory formerly controlled by the Palatinate and kept his electoral title. Elector John George of Saxony was confirmed in his possession of Lusatia, and Sweden received half of the duchy of Pomerania on the Baltic coast; the other half went to a shrewd military enterpriser, Elector Frederick William of Brandenburg-Prussia (r. 1640–1688).

Finally, the religious configuration of the empire was brought more into balance by moving back from 1627 to 1624 the date from which the religious identity of the ecclesiastical principalities was to be regarded as fixed—re-Catholicization campaigns subsequent to 1624 were thus abandoned. At the same time, freedom of conscience was recognized by limiting the ruler's right to determine the religious identity of his territory (as defined by the 1555 Peace of Augsburg) to matters of external observance; subjects were not to be molested for their private beliefs. But Ferdinand III (r. 1637–1657) insisted on separating his hereditary lands from the new imperial law on this point; in Austria and in most of the lands of the Bohemian crown, the Habsburg ruler retained the right to determine what his subjects should believe.

But if the Austrian Habsburgs emerged from the Thirty Years' War much stronger than before in their hereditary lands, Ferdinand II's vision of ruling all Germany by decree was shattered once and for all in the grim final stage of the conflict. For the rest of its history, the Holy Roman Empire would remain as the 1555 Peace of Augsburg had envisioned it, a loose federation of independent states. This result was achieved mainly by French subsidies, to a lesser extent by French armies marching into Germany. Richelieu's "devout" critics had warned that the French people would suffer for the cardinal's dreams of glory, and so they did; to pay for the armies that ravaged Germany's peasantry, France's peasants were squeezed to the point of rebellion. But Richelieu's dream was realized, even if the cardinal was no longer alive to see it. France emerged from the Treaty of Westphalia as Europe's preeminent power, a status confirmed by eleven more years of fighting along the Spanish frontier (1648–1659). By contrast, Spain sank to the status of a second-rate power: more than a century of nearly continuous wars (tracing back to the time of Charles V) had exhausted Castile's treasury and distorted its economic development. Under France's King Louis XIV (r. 1656–1715), Catholic Austria would have to band together with Europe's Protestant powers in a series of coalitions aimed at forestalling French hegemony.

Like Richelieu's campaign against the Habsburgs, wars of the century or so after 1650 were fought for reasons of state; the age of religious wars was over. Yet the conflicts of the period between 1560 and 1650 had left a mark on European society. Paradoxically, wars that were in part motivated by the desire to suppress false religion achieved a result that was nearly the opposite, for each of these conflicts ended by providing Christian minorities a modicum of religious liberty. Ardent Catholics in France were angered by the fact that heretics still controlled two hundred towns in the kingdom. Ardent Calvinists in the Dutch Republic were angered by the fact that town magistrates were not punishing popish idolaters as the law required when they celebrated mass in private houses. In the empire too there was grumbling from zealots on both sides about provisions of the final settlement that limited a ruler's rights over the religious life of his territory to public worship, not private beliefs. In all three conflicts the moderates could take some satisfaction in the outcome: Catholic *politiques* in France; Reformed town regents in the Dutch Republic; and, in Germany, Lutheran princes like Elector John George of Saxony, loath to see the empire torn by further war. In all three wars the final settlements made a small but important crack in traditional European assumptions about the proper relationship between the civil and ecclesiastical spheres of Christian society. Government still identified itself with true religion by determining the terms and conditions of public worship. But so long as they did not challenge the government's claim to control the religious use of public space, citizens who happened to hold heterodox beliefs were not to be molested. It was not that the coexistence of different confessions in one society was thought to be a good thing. Rather, dogged fighting between armed factions adhering to opposing beliefs had made some kind of compromise a requirement for peace. This limited recognition of the civil rights of religious minorities emerged not from the idea of toleration, but from the fact of religious war.

10 | Politics

The European Reformations

In the history of European state-building, the Reformation era was a period of increasing centralization. Taxes that were novelties when first granted to their rulers by parliamentary bodies of the fourteenth and fifteenth centuries became routine, necessitating the creation of new or larger government bureaus for overseeing collection and auditing disbursements. The French idea of a standing army was adopted by all states that could afford it and some that could not, meaning a standardization of expectations as to how soldiers were trained and equipped. Maintaining a permanent force and keeping up with rapid improvements in military technology—including siege artillery, and the costly new-style fortifications needed to defend against it—required more expenditures, even in peacetime. Territorial parliaments accepted additional forms of taxation with the greatest reluctance, in part because they often required compiling information about wealth and business activities that was precious to the ruler and dangerous for his subjects. Meanwhile, the prince's courts were using the natural litigiousness of every European society to extend his authority in another sphere. Unable to abolish the various kinds of courts that competed with their master's tribunals, the prince's judges insisted on appellate jurisdiction, which in the long run encouraged plaintiffs to come to their courts directly.

In some territories the growing strength of the ruler meant that the parliamentary bodies that had been so important in former centuries were rendered powerless or even abolished altogether. But we must not exaggerate the control rulers of this period were able to exercise over the lives of their subjects. Even the most closely governed territory still had enclaves where the ruler's writ did not run, and even the most powerful prince still depended on the collaboration of important men who were strong enough to obstruct his will on issues that mattered to them. At least for Western and Central Europe, there are now few defenders of the once popular idea that certain kings were able to achieve in practice the "absolute" or unlimited monarchy written about by theorists.

There was, however, an unmistakable trend toward consolidation of princely authority, and it was powerfully abetted by men who served the prince. The actual business of governing, once tended to by nobles and bishops who also had other duties, was by the sixteenth century firmly in the hands of career officials, recruited either from the nobility or from wealthy burgher families. Such men did not forget to look after their own kinfolk, but they saw themselves more as servants of the crown than as defenders of the interests of their native cities or regions. This esprit de corps, combined with university training in the law, imbued professional bureaucrats with a sense of mission. Faced with a labyrinth of local control, manipulated by powerful subjects for their own purposes, the officials had a glimmer of a new and better order in which all would be equally subject to the law that a wise prince imposed all across his territory. As a common French saying has it, these men were more royalist than the king.

In an age when religion was such a volatile and divisive issue, strong-willed rulers and their activist officials could not fail to take interest in the beliefs and practices of the prince's subjects. No one of any consequence disputed the common belief that it was the sovereign's highest duty before God to care for the spiritual as well as the material well-being of his subjects. Besides, how could there be peace in the realm if Christians nurtured fratricidal hatred of one another? And how could public order be maintained without good preachers and teachers to instruct citizens in their moral duties? Usually, decisions about religion were not made by the prince and his officials acting alone; persons of some political weight—nobles and magistrates of important towns—had to be brought into the discussion. But no one gave much thought to the opinions of the illiterate common folk who made up the great majority of the prince's subjects. On a matter of such importance as religion, the people at large were to be governed, not consulted.

To give an idea of how governments attempted to determine the religious lives of their subjects, this chapter discusses four outcomes: the Lutheran settlement in Scandinavia, the Calvinist settlement in the Dutch Republic, the Catholic settlement in Habsburg Austria, and in the Commonwealth of Poland-Lithuania. England's many different settlements are discussed in chapter 11.

Outside of Germany, Martin Luther's teachings became the basis of established churches only in the neighboring realms of Denmark (including

Norway) and Sweden (including Finland). Humanist scholars like Paule
Helie (1480–1534) of Copenhagen awakened interest in religious reform,
and former Wittenberg students like the Dane Hans Tausen (1494–1561)
and the Swede Olaus Petri (1493–1552) spread Luther's message. By the
early 1530s there were strong evangelical movements in the largest cities
in Denmark, Malmö (now part of Sweden), and Copenhagen, and in
Bergen (Norway), a port of call for German merchants. But the Reformation in Scandinavia owed its success to the fact that rulers of Denmark and
Sweden had a common problem: They needed cash, and the wealth of politically troublesome bishops was an inviting target.

Christian II, last king of the Scandinavian Union (r. 1513–1523), was no
friend of the aristocracy. In Sweden he arranged a massacre of leading nobles, provoking a rebellion led by Gustavus Vasa, son of one of the victims, who gained recognition as king of Sweden (1523–1560). The great
merchant city of Lübeck (fig. 10.1)—a bitter foe of Christian II—provided
Vasa with money for hiring troops, and ships to convey them from Germany. The new king could not ignore Sweden's debt to the Baltic's major
naval and financial power, but neither could he find money to pay
Lübeck. The property of the church attracted his attention, partly because
of his enmity with the former archbishop of Uppsala, ousted on suspicion
of complicity in the murders arranged by Christian II, and now demanding restoration, with papal support. At the Diet of Västerås (1527), Vasa

Figure 10.1. The free imperial city of Lübeck. From Matthaeus Merian, Martin
Zeiller, Topographia Germaniae (17 vols. facsimile reprint of second edition
[Frankfurt, 1655], Kassel: Bärenreiter, 1959–1967), vol. XIV, following p. 154. *Cour-
tesy of University Libraries, University of Minnesota, Minneapolis.*

pressured Sweden's nobles and town deputies to agree to place the wealth of the church at his disposal. The diet also decreed that clergy were to preach "the pure word of God, without human inventions and fables." This was the Swedish Reformation.

Denmark did not have a parliament or diet. Here, Christian's attack on noble privileges, though popular in the cities, led the otherwise fractious bishops and nobles who made up the Council of the Realm to join forces. Christian fled into exile, and the council elected the duke of neighboring Holstein as King Frederick I (1523–1533). Because the bishops had a strong position in the council, Frederick moved warily in matters of religion, despite the presence of Lutheran preachers in his entourage. But Frederick's son and presumed heir, the future King Christian III, was organizing a full-blown Lutheran reformation in Schleswig and Holstein, the territories he controlled. Thus, Frederick's death ushered in a three-sided civil war, lasting from 1533 to 1536. Emperor Charles V claimed Denmark for one of his nieces, a daughter of his brother-in-law, Christian II, but the troops he was finally able to get shipped to Denmark came too late. Meanwhile, the Lutheran towns of Copenhagen and Malmö were fighting in the name of their old ally, Christian II himself. But since Christian was the worst of all choices for Denmark's noble families, the aristocratic bishops and their kinsmen on the council rallied behind Duke Christian of Schleswig-Holstein, son of the late king. Having made his triumphal entry into Copenhagen, King Christian III (d. 1559) declared the bishops responsible for the turmoil of civil war. The bishops themselves were imprisoned; their property was forfeit to the crown. Denmark (with Norway) was now Lutheran by decree.

In Denmark the consolidation of the new religion over the next few generations was relatively tranquil. Neither King Christian III nor his son Frederick II (r. 1559–1588) found it necessary to prescribe the 1530 Augsburg Confession as a binding statement of belief. Instead, efforts were made to keep out heretics (meaning Calvinist or Anabaptists). The so-called Strangers Articles of 1569 were based on the Augsburg Confession, but only "strangers"—foreigners wishing to take up residence—were obliged to swear to believe as the articles prescribed. The intra-Lutheran quarrels between Philippists and Genuine-Lutherans surfaced in Denmark when a prominent professor at the University of Copenhagen was forced to recant his Calvinist teachings on the Lord's Supper and was eventually dismissed from his post (1576–1579). Early in the reign of Christian IV (r. 1588–1648) danger came from a different quarter. Young Danes and Norwegians were crossing the Baltic to attend Jesuit colleges, and some converted to Catholicism before returning home. When a Jesuit graduate who had become headmaster of the Latin school in Malmö openly professed his sympathy for Catholicism, the government prohibited Jesuit alumni from serving as ministers or schoolteachers. In Norway, six crypto-Catholics (including four preachers) were ferreted out and banished. Denmark and Norway, open to the world along long coastlines, were not open to un-Lutheran doctrines.

Sweden followed a different path. Here some years went by before any formal condemnation of Catholic belief and ritual occured; only in 1544 did an assembly of the clergy repudiate such practices as the veneration of saints and the saying of masses for the benefit of souls in purgatory. Unlike Denmark's monarch, Gustavus Vasa's son and successor Erik XIV (r. 1560–1568) welcomed Calvinist refugees from France and the Low Countries and was suspected of sympathizing with their views, even though he prohibited them from proselytizing. Laurentius Petri, the first Lutheran archbishop of Uppsala (1531–1573), stood for a high church Lutheranism; he was orthodox and anti-Calvinist in matters of doctrine, but he asserted the independence of the church from state control and sought to retain as much as possible of the old ceremonies. The church order written by Petri, not accepted during Erik's reign, was adopted by king and parliament under his brother and successor, John III (r. 1568–1592).

Influenced by his wife, Catherine Jagiello, the daughter of Poland's King Sigismund II, King John (fig. 10.2) was attracted to Catholicism, but not of the Tridentine variety. This theologically sophisticated monarch envisioned a national church worshiping according to the ancient Catholic liturgy, in the language of the people. He drafted his own liturgy, the so-called Red Book, which Sweden's Lutheran bishops accepted with some misgivings (1577). Jesuit missionaries were allowed to enter the country, and John himself secretly converted to Catholicism. He would make his conversion public if Rome approved three concessions: the laity must be allowed to receive the wine as well as the bread in communion; priests must be allowed to marry; and the language of worship must be Swedish, not Latin. But Pope Gregory XIII (r. 1572–1585) refused to countenance any such departures from the norms Trent had decreed for the universal Catholic Church, at least in its Latin Rite (see below). King John expelled the Jesuits and ended his days as a Lutheran.

Meanwhile, Sigismund Vasa, the son of King John and Catherine Jagiello, had been raised a Catholic and was now attempting to promote a Tridentine agenda as king of Poland (1587–1632). Hence, when John III died, his brother Charles persuaded the royal council to convene a church synod, which for the first time adopted the Augsburg Confession as Sweden's confession of faith. Since the synod's decision was endorsed by many of the leading men who made up Sweden's Diet, or Parliament, Sigismund Vasa had to accept it as a condition for his coronation (1593).

Figure 10.2. Sweden's King John III (r. 1568–1592). Portrait of John III Vasa, King of Sweden by Lambrecht Ryckx (?) ca. 1569–1570. *Swedish Portrait Gallery.*

Several years of friction between the Catholic monarch and his Lutheran estates led to a few military skirmishes, after which Sigismund abruptly returned to Poland. The Parliament deposed Sigismund (1599), and eventually acclaimed his uncle as King Charles IX. We may conclude that over the course of nearly three generations Lutheranism had taken hold in Sweden, certainly among the clergy and the political elite. In 1527, Gustavus Vasa was able to impose a change of religion on the kingdom; in 1593, Sigismund Vasa was not.

The Dutch Republic was the most important European state to adopt Calvinism as its official creed. But only a tiny fraction of the population were members or sympathizers of the Reformed Church. As late as 1586, though the numbers were rising, it was estimated that no more than 10 percent of the Dutch people were adherents of the "evangelical Reformed religion." Moreover, the leaders of the church were in no hurry to change things; to them, quality of membership counted more than quantity. Nonetheless, the "public church" was vested with exclusive control of all churches that still functioned as houses of worship—the others were closed or converted to other uses. Town governments also endowed scholarships for ministerial students in the theology faculty at the new University of Leiden. This was because the Dutch government and the church needed each other. No government of this age could function without invoking God's blessing, and no clergymen could be more fervent than the Reformed ministers in calling upon the Lord to bless those who guided the Revolt against Catholic Spain.

Especially in the provinces of Holland and Utrecht, urban magistrates were usually Protestant, but not necessarily Calvinist in their beliefs. In these provinces there was something of a marriage of convenience between church and state, and it was rife with friction. The church had a cohesive organizational structure: a church council (pastor and elders) for each parish, a *classis* for each town and its hinterland, and provincial synods to which each *classis* sent deputies. As far as ministers and elders were concerned, town regents had a right to be notified when the *classis* chose a minister, but no right of appointment; and decisions by the synods of the public church ought to be recognized by the government as having the force of law. The regents saw things quite differently. Many would have preferred a broader church in which Christians of differing beliefs could worship together. Remembering the radical Calvinists whose seizure of power in cities like Ghent and Antwerp had fractured the unity of the Revolt, they also mistrusted the south-Netherlands exiles who were so prominent among Reformed ministers and elders. To prevent hotheads among the clergy from causing trouble among the people, it was essential that magistrates keep the church in hand by sending "commissioners" to observe the meetings of the local *classis* and by exercising their rights to appoint or dismiss ministers.

During the 1580s these conflicting principles led in half a dozen cities in Holland and Utrecht to bitter struggles that followed a similar script. A preacher built up a large following, but fellow ministers making up the local *classis* attempted to remove him because he questioned Calvinist doctrine, often in regard to predestination. The preacher then appealed to what he deemed the superior authority of the town magistrates, who gladly maintained him in office, at least until a compromise was reached. Meanwhile, deputies to the provincial parliaments studiously ignored the decisions regarding the governance of the church promulgated by provincial synods or by the national synod of 1584. Instead, the States of Utrecht (1590) and the States of Holland (1591) approved their own plans for church governance, explicitly recognizing the rights of magistrates. In most places these resolutions of their "high mightinesses" were studiously ignored by the church.

In the early years of the new century, a dispute within Leiden's theological faculty turned these issues into a crisis of national proportions. Jacobus Arminius (1559–1609) was trained at Geneva, still the center of Calvinist orthodoxy. During his tenure as a pastor in Amsterdam (1588–1603), his views on predestination were questioned by some colleagues in the ministry, but Arminius's wife was from one of the city's leading families, and he enjoyed the favor of the magistrates. In 1603 he was named a professor of theology at Leiden, despite opposition from another member of the faculty, a south Netherlands refugee named Franciscus Gomarus (1563–1641). Arminius proved a popular lecturer, in part because among the theology professors he alone was a native of the provinces that now comprised the Dutch Republic. In the public debates that Gomarus now demanded, Arminius contended that God's final decree of salvation depended on which individuals freely chose to accept His grace. This doctrine put Arminius squarely at odds with Calvin, and, as he acknowledged, with the article on predestination contained in the Belgic Confession, a statement of faith that church rules required every minister to sign. Arminius proposed that the states of Holland convene a special assembly to consider revising the Belgic Confession—but for Gomarus, a strict Calvinist, such a subordination of matters of doctrine to state authority would be if anything even more of an abomination than Arminius's repudiation of orthodox teaching on predestination. This was the theological equivalent of war.

As graduates trained by Gomarus and Arminius filled ministerial posts, their mutual recriminations percolated through Holland's towns, transforming an academic debate into partisan strife (fig. 10.3). In the vibrant printing culture of the Dutch Republic, the debate among learned men quickly became a war of pamphlets aimed at a broader readership. City councils and church councils alike divided along factional lines, and preachers built up a popular following by denouncing the heresies or the narrow-mindedness of their opponents. When the *classis* of Alkmaar dismissed a preacher who had refused to sign the Belgic Confession (1608),

Op de WAAG-SCHAAL.

Figure 10.3. A Calvinist lampoon of the false doctrines of Arminius. Anonymous cartoon showing the true doctrine of Calvin (and of Gomarus) outweighing the ragbag doctrines of Arminius—a small glimpse of the extensive pamphlet and broadside campaign waged by rival Gomarists and Arminians. *Rijksmuseum, Amsterdam.*

Arminius's disciples grasped how precarious their position in the church was. In 1610, shortly after Arminius himself had died, forty-four ministers (many of them his former students) presented a "Remonstrance" to the States of Holland, requesting protection from harassment by orthodox Calvinists. This petition was sympathetically received by the states, but the recourse to state authority only intensified the hostilities between those who now called themselves "Remonstrants" (Arminians) and "Counter-Remonstrants" (Calvinists).

Where one faction gained control of a *classis* and filled the pulpits with its own men, adherents of the opposing faction seceded and formed their own church, recognized and supported by fellow believers in other towns.

With Holland in an uproar, the Calvinist party demanded the convening of a national synod of the church, the first since 1584; but Holland had always blocked this idea in the States General. Holland's leader, Oldenbarnevelt, decided the time had come to teach the *dominees* (preachers) their place. At his urging, the States of Holland convened a theological colloquy and, when this failed to bring agreement, commanded both sides to stop quarreling and live at peace. The outnumbered Remonstrants were quite willing to do so; the question was whether their "high mightinesses" could lay down the law to Holland's Calvinists.

In fact, Oldenbarnevelt badly underestimated the opposition. In some places where Remonstrant preachers were maintained in their pulpits by sympathetic magistrates, worshipers in the local church were outnumbered by secessionist Counter-Remonstrant congregations meeting outside the town walls. Meanwhile, political winds were shifting. Oldenbarnevelt's ideas on lay control of the church had always been strongly supported by deputies from Amsterdam, Holland's greatest and richest city. But now the ruling faction whose members had treated Arminius as one of their own was giving way to a new group who were strong Calvinists and whose overseas commercial ambitions were hampered by the Twelve Years' Truce Oldenbarnevelt had concluded with Spain. Thus Oldenbarnevelt found himself facing powerful opposition in the States of Holland. The final blow came from the prince of Orange, Maurits of Nassau, who was glad to see signs of interest in renewing the war with Spain—the Twelve Years' Truce had been approved over his protest. When Maurits announced his support for the Counter-Remonstrant cause (1617), opposition in the States of Holland to the convening of a national synod began to crumble. As preparations were being made for the Synod of Dordrecht (1618–1619), Oldenbarnevelt was arrested by order of the States General on vaguely worded charges that he had betrayed the fatherland to its enemies. The fact that no proof of treason was forthcoming did not prevent his execution (May 1619). Meanwhile, the Synod had completed its work. The Calvinist doctrine of double predestination was forcefully reasserted in its most extreme form; the teachings of the Remonstrants were explicitly condemned. Following the Synod, some two hundred Remonstrant preachers were dismissed and forced into exile.

In some ways the Synod of Dordrecht (fig. 10.4) marked a decisive turn in the religious history of the republic. The theology of the church was now unambiguously Calvinist, and no parliamentary body would ever again challenge the principle that doctrinal decisions were to be made by the church. Moreover, the fact that ordinary believers had some influence on the outcome—voting with their feet if confronted with a preacher not of their liking—reflected a steady growth in church membership. This trend

Figure 10.4. The Synod of Dordrecht, 1618/1619. Frederick Muller, "The Synod of Dordrecht." *Rijksmuseum, Amsterdam.*

continued through the remainder of the century, partly because the restriction of certain civil privileges to church members was for some an inducement to conversion, and partly because many believers were attracted by the distinctive teachings of Calvinism.

But the victory of Calvinism was not so complete as it seemed. When the political constellation that had made the convening of the synod possible changed, so too did the country's religious climate. Frederick Henry, Maurits's son and successor (1625–1647), let it be known that Remonstrant leaders who returned to their native country would not be persecuted. By the 1630s, Remonstrants were even allowed to build new spaces for their services, so long as they did not violate the Reformed Church's monopoly on public worship by erecting structures that had the appearance of churches. In Amsterdam, where a new and less ardently Calvinist ruling faction was taking control, the same courtesy had already been extended to Mennonites and Lutherans, and also to Sephardic Jews from Portugal. Catholics were usually not allowed to build houses of worship—this would have been too much of an affront to Calvinists—but it became less and less likely that illegal Catholic services in house-churches would be raided by the local sheriff. The end result was a paradox. Just when Calvinism was finally becoming the majority religion (around 1650), the place of non-Calvinist communities was becoming anchored in the daily life of the republic, if not in its public law. If one may describe as pluralistic a society that recognizes one religion formally and many others informally, this was Europe's first pluralistic society.

In the six duchies that made up the core of the Austrian lands, Emperor Ferdinand I (d. 1564) and his nobles had an informal understanding: They supported his campaigns against the Ottomans; he did not inquire into their beliefs, which were increasingly Lutheran. By the time of Ferdinand's death only Tirol remained largely Catholic. Upper and Lower Austria along the Danube (the latter having Vienna as its capital) and the three duchies to the south—Styria, Carinthia, and Carniola—all seem to have had Lutheran majorities at all levels of society. In his will Ferdinand provided for a division of the Austrian lands among his sons: Ferdinand (d. 1595) was to have Tirol; Charles (d. 1590) was to have the three duchies of Styria, Carinthia, and Carniola—now called Inner Austria; and Maximilian II (d. 1576), his designated successor as Holy Roman Emperor and king of Bohemia, was to have Upper and Lower Austria. Of the three brothers, it was Archduke Charles in Inner Austria who initiated the Catholic counteroffensive.

By this time the great Benedictine monasteries of the Austrian lands were moribund, some having only a few monks left. Ferdinand I appointed commissions of visitation that documented these conditions; Maximilian II appointed a "cloister council" to impose discipline on the monasteries, but this was a work of decades, not years. The state of the secular clergy was hardly any better; bishops who visited the parishes of Inner Austria during Charles's reign found many priests who had come there to escape their evil reputations elsewhere. Help could only come from the new orders flourishing in other parts of Catholic Europe. Ferdinand I showed the way by calling Jesuit priests to Vienna (1551) to serve as professors at the moribund university and as preachers at St. Stephen's Cathedral. Starting with but a handful of listeners, Peter Canisius (1521–1597) in a few years' time filled the cathedral—a result that led Lutherans elsewhere to be on guard against the Jesuits. Hence, when Archduke Charles invited the Jesuits to Graz (1572), Styria's capital, Graz's solidly Lutheran town council decreed fines for all who attended Catholic services, prohibited burghers from sending their sons to the new Jesuit school, and ordered local printers not to print its textbooks. But prominent families were not to be prevented from signing up their sons for a first-rate classical education. The school had 200 pupils by 1580 (though mostly not from the area), and according to Jesuit reports the town of some 8,000 people had 1,000 Catholic communicants, as opposed to about twenty in 1570. There was now some basis of support for a more aggressively Catholic policy.

Meanwhile, however, the estates of Inner Austria had compelled Archduke Charles to issue a sworn guarantee of freedom of worship for nobles (1578); he refused to say whether the same guarantee applied to the towns as well, and the nobles who dominated the estates did not press the matter. This concession to Lutheran nobles was protested by the papal nuncio and by Charles's brother-in-law, Duke William V of Bavaria; Charles, though bound by his word to the nobles, agreed to interpret the concession narrowly. In 1580 he began a step-by-step attack on urban Lutheranism. He decreed a ban on Lutheran worship, first in a few newly acquired cities, then in all the cities of Inner Austria, which would have forced Lutheran burghers to attend services on noble estates outside the walls or in rural parishes whose pastors were appointed by the nobles. It is not clear that the archduke's officials were able to enforce this decree, but he kept up pressure on the towns by, for example, promoting the election of Catholic burghers to town councils. In 1586, the flourishing Jesuit school in Graz was recognized by the pope as a university; Archduke Charles's son, the future Emperor Ferdinand II, enrolled as its first student (fig. 10.5).

Following his father's death, while a regency council ruled Inner Austria in his name, young Ferdinand pursued his studies at the now Jesuit University of Ingolstadt in Bavaria (1590–1595). When he took the reins of government in his own hands (1596), Archduke Ferdinand picked up the threads of the program of Catholic restoration. He used the receipts of his treasury to endow three more Jesuit colleges in Inner Austria, and he let nobles in the estates know that, while he respected their freedom of conscience, he did not feel bound by his father's oath to guarantee them freedom of worship. Like his father, Ferdinand decreed a ban on Lutheran worship in the towns. Unlike his father, he enforced it through "reform commissions" made up of high church and state officials, with a mandate to interrogate urban pastors and schoolmasters as to their beliefs; adherents of the Augsburg Confession were dismissed from their posts and ordered to leave the territory within two weeks. Lutheran nobles in the estates protested but took no action, perhaps because the peasant uprising in nearby Upper Austria (see below) made them fearful of challenging the

Figure 10.5. Emperor Ferdinand II (r. 1622–1637). Portrait by Justus Sustermans (1597–1681), Palazzo Pitti, Florence. *Bridgeman Art Library.*

ruler's authority. By 1601 Ferdinand felt strong enough to issue a general mandate prohibiting Lutheran worship throughout Inner Austria; the reform commissions now questioned Lutheran pastors in the countryside who had been appointed by Lutheran nobles who had patronage rights over the churches. Additionally, Ferdinand began purging territorial administrations and town councils of Lutherans. Soon Lutheran burghers of key cities like Graz were required either to convert to Catholicism or sell their goods and go into exile. Between 1598 and 1605, some 11,000 Inner Austrian subjects chose exile over conformity.

By the time Archduke Ferdinand was elected king of Bohemia (1617), the re-Catholicization of Inner Austria had been brought to a more or less successful conclusion. But in Upper and Lower Austria, which Ferdinand inherited from his uncle Mathias in 1619, the estates were not minded to accept meekly whatever their new ruler might decree. In both duchies Emperor Maximilian II had struck a bargain with the estates (1568–1571): in return for sizable grants to pay off his debts, he guaranteed freedom of worship for Lutheran nobles. By the early years of Rudolph II's reign, as many as 90 percent of the nobles in Lower Austria were Lutheran. In Vienna, the Landeshaus, the headquarters of the estates of Lower Austria, served also as the city's principal Lutheran church. In Upper Austria the situation was similar. Emperor Rudolph, in Prague, had entrusted the governance of Upper and Lower Austria to his brother, Archduke Ernest (d. 1595), who had hopes of imitating the Counter-Reformation policy of Archduke Charles in Inner Austria. He prohibited Lutheran services in the Vienna Landeshaus. To make it clear there would be rewards for having the correct belief, he dismissed Lutherans from the city council and appointed Catholics instead and ceased appointing Lutheran nobles to posts in the territorial administration. Lutheran and especially Calvinist nobles opposed these measures, but the nobility's dependence on their Catholic rulers was made clear by a peasant rebellion in Upper Austria (1594–1597), directed against new obligations the noble landlords were imposing on their peasant tenants. Peasant armies fought the troops raised by the estates to a standstill but accepted a compromise dictated by Emperor Rudolph II.

Archduke Mathias, who followed Archduke Ernest as administrator of Upper and Lower Austria, pursued the same strategy of giving leading families incentives to convert to Catholicism. But Mathias's plans for easing Emperor Rudolph from his throne forced him to negotiate for the support of the estates, in Austria as well as Bohemia. He guaranteed freedom of worship for the nobles of Upper Austria in 1609 and for the towns in 1610. From this time forward the cause of Protestant nobles in Upper and Lower Austria was connected to that of their confreres in Bohemia. Hence when Bohemia's estates revoked their election of Archduke Ferdinand and chose Frederick V of the Palatinate as their king instead (1619), the estates of Upper and Lower Austria let Ferdinand know that hereditary succession did not mean what he thought it did—he would be their ruler only if they chose to accept him as such. In Vienna, Ferdinand had the fortitude to refuse the estates' demands—including the expulsion of the Jesuits and the building of a Lutheran church in Vienna—even as an army sent by the rebel estates of Bohemia neared the city gates. He was saved from a likely disaster only by the timely arrival of a cavalry troop from Catholic Tirol, which bolstered Vienna's defenses.

Ferdinand deputized Maximilian of Bavaria, head of the Catholic League, to deal with Upper Austria. En route to Bohemia, Maximilian, backed by Tilly's army, forced the submission of the rebellious estates in Linz, the capital city (August 1620). Since Maximilian and the league had borne the expense of this campaign, Ferdinand named him interim administrator of Upper Austria. For six years the occupying Bavarian officials collected taxes with great punctiliousness and ousted Lutheran pastors as soon as they could find suitable Catholic priests to serve in their stead. Replacement of a Lutheran pastor was the spark that touched off the last great peasant rebellion of the early modern era (1626–1627). A peasant army defeated Bavarian forces in the field and confined them to Linz and one other fortified town. Mindful of the historical record, their leaders reissued the Twelve Articles of the 1525 Peasants' War as a basis for negotiation. Their specific demands included expulsion of the Bavarians, reinstatement of dismissed Lutheran pastors, and the admission of peasant deputies to the estates of Upper Austria. But the arrival of a new and more skillful Bavarian commander meant defeat once more for the recurring dream of peasant freedom.

Only now did Emperor Ferdinand decree for Upper and Lower Austria (1627) the enforced re-Catholicization he had put in place some years earlier in Inner Austria: all Protestant pastors and teachers were to be expelled from the territory, no matter by whose authority they held their position. Meanwhile, Ferdinand's efforts to change the beliefs of the all-important nobility were beginning to show results, partly because administrative positions were open only to Catholics, and partly because of Jesuit preaching and the quality education offered by Jesuit schools. Under Ferdinand II (d. 1637) and Ferdinand III (d. 1657), burghers in Upper and Lower Austria were given the choice between conversion and exile; between 1620 and 1660, some 50,000 people chose exile. Though small communities of "hidden Protestants" survived into the eighteenth century, especially in the remote mountain valleys of Tirol and Inner Austria, Habsburg Austria was becoming solidly Catholic.

One can see now why Ferdinand III insisted on exempting the Austrian lands from the clause in the Treaty of Westphalia that abrogated the ruler's prerogative (according to the 1555 Peace of Augsburg) of compelling his subjects to profess the religion of his choice. Charles V had fought, ultimately in vain, to prevent the empire's Lutheran princes from exercising the so-called "right of reformation" to determine the religious identity of their subjects. In the years subsequent to 1555 there were certainly Lutheran and also Calvinist princes who made use of the right of reformation to change the confessional character of their lands. But one of the historical ironies of the Reformation era is that no princely dynasty in the empire made better use of this prerogative than the Catholic Habsburgs, in their own hereditary lands.

The Commonwealth of Poland-Lithuania, covering a large swath of northeastern Europe, dated from the 1385 union of two crowns: the Kingdom of Poland and the Grand Duchy of Lithuania, Europe's only remaining pagan principality. Upon the death of King Louis of Anjou (1384), Poland's barons recognized as their queen his young daughter Jadwiga; suspicious of Jadwiga's German fiancé, a member of the Habsburg family, they compelled her to break the engagement and marry instead Jagiello, Grand Duke of Lithuania (r. 1377–1434). In return for a crown in Poland, Jagiello agreed that he and his pagan subjects should convert to Catholicism (many of his subjects, like many of Poland's, were Eastern Orthodox Christians who spoke Ruthenian, related to modern Byelorussian and Ukrainian). Union with Lithuania strengthened Poland against its worst enemy, the Teutonic Knights of Prussia, a territory that blocked Poland's access to the Baltic Sea. This largely German military order, dating from the era of the Crusades, presented its military campaigns as godly struggles against the pagans of Lithuania; Poland, a land that tolerated schismatics—that is, Eastern Orthodox Christians who rejected the papacy—was not much better. To counter the propaganda of the Knights, fifteenth-century canon lawyers in Poland developed arguments as to why a Catholic ruler ought to tolerate people of different faiths in his lands—an interesting anticipation of sixteenth-century debates.

Politically, public life in both parts of the new Commonwealth was dominated by an unusually numerous nobility. By the end of the fifteenth century, Poland's *Sjem* (diet) had two houses, a senate for the higher nobility and a Chamber of Deputies for the lower nobility. Bishops of the Catholic Church had seats in the senate, as did bishops of the Ruthenian Orthodox Church. But neither Catholic nor Orthodox bishops had power to inhibit the spread of Protestant ideas from about 1550, especially among Polish or Lithuanian noblemen whose humanist education encouraged them to look for a dawning age of church reform. In 1556, the Commonwealth's Calvinists organized a synod on the estates of a leading nobleman, not far from Cracow, then Poland's capital. For two or three decades there were more Calvinists than Catholics among nobles in the senate. Moreover, even lay Catholic senators joined in blocking the bishops from enforcing the antiheresy verdicts of church courts, especially if directed against fellow nobles. Poland's kings were equally averse to constraint in matters of religion. Sigismund II, last of the Jagiellonian dynasty (r. 1548–1572), understood himself to be "king of the people, not of their consciences."

Early in 1573 the *Sjem* voted approval of the Confederation of Warsaw, declaring that freedom of conscience and religious toleration were inviolable principles of law. Then 40,000 noblemen gathered on a field near

Warsaw to elect a new king, Henry of Valois, younger brother of France's King Charles IX; before his enthronement, Henry, suspected of complicity in the hideous Massacre of St. Bartholomew's Day (1572), had to swear his personal allegiance to the Confederation. Henry left Poland soon afterward and returned to France as King Henry III, succeeding his late brother (1574). His successor, Stephen Bathory of Transylvania (r. in Poland 1576–1586), devoted himself to war with the Grand Duke of Muscovy, who now styled himself Tsar (Caesar) Ivan IV, better known as Ivan the Terrible (r. 1533–1584). Ivan had sent out his armies to "gather" under Muscovy the "Russian" lands, that is, the Ruthenian lands of Poland-Lithuania; Bathory's offensive stalled, for a time, Russia's push to the west. In religion, Bathory was both an ardent Catholic and a strong believer in toleration.

Poland-Lithuania was not the only land where nobles were prominent among those attracted to Calvinism, but it was unusual in that almost no one else felt the same attraction, apart from burgher churches in the towns of southern Poland. As in Transylvania, the Polish Reformed Movement suffered also from internal divisions, due to the success of Anti-Trinitarian doctrines propagated by Italian expatriates. The Arians, as Polish Anti-Trinitarians were known, formed their own synod in 1565; when Calvinists, Lutherans, and Bohemian Brethren (Hussites) in Poland formed a common doctrinal front against Catholicism in the 1569/1570 Consensus of Sandomierz, the Anti-Trinitarians refused to join. By the 1570s, it seems Polish Calvinism had passed its peak.

One thing Poland's bishops could do was to bring in Jesuit fathers to open secondary schools; by about 1600 there were twenty-five large "colleges," with over 10,000 students. Their pupils included many sons of elite Calvinist families who themselves converted to Catholicism. As elsewhere, the Jesuits also promoted a revival of devotion. The *Lives of the Saints* by Sigismund II's Jesuit confessor became one of the most popular Polish-language books of the era. For those yearning for a deeper kind of prayer, there were translations of the classics of Spanish spiritual writing, like Luis de Granada's *Guide for Sinners* (1564) and the *Spiritual Exercises* of St. Ignatius Loyola. By the seventeenth century, popular Catholicism had a momentum of its own, centered on the Commonwealth's thousand or more shrines devoted to the Blessed Mother, of which the most famous was that of the "Black Madonna" of Czestochowa, an icon dating from the fifteenth century.

Sigismund Vasa, King of Sweden by hereditary right, was also elected in Poland-Lithuania as King Sigismund III (r. 1587–1632). If Sigismund's attempt to impose a Tridentine Catholicism on Lutheran Sweden was utterly rejected, as noted above, in Poland-Lithuania his freedom of action was limited by the Commonwealth's deep-rooted tradition of toleration.

Also, the influential men who backed his election had wanted a plausible alternative to a Habsburg candidate for the throne, not a Catholic prince of the Tridentine stamp. But over what proved to be a long reign, Sigismund was able to promote the Catholic cause indirectly, and probably more effectively than he could have done by royal fiat. Noblemen needed the king's approval for admission to the senate, and Sigismund rarely named a Protestant senator; gradually, the confessional identity of this important chamber shifted. He also made it clear that Catholic nobles would have privileged access to such favors as the court could dispense. In Lithuania, Ruthenian noble families that had converted to Calvinism now converted again, to Roman Catholicism.

Meanwhile, change was astir in the Ruthenian Orthodox Church. In 1589 Ivan the Terrible's successor created a Patriarchate of Moscow that was to be equal in status to the Patriarchate of Constantinople. To many Ruthenians, this looked to be a continuation in a different guise of Tsar Ivan's campaign for a "gathering" of the "Russian" lands. Might it not be better to strike a bargain with a more distant Patriarch, in Rome? Not many years earlier, Pope Gregory XIII had rejected King John III's appeal for a Swedish version of Latin Rite Catholicism, in which married priests would say mass in Swedish. Uniate or Eastern Rite Churches that recognized papal authority, while preserving their long tradition of having a married clergy and worship in the language of the people, were a different matter. Hence when the Metropolitan of Kiev petitioned for union with Rome under these terms, Pope Innocent IX (r. 1591–1605) gave his approval, sending representatives to Poland-Lithuania to celebrate the Union of Brest (1596). The Union was, however, immediately rejected by many Ruthenian Orthodox bishops, and by large segments of the laity, including the Cossacks of the Dnieper River basin, an independent-minded federation of borderland warriors. King Sigismund III sought to promote the Uniate Church by refusing to admit to membership in the senate those Ruthenian bishops who rejected the Union. But Piotr Mohyla, Metropolitan of Kiev (1632–1647), forged a powerful weapon against the Union by founding an academy that became the center for a Ruthenian Orthodox intellectual and spiritual revival—rather like a combination Tridentine seminary and Jesuit college. In 1648 the Dniester Cossacks launched a successful revolt against the crown of Poland-Lithuania, which ended by their accepting the suzerainty of the tsar in 1654. Though it was not by Muscovy's initiative, the Ruthenian lands were now "gathered" under Muscovy.

Sigismund Vasa believed that it lay within his power to determine the religious complexion of his realms, first in Sweden, then in Poland-Lithuania.

So did Archduke Charles and Emperor Ferdinand II in their Austrian lands. Oldenbarnevelt and Holland's town regents believed that wise government could steer the Dutch Republic safely past the dogmatic storms stirred up by (as they thought) a few Calvinist agitators. Sigismund Vasa failed utterly in Sweden, where the elite of the country were united against him in their Lutheranism, but had better success in Poland-Lithuania, where he could offer inducements for the nobles to return to the Catholic fold, but not coerce them. Ferdinand II found that the peasants of Upper Austria had more stomach for resisting a Catholicism imposed from above than the Lutheran nobles of his territories. Oldenbarnevelt lost his life by failing to recognize the appeal that strict Calvinist doctrine had for ordinary believers. Each of these outcomes shows that doctrine and politics, even if taken together, are not enough to account for the religious changes of this era. We must also have a sense of how different social groups in different lands reacted to what the preachers said and what the princes did. This point will be reinforced by looking at the religious history of England (chapter 11), where each successive government found its vision of religious uniformity for the kingdom obstructed by one kind of resistance or another.

11 | Politics

England's Reformations, 1527–1660

Late medieval England had an underground dissenter tradition: the Lollards, who trace back to the condemned doctrines of John Wycliffe (d. 1384), an Oxford theologian. That Lollards became Protestants is not easy to document, but they prepared the ground for Reformation doctrines by rejecting many Catholic doctrines and by insisting that lay people nurture their faith by reading the New Testament in their own tongue.

Luther was told in 1519 that his Latin works were being reprinted and discussed in England. The earliest known center of this discussion was at Cambridge's White Horse Inn, where regular gatherings of students inspired by the humanist program of biblical study, presided over by an Augustinian friar named Robert Barnes, soon had townsfolk calling the tavern "Little Germany." Imprisoned for his heterodox beliefs, Barnes escaped to Wittenberg, where he studied with Luther. When England repudiated the papacy, Barnes became an English agent in Germany, but when he returned home he was burned as a heretic (1540) for preaching the doctrine of justification by faith. Though apparently not connected with the White Horse group, William Tyndale, a preacher and an Oxford graduate, proposed to translate the New Testament directly from Greek into English. Church leaders frowned on this "Lollard" idea. But Tyndale found backing from London merchants while he lived in the Low Countries and saw his English New Testament through the press (1525). He then produced polemical writings of a generally Lutheran inspiration, aided after 1528 by another English refugee, John Frith. Frith was martyred for his beliefs (1533) shortly after returning to England; Tyndale too was eventually caught, tried, and executed, not in England, but by Charles V's government in Brussels (1536). Though Barnes's theology was wholly Lutheran, Tyndale and Frith seem to have adopted some Zwinglian ideas during their years on the continent. Right from the start,

Figure 11.1. King Henry VIII (r. 1509–1547). Hans Holbein the Younger, "King Henry VIII of England." *Colección Thyssen-Bornemisza, Madrid.*

English Protestantism showed signs of the heterogeneous character that was to be its distinguishing feature.

During the first decade of the continental Reformation, England's King Henry VIII (r. 1509–1547; fig. 11.1) had no patience for heretics like Barnes and Tyndale. An amateur theologian, he won praise from the pope for a treatise in defense of the Catholic doctrine of the sacraments against Luther (1521). One of his councillors, the humanist Thomas More (1477/8–1535; fig. 11.2), matched Tyndale's polemics from the Catholic side book for book; as chancellor of England (1529–1532), More presided over a judicial apparatus

Figure 11.2. Sir/Saint Thomas More (1478–1535). Hans Holbein the Younger (1497–1543), "Sir Thomas More," 1527. *Copyright the Frick Collection, New York, NY.*

that sent Anabaptists to the stake, in keeping with antiheresy laws once enacted against the Lollards (1415). Yet in the end, as in Sweden and Denmark, it was the king and not the scholars who made the first of England's many Reformations.

This chapter briefly discusses Henry VIII's separation of the Church of England from the Catholic Church (1534–1547), Edward VI's establishment of Protestantism (1547–1553), the reestablishment of Catholicism under Mary Tudor (1553–1558), the reestablishment of Protestantism under Elizabeth I (1558–1603), the reassertion of episcopal authority and certain pre-Reformation practices under Charles I (1625–1642), and the Presbyterian establishment mandated by Parliament (1646–1649). While England was controlled by Oliver Cromwell (1649–1658), the Congregationalists or

Independents sought without success to have an established church according to their liking, while radical sects like the Quakers created their own religious communities.

In 1503 the future *Henry VIII* married his elder brother's widow, Catherine of Aragon, a younger daughter of Ferdinand and Isabella. In light of Old Testament warnings that the man who took his brother's widow to wife would have no issue, he sought and received from Pope Julius II a dispensation for the marriage. But Queen Catherine gave Henry no living child save for a daughter, Mary Tudor, born in 1516. Not having a son to carry on his line, King Henry feared he was under God's curse, a fear that took on a new edge when he determined (1527) on marrying one of the queen's young attendants, Anne Boleyn. Did the pope really have authority to dispense anyone from an obligation of divine law, as laid down in the Bible? And could the present pope not retract the papal dispensation of 1503, thus rendering Henry's marriage with Catherine invalid, so he could marry Anne? But in this year of the Sack of Rome, it was no time for Pope Clement VII to defy the wishes of Catherine's nephew, Emperor Charles V. Hence the papal legate, who after protracted negotiations finally came to England, immediately declared that he was remanding the matter of Henry's annulment to the curia in Rome.

While Clement VII sought excuses for further delay, an angry Henry VIII brought into play an antipapal statute of 1393 prohibiting appeals to any court outside of England. The king's chief adviser, who had also been exercising the judicial powers of a papal legate in England, was first to feel the sting of this new turn in royal policy. Henry seized on an idea that royal courts had been suggesting, namely that England's ecclesiastical courts were violating the 1393 statute by the mere fact of recognizing Rome's appellate jurisdiction. In return for his gracious pardon for this offense, the king forced a cowed Convocation (assembly of the clergy) to recognize him as "sole protector and supreme head" of England's church (1531). Parliament then approved a suspension of the payment to Rome of papal taxes on the income of English bishops.

At the same time, a petition purporting to come from members of the House of Commons (actually drafted by one of Henry's ministers) complained that bishops who swore an oath to the pope were not even proper subjects of the king; Henry professed to be shocked. Parliament specifically prohibited appeals to Rome in 1533, just as a new archbishop of Canterbury, Thomas Cranmer (1489–1556), granted Henry the annulment he had sought and solemnized his marriage to Anne Boleyn. The 1534 Act of Supremacy declared the king to be "supreme head of the church in England," and for good measure Parliament made it treasonous to say otherwise. In 1535 a few brave souls who refused commands to endorse the king's supremacy over the church, including Thomas More, the former chancellor, and Bishop John Fisher of Rochester, were beheaded at the Tower of London.

Since the Latin mass continued to be celebrated as before, the priest vested as before, parishioners had only a dim idea of the great changes afoot. But between 1536 and 1540 Parliament suppressed England's monasteries and confiscated their property to the profit of the king. This attack on the fabric of church life gave rise to rumors that parish churches too would be closed, which sparked a series of popular uprisings, mostly in northern England, known as the Pilgrimage of Grace (1536–1537). As one of their manifestos proclaimed, the rebels aimed at "maintenance of the faith of God, the right and liberty of his church." Though mobilizing sizable forces in places, they were talked into laying down their arms, and nothing changed. As in other parts of Europe, England's common folk were to be governed in matters of religion, not consulted.

What kind of church was England to have? Two court factions struggled over this question for the balance of Henry's reign. The group that sympathized with the doctrines of the continental Reformers was led by Thomas Cromwell (d. 1540), the architect of the king's Reformation legislation; Archbishop Thomas Cranmer; and Edward Seymour, duke of Somerset (1500–1552), the uncle of Henry's third wife, Jane Seymour. The group that sought to preserve as much as possible of Catholic doctrine and practice was led by Thomas Howard, duke of Norfolk (1473–1554), and Stephen Gardiner, bishop of Winchester (1497–1555). Various credal statements were drafted, sometimes influenced by the 1530 Augsburg Confession and sometimes not. Henry's preferences are evident in the so-called King's Book, adopted by Parliament in 1543, which asserts a Catholic interpretation of the eucharist and specifically defends human free will against the Protestant doctrine of predestination. When the confiscation of chantries was proposed (1545–1546), the measure was defended before a skeptical Parliament not on doctrinal but on fiscal grounds—the king needed money. But in 1546 Howard was accused of treason, and Gardiner's name was dropped from a proposed list of regency councillors for the king's nine-year-old son.

Policy in the reign of *Edward VI* (r. 1547–1553) was made initially by Seymour, the young king's great-uncle, and after 1549 by a more zealous Protestant, John Dudley, earl of Warwick (1504–1553). It was of great importance for England's subsequent religious history that Seymour and Dudley took their doctrinal cues from Zurich and Geneva, not from the Augsburg Confession. The new reign began with a royal decree (1547) banning all emblems of "superstition," including altars, all religious images, candles, and processions. Royal commissioners made a circuit of the kingdom's parishes over the next few years to enforce the decree, though they met a good deal of resistance.

Meanwhile, a committee under Cranmer's direction was preparing an English-language liturgy, with texts for the traditional monastic hours as well as for the mass. The *Book of Common Prayer* was endorsed by Convocation (1549), after Seymour intimidated conservative bishops into abstaining. Introduction of the Prayer Book liturgy provoked a brief uprising in the west of England, where rebels demanded that every priest at mass pray for the souls of the dead by name, "as our forefathers did." Three years later Convocation approved a credal statement, the *Forty-two Articles*, which repudiated Catholic teaching on the presence of Christ's body in the eucharist but did not endorse the Reformed doctrine of predestination. Under Dudley's influence, Convocation issued a second *Book of Common Prayer* (1552), which confirmed the Reformed understanding of the rite that was now called holy communion, no longer the mass. The legislation of Edward's reign thus amounted to a revolution in belief and worship going well beyond Henry VIII's revolution in the governance of the church. Whether changes of this magnitude could have been successfully imposed on an unwilling populace remains uncertain. When Edward VI died of an illness (1553), England's new ruler was the Catholic daughter of Henry VIII and Catherine of Aragon.

Mary Tudor (r. 1553–1558; fig. 11.3) easily overcame a Protestant conspiracy mounted by Dudley, in the name of his daughter-in-law, Lady Jane Grey, a descendant of Henry VII. There was also a brief rising in favor of Mary's Protestant half sister, Anne Boleyn's daughter Elizabeth, which was provoked by Mary's marriage to a foreign prince, Spain's Philip II (1554). But her restoration of Catholic worship and of England's ties to Rome evoked no more resistance than Henry VIII's Act of Supremacy in 1534. Some of Henry's conservative bishops—those who opposed a Protestant theology for the new church and were deprived of office under Edward VI—had by now accepted papal supremacy and regained their positions under Mary; Stephen Gardiner and others carried on learned polemics with continental Reformers. To deal with the convinced Protestants whose numbers had grown appreciably during the previous reign, the heresy laws of

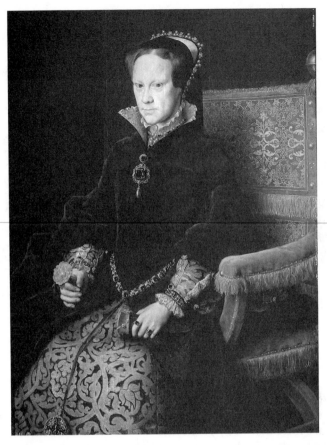

Figure 11.3. Mary Tudor. Anthonis Mor, "Mary Tudor, Princess of England." *Scala/Art Resource, NY.*

old were also reinstated. Among the roughly three hundred victims during Mary's reign, many were Anabaptists. Some were leaders of the Protestant wing of England's clergy who had not gone into exile on the continent, like the preacher Hugh Latimer (1485–1555); they met their deaths as bravely as More and Fisher under Henry VIII (fig. 11.4). Meanwhile, churchwardens around the country brought out altars and statues and restored them to their places of honor. The fact that these and other church furnishings had been carefully hidden away, not destroyed, suggests parish leaders were hoping that the changes dictated from on high under Edward VI would not last. In fact, change was only beginning. In 1558 the ailing and childless Mary recognized her Protestant half sister as her lawful successor.

Figure 11.4. Protestant martyrs under Queen Mary. The Burning of Bishops Hugh
Latimer and John Ridley, John Foxe, Book of Martyrs (London, 1776). *Courtesy of
University Libraries, University of Minnesota, Minneapolis.*

Elizabeth I (r. 1558–1603) was recognized by the 1559 Act of Supremacy
as "supreme governor" of the Church of England (fig. 11.5). Insofar as the
new queen's intentions may be divined (she kept her thoughts to herself),
it seems Elizabeth envisioned a straightforward restoration of the *Book of
Common Prayer* and the *Forty-two Articles* of 1552. Note, however, that a
church governed by bishops was an unlikely spiritual home for the zealous preachers who now returned from exile in the continental centers of
Reformed Protestantism. Elizabeth's Reformation statutes also blurred
some doctrinal and liturgical distinctions. The 1559 Act of Uniformity reinstated the *Book of Common Prayer* of 1552, but with new language permitting a Catholic as well as a Reformed understanding of the eucharist
and an "Ornaments Rubric" requiring clergy to wear the traditional vestments. When thirty-seven London clerics of a Reformed Protestant temper
ostentatiously refused to don "popish rags" for their services, Elizabeth insisted on their removal from office. The queen's concessions to Catholic
sentiment were dictated by the politics of getting her statutes accepted in
the House of Lords, but they also reflected her fears of the kind of popular
resistance to radical changes in worship that had been evident in the two

Figure 11.5. Elizabeth I (r. 1558–1603), standing on a map of England. Marcus Gheeraerts the Younger (1561/2–1636), "Elizabeth I." *National Portrait Gallery, London.*

previous reigns. If England's people were still in some sense Catholic, Elizabeth and her officials took well-considered steps toward creating a Protestant sensibility. Royal commissioners who now made a circuit of the parishes ensured that altars and statues and other "superstitious" church furnishings were destroyed—not hidden away for future use, as in Edward VI's time. Copies of the English-language Great Bible compiled under Henry VIII (1539) were placed in every parish church; the popular *Book of Martyrs* by John Foxe (1517–1587), recounting in particular the gruesome torments suffered by faithful Christians under "Bloody Mary" Tudor, was also given wide distribution.

Partly in hopes of preserving amity with Spain, Elizabeth was at first loath to see Catholics punished for their beliefs—but not after a series of Catholic plots against her were sparked by Pope Pius V's declaration (1570) that she was excommunicated and that faithful Catholics must no longer recognize her as queen. In 1574 she authorized the first executions of "seminary priests," trained at a seminary for English Catholic exiles at Douai in the Low Countries. A 1582 statute declared seminary priests and Jesuit missionaries automatically guilty of treason, a crime punishable by death. By the 1580s Catholic "Recusants," willing to accept the penalties for their form of dissent, were a dwindling minority.

Meanwhile, Spanish backing for Catholic plots in England helped persuade Elizabeth to support the Dutch Revolt. This in turn provoked Philip II to send against England his "invincible Armada" (1588), the defeat of which stoked an English national pride that was by now firmly identified with the Protestant cause (fig. 11.6). But a Protestant foreign policy was of little consolation for those frustrated by the queen's apparent unwillingness to "complete" England's Reformation. When Elizabeth's Protestant bishops presumed to endorse a new version of the *Forty-two Articles* (1562–1563), they were sharply reprimanded; only in the queen's good time were the *Thirty-nine Articles* approved, and by Parliament, not Convocation (1571). When groups of devout Protestant clergy and laity formed biblical study groups known as "prophesyings," Elizabeth ordered the archbishop of Canterbury to suppress these divisive gatherings; when he refused (1576), she placed him under house arrest, waited for him to die, and found a successor, John Whitgift (1583–1604), who was more than willing to carry out her wishes. To silence those among his clergy who were now calling openly for a presbyterian rather than an episcopal form of church governance, Whitgift required all clergy to swear to the *Thirty-nine Articles,* which included a defense of the authority of bishops. Eventually, some three hundred clergy were dismissed for refusing the oath. Such pressures from above provoked a series of bitterly satirical anonymous pamphlets (1588–1589) under the name of Martin Marprelate (that is, Martin the foe of prelates, or bishops). An angry Elizabeth authorized a roundup of zealous Protestants, of whom a few were executed. The Conventicle Act of 1593 threatened death for anyone (not just Catholics) who refused to attend Church of England services.

By the end of Elizabeth's reign the ambiguities of her religious legislation were causing serious dissension. For example, the *Thirty-nine Articles* took no position on the key question of predestination. Hence a group of young

Figure 11.6. Defeat of the Spanish Armada, 1588. The *Ark Royal*, flagship of England's Admiral at the time of the Armada, Lord Howard of Effingham (1536–1624); engraving, English school, sixteenth century, private collection. *Bridgeman Art Library.*

professors and students at Cambridge felt at liberty to espouse publicly the doctrine of human free will. To set these errant youngsters straight, Archbishop Whitgift convened a synod that approved the Calvinist doctrine of predestination in its most extreme form (1595). But the queen ordered the withdrawal of this new statement, precisely because it went beyond the *Thirty-nine Articles*. Meanwhile, and without rejecting the authority of their bishops, clerics sympathetic to presbyterian ideas on church governance were forming Netherlands-style *classes* with like-minded colleagues in the same district. Sympathetic lay patrons were endowing preacherships, earmarked for orthodox Calvinists, to make up for a lack of preaching by the poorly paid and sometimes poorly educated parish clergy. The earlier controversy over "popish rags" was not forgotten either. Indeed, there was now a more general demand for purging the liturgy of a long list of "popish" elements, like saints' days, candles, the exchange of rings at marriage, prayers at the graveside, and the celebration of Christmas. Finally, many earnest Christians were offended by the fact that most people in England did not properly observe Sunday, the Lord's day: afternoon and evening were mainly given over to such lewd entertainments as drinking, dancing, and plays; traditional parish festivals continued as before, with the same pagan overtones, like dancing around the Maypole.

Those expressing such sentiments had come to be known as Puritans. But Puritans, in the latter years of Elizabeth's reign, represented a current of opinion within the Church of England, not a separate church body. Puritans had a distinctive tendency to personalize the doctrine of predestination, searching within their own experience for a moment of conversion at which God's grace had entered their lives. Still, on the doctrinal formula of predestination, and also on a more proper observance of the sabbath, most bishops were of the same mind as the Puritans, although many Puritans would have preferred a presbyterian form of church governance.

Not all of those who hoped to see the church some day "purified" of episcopacy, as well as popish ritual, had presbyterian views on church order. Refusing to recognize any larger church body, Separatists believed decisions on all important matters must be made by each congregation. Searching their consciences for evidence of God's grace in their lives, like other Puritans, Separatists also concluded that baptism must be the expression of the precious experience of conversion—and hence not a ritual suitable for infants. Harassed by Church of England authorities, in part because of their views on baptism, some Separatist or "Baptist" congregations took refuge abroad. Among them were those known in American history as Pilgrims, who found a home in Leiden before crossing the Atlantic to Massachusetts. Within the broad Puritan current there were thus numerous countercurrents flowing in different directions. The demarcation between defenders of the established church and a Puritan opposition, overly simple for Elizabeth's reign, did eventually become a battle line, but only because of the events of the next two reigns.

King James I (r. in England 1603–1625) made promises to relax the laws against Catholic Recusants but backed down in the face of pressure from a solidly Protestant Parliament. James was perhaps never more in harmony with his subjects in England than in the months following the foiled Gunpowder Plot (November 1605), in which Guy Fawkes and several other Catholics secreted thirty-four barrels of powder beneath the House of Lords. For Protestants this was not just the act of a few men; it was a diabolical popish plot directed from abroad, with the complicity of people whose foreign allegiance prevented their being true Englishmen. The growing sense of a distinctive English identity included a streak of rabid anti-Catholicism; England's greatest writer of the next generation, John Milton, could speak of Catholicism not so much as a religion as a "[foreign] priestly despotism under the cloak of religion." The penal laws now multiplied: Recusants were forbidden to practice law, take a university degree, or vote in local or parliamentary elections. A bill for making Catholics wear red hats (as Jews were made to do in papal Rome) was discussed but failed to pass.

In just about every other respect James's reign sowed mistrust of the crown among ardent Protestants. Because of his experience as king of Scotland, he made it clear he was no friend of those who wanted a presbyterian Church of England. As the author of a treatise on monarchy, he believed a king was answerable only to God, not to his subjects—he once shocked the House of Commons by referring to himself as an "absolute" monarch. Under Elizabeth, members of the privy council formed a faction in Commons, helping to guide the House's deliberations; James elevated his councillors to the upper nobility, leaving himself no organized party in the lower House. James's queen, Anne of Denmark, converted to Catholicism, creating at the court an island of toleration for Catholicism, which made Puritans in particular deeply suspicious.

Also, the expenses of James's household much exceeded those of the frugal Elizabeth. Critics made no allowance for the fact that Elizabeth did not have a family to maintain in royal state, but they did note that some of the king's largesse went to two handsome male favorites, each in turn raised to a high place in his council. Since Parliament refused to increase the subsidies granted during Elizabeth's reign, James and his council made do with customs revenues, which grew as foreign trade increased. Between 1611 and 1621 James governed without summoning Parliament, save for one brief and contentious session (1614). This was not illegal, but it was unprecedented, and men with experience in Parliament pondered what it meant when the king had no need for his subjects' consent.

The separate issues of religion, governance, and state finance fused together in debates on foreign policy. During the early stages of the Thirty Years' War, there was wide support for the popular Princess Elizabeth, James's daughter and wife of the embattled Frederick V of the Palatinate—but little appreciation of what going to war would cost. Meanwhile, seasoned Spanish diplomats dangled before the king hopes of a Spanish bride for his son and heir, Prince Charles. The idea of a Spanish Catholic match was deeply unpopular, but James had visions of a Spanish dowry that would solve his financial problems. After years of fruitless discussions, Prince Charles and the duke of Buckingham, his father's current favorite, crossed the English Channel and rode incognito across France to reach Madrid, only to learn Spain was not interested in a marriage under conditions England could accept (1623). Summoned the following year, Parliament readily accepted proposals to break England's treaties with Spain. For a moment, it seemed that James's heir and Parliament would unite behind an anti-Spanish policy.

Figure 11.7. Charles I of England and Scotland (r. 1625–1646). Anthony van Dyck, "Portrait of Charles I," 1637–1638. *National Gallery.*

But *Charles I* (r. 1625–1646; fig. 11.7) and Buckingham concealed from Parliament the true costs of an ambitious policy that included subsidies for Protestant armies in Germany and naval expeditions against Spain. This left the new king hungry for money and Parliament puzzled by his need for it. Moreover, none of the ventures that England now undertook or helped sponsor met with success; for example, the English fleet that raided Cadiz captured the wine stores of the Spanish navy, leading to a few days of merriment during which the Americas treasure fleet slipped into port unmolested. Finally, an anti-Spanish policy was not necessarily a Protestant policy. France's Cardinal Richelieu was promoting anti-Habsburg coalitions well before the time he was free to mobilize France's resources toward this end. It was in this context that Buckingham arranged for Prince Charles to marry Henriette Marie, daughter of France's Louis XIII. Many English Protestants were offended by the new queen's Catholic chapel, and despite the king's denials they rightly suspected from his actions that some relaxation of the anti-Recusant laws had been part of the bargain. When Charles at Parliament's behest ordered stricter enforcement of the laws, Richelieu responded to this breach of faith with one of his own: English ships lent to France for the war against Spain were used instead in the successful siege of the Huguenot port of La Rochelle. Protestant England was outraged.

Meanwhile, in the Parliament of 1626, the House of Commons raised the novel idea that the king should respond to grievances presented by Parliament before Parliament voted on his fiscal requests. Members demanded among other things that Buckingham, the architect of Charles's policies, be impeached before the House of Lords on a long list of treason counts, including a fantastic accusation that he had poisoned the late King James. To save Buckingham from being tried on trumped-up charges, Charles dismissed Parliament without getting approval for the subsidies and customs duties he so desperately needed. Charles presumed the right to continue collecting the usual customs duties, and to make up what was lacking he levied a forced loan on his wealthy subjects. A number of knights and burghers refused to pay, appealing to the king's courts for vindication. But Charles and his councillors pressured judges to make sure no one escaped his quota in the loan. In one instance, the king's attorney general had the court record falsified to make it appear that a case actually decided on procedural grounds had established a precedent allowing the king to imprison his subjects without showing cause. As word of these tactics leaked out, there was widespread public discussion of the king's unprecedented attack on the rights of Englishmen.

When Parliament was again summoned in 1628, Commons refused to vote the requested subsidies until Charles accepted the Petition of Right, stating that no English subject could be forced to pay a loan or tax without approval by Parliament or held in prison without a showing of cause. But Charles's insistence that the customs duties he continued to collect were not a "tax" subject to parliamentary approval led to bitter disputes in the Parliament of 1629; members of Commons also claimed that the king's "Arminianism" in religion (see below) portended a Catholic and Spanish "tyranny" for England. When Charles ordered Parliament dissolved, two members of Commons held the speaker in his chair, while others barred the doors against those wishing to leave, until a resolution was passed declaring that anyone who paid customs duties or promoted Arminianism was a "capital enemy" of England. Charles decided that he, like his father, could govern England without Parliament.

England had by now made peace with Spain, relieving the pressure on the king's budget, while Buckingham's assassination by an unknown hand removed the most obvious target for popular hatred. Charles still needed revenue for the navy (he was properly concerned by the growth of Dutch naval power), but his lawyers contrived a novel means of raising it. By tradition, five cities along the Channel were required to supply ships for the king's needs. Charles now commuted this nearly forgotten obligation to a payment for ships and extended "ship money" from the five ports to the whole kingdom (1634). As in the previous disputes over customs duties and forced loans, this novel practice was denounced in numerous pamphlets and tested in the royal courts. But the combination of ship money and the still increasing customs revenues enabled the king and his council to manage for eleven years (1629–1640) without summoning a Parliament, where Charles would have to confront the opposition to his policies head-on. Indeed, the king might have ended his days without ever calling a Parliament, had it not been for the religious policies that provoked war in Scotland.

Under James, a king who strongly defended episcopal authority against the presbyterian challenge, some bishops presented episcopacy as a matter of divine law, not mere human law; England's bishops were true successors of the Apostles, as were Roman Catholic and Eastern Orthodox bishops. This doctrine of the apostolic succession of bishops implied that the Catholic Church was a true church, albeit misguided on some points—an idea deeply offensive to Puritans, but not to King James. Indeed, he saw the Church of England as a "middle way" or happy medium between the excesses of papal tyranny and presbyterian fanaticism. In keeping with this conception of the church, some bishops and clergy pressed for restoring a solemnity of worship comparable to Catholicism, to complement the traditional Protestant emphasis on preaching. Among other things, they proposed moving the communion table from the center of the church to the east end, where once the altar had stood, and surrounding it with a railing, where those who wished to do so might kneel for reception of communion.

Meanwhile, Puritans also vigorously attacked the doctrine of free will, which had been given a new lease on life by Elizabeth's refusal to sanction the bishops' condemnation of it (1595). They denounced with equal vigor the doctrine of the apostolic succession of bishops and any effort to revive liturgical practices of the pre-Reformation era. Puritan opposition helped fuse these otherwise disconnected issues into a coherent point of view. By the end of James's reign, Puritans were convinced that backsliding on the doctrine of predestination—"Arminianism"—was a dangerous stalking horse for that cesspool of iniquity, "popery" itself.

William Laud (1573–1645; fig. 11.8), whom James I named bishop of St. David's, was one of a number of influential clerics eager to counter Puritan polemics point by point. Charles I signaled from an early date his backing for Laud and like-minded clerics in the Church of England. He protected from parliamentary censure a cleric who wrote against Jesuit tracts but without including the (for Puritans) obligatory denunciation of Catholicism as the religion of the Antichrist. The king baffled his subjects by his leniency to Recusants, repeatedly promising Parliament to enforce the penal laws more strictly but not doing so in practice; that some of his

Figure 11.8. Archbishop William Laud. Anthony van Dyck, "Archbishop William Laud," 1633. *Courtauld Institute of Art, London.*

aristocratic advisers were known to be Catholics only made things worse. Finally, he promoted Laud through the ranks of the hierarchy, making him bishop of London (1628) and archbishop of Canterbury and leader of the church (1633). Despite increasingly vocal opposition from Puritan clergy and laity, Laud and other like-minded bishops worked to promote liturgical reform throughout England. If churchwardens of former times were badgered for not having gotten rid of their altars, they were badgered now for not setting the communion table "altar-wise" in the east end of the church and surrounding it with a railing at which those receiving communion were to kneel.

Charles and Laud decided that Scotland too must have the benefit of this new order. Under King James a weak form of episcopacy was superimposed on the Scots Presbyterian Kirk in 1570. He later demanded that the Scots conform to certain usages in England's *Book of Common Prayer* (1614) but had the good sense to back down on further changes that evoked opposition. The version of the *Book of Common Prayer* now decreed for Scotland, following perfunctory consultations in the northern kingdom, was slightly modified to suit Scottish sensibilities. But when the new service was introduced at Edinburgh's cathedral of St. Giles, a woman threw a stool at the officiating cleric; this led to a riot, which served to galvanize opposition in much of the country. Early in 1638, a National Covenant demanding a General Assembly of Scotland's Presbyterian Kirk was signed with great ceremony by nobles, preachers, and burghers. The General Assembly duly met, voting in large majorities to abolish all changes in worship imposed by James I and Charles I, as well as the office of bishop.

Meanwhile, the Catholic faction among the king's advisers urged him to be bold in facing down the Scots. This was bad advice, but Charles was not accustomed to seek counsel from men who failed to tell him what he wanted to hear. He marched to Scotland with an army, but lacking funds to keep his men in the field he accepted an inconclusive treaty. By refusing in subsequent discussions to abandon episcopacy in Scotland, he in effect prolonged a war for which he had no resources. The so-called Short Parliament (April 1640) was quickly dissolved when Charles found that appeals to English patriotism against the Scots were of no avail; in fact, opposition leaders in Parliament were already in contact with Scottish Covenanters. When the Covenant Army entered northern England, Charles had to agree to buy them off; but the invaders pointedly refused to withdraw until they had their money in hand. Charles had to summon what came to be known as the Long Parliament (1640–1649).

Even now, Charles and the opposition in Parliament might have reached an accommodation had it not been for unforeseen events in Ireland. Since the twelfth century, the descendants of a conquering English aristocracy based in the area around Dublin had gradually extended their authority to the rest of the country, save for the northern region of Ulster, where native Irish chieftains still ruled. The Reformation was officially proclaimed when a docile Irish Parliament created the Church of Ireland (1534). But strong support for the Church of Ireland was not evident until "new English" settlers occupied land that was confiscated from Irish chieftains during Elizabeth's reign and regranted for "plantation" or colonization by English entrepreneurs. By the late sixteenth century, as seminary priests trained in the Low Countries ministered to the "Old English," and bards created a new Catholic literature in Irish, the Counter-Reformation was well underway. From 1594 until 1603 Ulster's chieftains fought an ultimately futile struggle against England's political control of the country; their flight to France in 1607 created an opportunity for more extensive "plantations." In parts of Ulster groups of English or Scottish colonists settled solid blocks of land from which Irish Catholic landholders and tenants were forcibly removed. England's government in Ireland, represented from 1632 to 1641 by Thomas Wentworth, earl of Strafford, did not shrink from stern measures to quash resistance. But in October 1641, Old English nobles and Irish chieftains conspired to seize fortified posts in Ulster; their declared goal was the defense of Irish and Old English rights, not rebellion against the crown—one leader even claimed to be acting in the king's name. This carefully orchestrated rising among the elite sparked a very different kind of rebellion, as local groups of Catholic Irish, often led by women, spontaneously vented their fury on Protestant colonists, leaving perhaps four thousand dead and many more expelled from their lands. This was the desperate violence of the dispossessed, comparable in some ways to Indian uprisings against English colonists in North America. Indeed, Protestant Englishmen saw the "Wild Irish" and the "Savage Indians" of North America as equally dangerous to civilization.

King Charles had found himself virtually powerless as Parliament convened in November 1640. He accepted Commons' condemnation of ship money as illegal, as well as a bill providing that Parliament must meet at least every three years. But Commons also voted to impeach the king's two most detested councillors, Archbishop Laud and the earl of Strafford. Despite solemn assurances from the king that the charges against Strafford were baseless, the House of Lords voted a sentence of death. After an attempt organized by the king to break Strafford out of prison was foiled, a mob outside the palace howled for Strafford's blood; Charles did as he had to, signing an innocent man's execution warrant. Still mistrustful of the king's intentions (not without reason), the opposition leadership forced him to accept a bill providing that Parliament could not be dissolved without the consent of the members.

At this point Charles made a surprise trip to Scotland (August 1641), where he first attempted (again without success) to organize the overthrow of the Covenanters and then accepted a treaty abolishing episcopacy in Scotland. Hoping to return to London with some measure of prestige restored for having made peace with his Scottish subjects, Charles was instead engulfed by a wave of anti-Catholic hysteria touched off by lurid reports of the rebellion in Ireland. By a vote of 159 to 148, Commons passed the so-called Grand Remonstrance, declaring that all the evils England had suffered for many years past were part of a vast popish plot, fomented by Jesuits and bishops, that had now reached its horrid climax in the slaughter of law-abiding English settlers in Ireland. In the House of Lords, twelve conservative bishops declared that angry crowds in the streets were making it dangerous for them to attend sessions. Commons impeached the bishops and placed them under arrest, depriving the king of twelve votes in the Upper House. Charles retaliated by presenting a bill of impeachment for six leaders of the opposition (January 1642), but the Lords balked; by tradition, bills of impeachment were presented by the House of Commons, not by the king. Charles's efforts to carry out the arrests himself roused great anger. The king and his entourage soon had to quit a capital he no longer controlled. Negotiations between the two sides continued for several months, but when Charles was presented with an ultimatum that would have stripped him of all effective authority, he chose instead to raise an army, as Parliament did the same. England was at war.

The Presbyterian settlement was a consequence of Parliament's victory in England's Civil War. In 1645 Parliament created a New Model Army, based on egalitarian principles: the officer ranks were for the first time opened to men not of noble birth. Though Oliver Cromwell (1599–1658; fig. 11.9), one of the army's more successful leaders, was of the lesser nobility, most commanders were commoners. It was not the Parliament but this new and effective fighting force that defeated the king's armies in several crucial battles. The Parliament was made up of respected and propertied gentlemen; the army had a good sprinkling of social upstarts. More important, Parliament had legitimacy, but the army had power.

Most members of the Long Parliament, by now Presbyterians, favored an alliance with the Scottish Covenanters (concluded in 1644) and a national Presbyterian church, free of bishops, similar to Scotland's. A national synod of Presbyterian clergy (the Westminster Assembly, 1645) adopted an orthodox Calvinist creed, but it was only in 1646, after the king's armies had been decisively defeated, that Parliament abolished episcopacy and created

Figure 11.9. Oliver Cromwell. Robert Walker, "Oliver Cromwell, Lord Protector of England," ca. 1649. *National Portrait Gallery, London.*

a Church of England governed along presbyterian lines that everyone was required to attend. Puritan austerity in worship and Puritan morality were the new orthodoxy. Churchwardens were now badgered if they failed to bar the church door on Christmas day, lest parishioners sneak in for Christmas carols and other popish ceremonies.

But the army's leading officers, Cromwell included, were Independents, not Presbyterians. Rather than having Parliament impose on the country a national church, they favored congregational autonomy and toleration for Protestant sects (like the Anabaptists) condemned as heretical by the Presbyterians. This diversity of opinion was important for the army, because Anabaptists could make good officers, and so could the adherents of political factions like the Levellers, who demanded abolition of the monarchy and a broadening of the franchise for parliamentary elections. But once Charles I surrendered (1647), Presbyterians viewed the army and its heretical friends as a liability; Parliament voted to dismiss the army without pay. Instead, the army occupied London and dictated the impeachment of eleven Presbyterian leaders. Following a confusing year (1648) in which Charles I escaped from captivity and opened discussions with a Parliament that now feared the army more than the king, the army triumphed once more. Charles was recaptured, and roughly one hundred Presbyterians were purged from the Long Parliament. The remaining "Rump Parliament" agreed to try the king and order his execution as a traitor (1649). Monarchy and the House of Lords were now abolished.

From 1649 until the restoration of monarchy in 1660, England was a *Commonwealth,* not a kingdom. Lavish revenues from the seizure of church lands and the properties of the late king's supporters now supported ambitious campaigns by the army. In Ireland, where leaders of a reorganized rebellion had now joined forces with royalists, Cromwell's campaign of 1649–1650 was decisive. At Drogheda and Wexford, he calmly sanctioned the slaughter of defeated soldiers and civilians alike, for in his eyes this was God's retribution on the Irish, "tainted" with the blood of English victims in 1641. In 1650–1651 he turned back two armies loyal to the late king's son, whom Scotland had acclaimed as King Charles II. But neither the "Rump" of the Long Parliament (finally dismissed by Cromwell in 1653) nor the "Parliament" whose members were handpicked by the Independent or Congregationalist churches (1653) was able to agree on a form of government for the now kingless England. In 1654 power was returned to the army, and in a constitution written by leaders of the army, the Instrument of Government, Cromwell was named Lord Protector of the Commonwealth. But when the Parliament elected according to this new constitution refused to accept the supremacy of the army, it too was dissolved by Cromwell (1655). The next Parliament (1656–1659) offered the crown to Cromwell; he declined, but he did designate his son Richard to succeed him as Protector, as Parliament had also suggested. Yet upon the death of Oliver Cromwell (1658), the new Protector had little support either in Parliament (which he dissolved) or in the army. As leaders of the army conducted contentious discussions with members of the recalled Rump Parliament, royalists and Presbyterians joined forces to raise an army in Scotland that marched south and entered London. A newly elected Parliament (including a revived House of Lords) negotiated the terms by which Charles I's son returned to England as King Charles II (r. 1660–1685).

During the Commonwealth years the army leadership also had plans for a new order in England's religious life. Cromwell favored a unified national Protestant church, with full toleration for all of the disparate tendencies that might loosely be grouped together as Puritan. To an important degree, toleration of this kind already existed. The abolition of episcopacy (1646) meant that the episcopal courts that had traditionally exercised censorship over the publication of religious tracts no longer existed. The expulsion of the Presbyterians from Parliament (1649) undermined the authority of the orthodox Calvinist clerics who now filled most pastorates. Hence under Cromwell there was an explosion of sectarian opinions such as had not been seen anywhere in Europe since the early years of the German Reformation. The Congregationalists or Independents were Calvinist in their theology of predestination and the sacraments, but not in their conception of church order. The Baptists or Separatists, whose theology was Calvinist in origins, had by now split into two warring camps over the interpretation of Christ's redeeming death. Other Separatists, known as Seekers, were not so much an organized sect as a loose grouping of believers who rejected any organized worship, gathering instead in small groups to read the Bible and seek illumination from the Spirit of God moving within them. The Seekers in turn gave rise to still other groups. One was the Ranters, whose preachers derided the idea that there was any such thing as "sin" for those truly possessed by God's grace. Another, popularly known as the Quakers, developed from the life and teaching of George Fox (1624–1691), an itinerant cobbler who believed that Christ had commissioned him to "turn people to that inward light, spirit and grace . . . that divine Spirit which would lead them all into Truth." The Friends (as Fox's followers called themselves) gathered in silence, waiting until someone among them was led by the Spirit within him or her to offer a word (fig. 11.10).

This proliferation of conflicting opinions about the ultimate nature of reality was as alarming to many seventeenth-century Englishmen as it had been to many Germans of the sixteenth century, all the more so because radical preachers were often (like George Fox) of humble background, and some called for an overturning of the social hierarchy as well as the hierarchy of the church. Yet Cromwell remained a consistent advocate of toleration for all Protestants; he also ended a ban on Jewish settlement in England that dated back to the 1290s. The Rump Parliament agreed (1650) to a Toleration Act abolishing the requirement to attend services of the national church, but it also tightened existing laws against blasphemy and adultery, a reflection of Congregationalist fears about the unheard-of sects (like the Ranters) that now seemed to be sprouting like mushrooms. In fact, Congregationalist churches were just as eager to suppress the heretical

Figure 11.10. A Quaker meeting. "Reunion of Quakers," seventeenth-century engraving from the school of E. Heemskerk. Note that it is a woman who speaks as worshipers listen. © *Copyright The Trustees of the British Museum.*

doctrines of the Separatists as the Presbyterians had been to suppress the heretical doctrines of the Congregationalists. Cromwell persuaded the Congregationalist Parliament of 1653 to pass legislation enabling each parish to name "Tryers and Ejecters" to test the doctrine and qualifications of current or would-be pastors; this measure strengthened the generally Puritan character of the pastorate, but did nothing to still the imprecations that different groups hurled at one another. In 1656 Parliament thumbed its nose at Cromwell's desire for toleration by insisting on trying and severely punishing a Quaker leader named James Nayler for "blasphemy."

In the end, toleration for Protestant Dissenters was promised in the terms that Charles II agreed to (1660), though not in fact implemented for some time. Some 1,750 Puritan clerics were dismissed from their posts and replaced over time by clergy who accepted the authority of the restored bishops. In the so-called Clarendon Codes of 1661–1665 Protestant Dissenters as well as Catholic Recusants were banned from taking part in elections or attending universities and subjected to heavy fines for nonattendance at Church of England services. But the king's Act of Indulgence (1672) authorized dissenting Protestant congregations (not Catholics) to purchase from the crown licenses to worship as they chose. Puritan preachers of various persuasions, including many dismissed from office when Charles II came to the throne, could now function as pastors of regularly organized churches rather than underground conventicles. After so many vicissitudes, after so many versions of Christianity had each had its hour on the stage of power, England too was a nation that recognized one religion formally and many others informally.

A moment's reflection on England's history between 1527 and 1672 corroborates two important points. First, politics and religion cannot be separated. It was not religion that made Henry VIII anxious for a male heir or gave him the force to cow his bishops, nor was it politics that made him reject the theological advice of the Protestant councillors who were the most natural supporters of England's break with Rome. The halfway house between Protestant and Catholic ideas of the church that Elizabeth I created for reasons of political prudence became, for King James I and Archbishop Laud, a principle of theology that allowed England to navigate safely between the contrary errors of Rome and Geneva. Charles I might conceivably have ended his reign without another Parliament, but Scottish Presbyterian resistance to his *Book of Common Prayer* forced him to confront the opposition in England. Again, the constitutional conflict between king and Parliament might possibly have been resolved short of war, except for the superheated English Protestant reaction to the rebellion in Ireland. Finally, the major Protestant parties involved in these conflicts seldom challenged the medieval principle that there must be only one law of belief for all of England. As in France, Germany, and the Dutch Republic, the limited toleration finally made available to Protestant dissenters was dearly bought. It was based not on a belief that subjects of the crown ought to be free to believe as they wished, but on recognition of the fact that all efforts to achieve by force the laudable goal of uniformity had failed.

Second, politics and religion by themselves do not provide a sufficient explanation for the flow of events. This is especially true for the years between 1640 and 1660. The respectable Presbyterian gentlemen of Parliament, much as they opposed Charles I, found a king more to their liking than the army and its lowborn clientele; it was the humbler folk who filled the army's ranks who wanted monarchy abolished altogether. Ireland's gentry, with a stake in the existing order, modulated their rebellion, but the dispossessed peasantry did not. Neither religion nor politics can be understood without an appreciation for the conflicts that divided people of differing wealth and status and for the visions of social harmony evoked to bridge such differences. This is the topic of part IV.

IV SOCIETY AND COMMUNITY

The words "society" and "community" have a shared range of meaning. But "society" usually refers to all who live in a given territory, while "community" usually refers to a smaller unit within the social body. Also, "society" describes the complex of social relations in a morally neutral way; "community" describes a moral unity that surmounts individual or interest group conflicts. The people of a community are thought capable of achieving harmony because they make up a relatively small, face-to-face group. Was the medieval town or village a community in this ideal sense of the term? Or was it merely a less complicated version of our own market-driven society? For most of the twentieth century, social theorists have debated whether the idea of community indeed describes an earlier phase of human social evolution or simply expresses a nostalgia, on the part of thinkers unhappy with modern life, for a harmonious past that never existed. Niccolo Machiavelli offered another alternative. He believed there could be a true community even in a large city like Florence, but only under two conditions: There had to be an external danger strong enough to overshadow normal tensions between haves and have-nots, and the common people had to have some share in political power.

While differing about whether to define society according to class (as understood by Marx) or merely according to status groups, Reformation historians have sought to explain religious choice in terms of economic conflicts. But the results have been mixed. Any social group one can name will be Lutheran in some areas, Catholic or Calvinist in others, and in still others impossible to classify as tending one way or the other. Literacy sometimes seems more important than economic status, as do political conflicts, like that which pitted the independent-minded Protestant magistrates of Toulouse against the Catholic judges of the Parlement of Toulouse, who naturally took the king's side in any dispute. In two other large French cities, Lyon and Rouen, what counted was not whether one was a rich master craftsman or a poor journeyman, but when one's guild had been established. Guilds long a part of urban life and ceremony, like the butchers or the bakers, remained Catholic; new trades, like the printers in Lyon or the bonnet makers in Rouen, found the new doctrine more attractive. A great number of local studies, by authors espousing very different views of society, have found group rivalries of one kind or another taking on a confessional coloration. There seem to be social explanations for religious choice, if not necessarily economic ones. In fact, early modern Europeans survived by the aid of their fellows—kindred, neighbors, members of the same guild or the same political faction. In a matter as complicated as religion, it was a mark of good sense to do as one's fellows did. This pattern of collective action has led scholars to ask what the different forms of group solidarity may have meant for the Reformation. "Society" and "community" have to be looked at together.

Chapter 12 offers a descriptive account first of tensions that divided the *society* of late medieval Christendom, then of the various ideals of *community* by which people were guided in efforts to overcome their divisions. Chapter 13 then examines interest group conflicts in the German and Swiss Reformation, together with Lutheran and Swiss Protestant ideas on how conflicts were to be surmounted in a true Christian community. Chapter 14 first considers the same questions for the Calvinist and Catholic Reformations outside the empire, then concludes with a look at a few of the religiously mixed urban societies that represent the greatest break from medieval conceptions of the social order.

12 | Society and Community

Late Medieval Background

The *society* of late medieval Christendom was riven by a myriad of conflicts: within the family, between husbands and wives; within rural society, between peasants and their noble landlords; between town and countryside; within the towns, between patricians and guilds and also among the guilds themselves; and within the church, between clergy and laity. Over against these tensions one may set different forms of the ideal of *community:* the family, founded by marriage; the parish; the village; and the town.

SOCIETY

Christendom in the late Middle Ages was predominantly rural, and its slow growth beyond the limits of subsistence farming was mainly due to incremental improvements in agricultural productivity. Yet the fraction of its people who lived in towns created the market conditions that helped stimulate innovation in the countryside. Town and countryside are often contrasted—townsmen certainly thought of their rural neighbors as mere bumpkins—but both were shaped in the medieval centuries by the same economic and social processes. Priests and the members of male and female religious orders were an even smaller fraction of the population. There are indications that lay people of the late Middle Ages were more willing than ever to follow the guidance of the clergy, but there is also evidence of growing resentment, in some parts of Europe more than others, of the privileges that set the clergy apart from lay people.

Since in all societies the *family* is the basic unit, some sense of how families are formed tells us a great deal about the larger society. In fifteenth century Europe, patterns of marriage differed from one area to another. In Venice and Florence, the patrilineal family was of paramount importance, especially in elite circles; the sons expected to carry on a father's name and divide his inheritance in equal shares, usually of greater value than the dowry that was a daughter's share. To be sure, the price of dowries rose steadily, because families measured their own standing in society by the prestige of the families from which their daughters-in-law came. Men typically married in their late twenties or early thirties, women in their late teens. A young wife learned over time to be mistress of her household—sometimes quite a large household—but she was never of equal standing with her husband; her family of origin, having once provided a dowry, had no further obligation to her, and in her family of marriage she was a temporary resident.

Elsewhere, especially in northwestern Europe—England, the Low Countries, northern France, and Scandinavia—scholars have found evidence as early as the fourteenth century for what is now called the European marriage pattern. In other parts of the globe parents commonly arranged marriages for their teenage children, who then lived with one set of parents. In the European pattern, couples deferred marriage until their mid- or even late twenties, then immediately established independent households. By the end of the seventeenth century, marriages of this kind seem to have become common for all of Latin Christendom, even in the east, where it had been the custom for teenage couples to live with one set of parents. The Catholic Church's long-standing insistence that marriage be based on the free consent of both parties was a necessary condition for the emergence of the European marriage pattern, though not a sufficient condition, for fifteenth-century Italy was no less a Catholic society than fifteenth-century England.

In the choice of a mate, women often found themselves at the center of an age-old conflict between private desires and family responsibilities. Could a young woman understand herself as an autonomous individual without necessarily being in conflict with her family? Prospective brides seem mostly to have found a way to satisfy their wishes as well as those of their elders. This delicate balance within the family, between personal choice and group pressure, seems fundamental for an understanding of the larger nodes of society to be considered here, like villages and towns. If it is plausible (as scholars now believe) to speak of individual self-consciousness in Europe as early as the thirteenth century, this may be because European society threw up so many kinds of tightly organized groups, and thus so many occasions for individuals to play out the game of deciding who they were.

The other important consideration underlying the European marriage pattern was that men and women chose their spouses not so much (it seems) for romantic inclinations as for practical reasons: To get by in the world, a man needed a woman who could "spin well" in addition to tending to the children, just as a woman needed a man who "worked hard" to provide for them. In European towns of the late Middle Ages, both craft production and small business were concentrated in shops where husband and wife worked side by side, as is often shown by artists of the period (fig. 12.1). In many German towns, guild regulations of the later Middle Ages stipulated that a master craftsman could not set up shop unless he were married; they also required documentation that the woman herself, now to be admitted to the guild in a formal or informal capacity, had been born of "honorable" parentage. Among the goldsmiths, wives were not just full members of the guild, they also (unusually) paid the fees (fig. 12.2). But from the sixteenth century, if not earlier, the world of small-scale production and small-scale enterprise came under threat from mercantile capitalism, with its organization of large-scale credit operations and large-scale enterprises (see below). In these circumstances, male members of the guilds took steps to protect their jobs: Wives were barred

Figure 12.1. A man and his wife at work. Quentin Metsys (1465/66–1530), "The Money-lender and His Wife." *Réunion des Musées Nationaux/Art Resources, NY.*

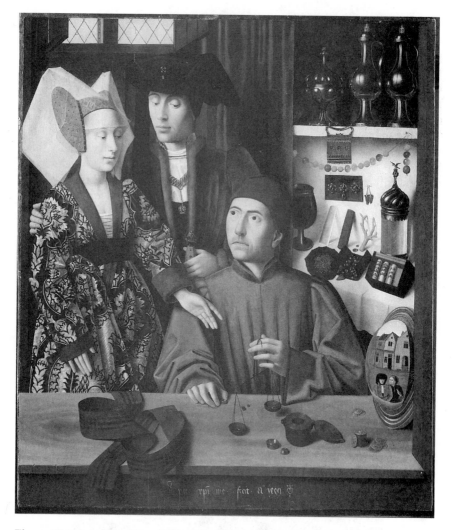

Figure 12.2. A goldsmith and his wife. Petrus Christus (1410–1472), "St. Eligius as a Goldsmith," 1449. Eligius of Noyon (d. 660), patron saint of goldsmiths, had been master of the mint for a Frankish king; as a widower, he became bishop of Noyon and Tournai. *The Metropolitan Museum of Art, Robert Lehman Collection, 1975 (1975.1.110), photograph. All rights reserved. The Metropolitan Museum of Art.*

from full membership and girls were no longer to be taken on as apprentices. Meanwhile, however, artisans' wives were finding reasons of their own to concentrate their energies on the household. Households were becoming larger, not because there were more children, but because the man of the house and shop needed more hands to keep up with the competition; wives had to provide for the accommodation of live-in apprentices, or unmarried kinfolk. The era of the Reformations was one in which the home was coming to be defined, more clearly than before, as woman's place. Would the woman of the house experience her new situation as a confinement, or as an opportunity?

From roughly 500, if not earlier, much of Europe's arable land was parceled out into large manors or estates, organized for the profit of great landowners who eventually came to be seen as Europe's *nobility*. Nobles liked to think of themselves as a superior breed of human stock, descended from valiant ancestors of the distant past, able to face unafraid the shock of battle that made ordinary men quake. Though the origins of these families were in fact quite heterogeneous, so long as success in war depended in part on a ruler's ability to deploy large numbers of the fighting-age landholders who alone could afford to equip themselves as heavily armed knights (horsemen), the nobility's dominant place in Europe's social order was secure. But the advent of new infantry tactics in the fourteenth century—including the Swiss pike and the English longbow—diminished the military importance of mounted warriors, just as men from burgher families, fortified by university degrees, were moving into judicial and administrative posts formerly monopolized by nobles. In many parts of Europe, these new men acquired titles of nobility, much to the disgust of the old nobility. Like their burgher cousins, who also invested in land, the new nobles were often better estate managers, introducing new crops, devising new ways to squeeze income from their peasants (see below), and making loans to spendthrift traditional nobles, which not infrequently led to foreclosure.

The one sphere in which the nobility doggedly maintained its dominance was the church. The great bulk of the church's landed income came from donations by rulers and especially by the nobility. Noble families endowed many of Europe's parish churches; they also alienated parcels of land to monasteries and convents, often presided over by their younger sons and daughters. Would-be reformers of the clergy had long demanded observance of the canon law requirement that a certain percentage of important positions be set aside for non-noble clerics with university degrees in canon law or theology. But the nobility fought off the reformers; in Strasbourg, for example, members of the cathedral chapter, from which bishops were often chosen, had to show sixteen quarters of nobility, documenting the nobility of their ancestors for four generations. Having made the church rich, noble families regarded the church's places of honor as the birthright of their surplus children. In a city like Strasbourg, the Reformation was in part a burgher protest against a church dominated by the rural nobility.

Peasants made up the pool of labor for the great estates. Until about 1150 most peasants had the legal status of unfree persons, or *serfs*. Serfs could not be sold by their noble or ecclesiastical lords, but in other respects their status was no different from that of slaves. Serfs could not leave the patch of ground tilled by their ancestors; they could not testify against a free man or woman; they had to marry off their daughters as dictated by the lord. Lords were free to demand from serfs a higher portion of the harvest, over and above what was theirs by custom, or extra labor on the demesne, the portion of land tilled entirely for the profit of the lord. This was not an agrarian economy that generated a large surplus. Serfs produced for their families and for the lord's portion; what was left they bartered for goods they needed. Money had not been widely used in transactions among rural folk for centuries. But after about 1150, the growth of cities (see below) generated a new, cash-based economy. Needing workers for their crafts, towns offered freedom to serfs. To avoid the trouble and expense of fetching back runaways, some lords granted their serfs freedom in return for annual lease payments in cash. To provide more grain for an expanding population, other nobles developed newly cleared land; to attract settlers, they offered inducements, including freedom for serfs. The fourteenth century witnessed a great population catastrophe due to famines as well as plagues like the Black Death (1347–1349). In some areas Europe's pre–Black Death population (about 80,000,000) fell by as much as one-third within the space of a few months. This was a good time for Europe's remaining serfs, as lords converted demesne lands to leaseholds for former serfs, rather than having to keep their peasants from running off to better opportunities elsewhere.

But other responses to the agrarian labor shortage were also possible. In the early fifteenth century, the prince-abbots of many south German monasteries forced peasants, under threat of arbitrary imprisonment, to sign documents acknowledging their status as serfs. This was the part of Germany marked by a series of rural uprisings, beginning in the 1440s. Some rebellions opposed departures from "old law," the customs regulating what landholders could demand. Others demanded "godly law," meaning that serfdom and other customs, no matter how old, were evil and must be abolished. The close connection between the enserfment of the fifteenth century and the great Peasants' War of 1524–1526 is indicated not only by the geography of the revolt, but also by where it did not occur. Though there were centers of the revolt to the west and east of Bavaria, there was no rebellion in the duchy itself, apparently because there had been no enserfment. Bavaria had a tradition of strong government— monasteries and nobles were simply not permitted to treat peasants in a way that curtailed their ability to pay taxes to the duke. After 1526, monasteries and other lords in the areas affected by the revolt made agreements with peasants recognizing the abolition of serfdom; this much was achieved by the rebellion.

Serfdom still had a future farther east. Beginning about 1450, Europe's population began a long period of recovery, reaching perhaps 120,000,000 by about 1600. To cash in on the growing demand for grain during this period, noble proprietors in east-central Europe compelled hitherto free peasants either to become serfs or to accept the burdens of labor service associated with serfdom. Rulers had a natural interest in protecting peasant wealth for purposes of their own taxation. But just as there was no superior to tell Germany's prince-abbots how to treat their peasants, rulers in Poland, Bohemia, Hungary, and the Austrian lands had little control over what nobles did on their estates. In some areas the nobility's normal contempt for the peasantry was enhanced by language differences: thus Polish peasants were enserfed by German lords in Prussia, Ukrainian peasants by Polish lords in southeastern Poland, and Slovak peasants by Hungarian lords in Habsburg Hungary. Czech peasants in Bohemia were enserfed by the polyglot aristocracy that won the battle of White Mountain. Thus by about 1650 there was a new line of division in rural Europe. West of the Elbe River, peasants might be poor or rich, but they were legally free and not bound by labor service. To the east, peasants were either unfree or bound by labor service.

Some peasants owned their land, but in most places they were a small fraction of those tilling the soil. As serfdom disappeared from Europe west of the Elbe, on different timetables in different areas, the *tenant farmer* became the "common man" of the countryside. Tenants leased their land, usually for lengthy periods, like seven to nine years. Their living standards varied enormously, depending on many different circumstances. One was the size of the holding; another was security of tenure. In Lombardy, lords had an incentive to renew their tenants' leases, because local law required a lord not renewing the lease to pay for improvements put in place by his tenant. In England, by contrast, tenant farmers faced eviction wherever the major landowners of a village determined on "enclosure," meaning that scattered fields were either consolidated or converted to pasture. This process began in the fifteenth century, as dwindling grain prices in an era of depopulation made the coveted wool of England's sheep a better crop, and continued into the nineteenth century.

Terms of the lease were another important consideration. As grain prices rose again after about 1450, tenant farmers prospered in the Low Countries (fig. 12.3) and northern France, where tenants owed landlords only the annual rent, but less so in much of Italy, where sharecropping was the common arrangement. Lords could demand higher rents as leases expired but not if tenants had the option of moving on to a better arrangement elsewhere. In southern France, for example, rents increased significantly only after about 1600, when there was no more new land to be

Figure 12.3. A peasant feast. Pieter Bruegel the Elder (ca. 1525–1569), "Peasant Wedding." *Kunsthistorisches Museum, Vienna.*

opened for cultivation by contractors and their tenant farmers. Demography and inheritance customs played a role as well. Especially in regions of partible inheritance, abundant families meant a splintering of tenancies that left the new generation without enough land to scrape out a living. Finally, beginning in the fourteenth or fifteenth century, depending on the area, the prince's tax collectors were a veritable scourge—peasants sometimes had to borrow at high rates to make the cash payments. More than anything else, it was the steadily increasing levels of taxation that drove peasants in late medieval and early modern Europe to take up arms against the existing order.

Despite all the vicissitudes that left a few men rich and their fellows not far from poverty, tenant farmers had an honorable status. They were the managers of the rural economy. Looked down on by their social betters, they were the solid citizens of the village communities to be discussed below. The people on whom tenant farmers could look down were the hired hands, known in England as *cottagers*. These relative newcomers to the local scene supplemented the wages they received from landlords or from wealthy tenant farmers by growing what their could on tiny patches of ground attached to their cottages. Their time of opportunity was dur-

Figure 12.4. A poor vagabond. Hieronymus Bosch (d. 1516), "The Prodigal Son." *Museum Boijmans Van Beuningen, Rotterdam.*

ing the agricultural depression of the late Middle Ages, when labor was at a premium. Despite laws enacted in response to the clamor of land-holders, wages could not be kept at pre–Black Death levels. According to scholars who have examined records of the meals provided to day labor-ers in some areas, the rural working man had a richer diet in the late four-teenth century than at any time until the twentieth century. But as rural population rose again, especially after about 1500, wages were locked in while prices for basic necessities steadily rose. Soon there were too many working folk for the rural economy to support. Mercenary warfare was an option for young men, especially in Switzerland and south Germany, the favored recruiting grounds for military entrepreneurs. Other options were to wander the roads as vagabonds (fig. 12.4) or to migrate to the nearest town. Cities in this era were hothouses of disease, never able to maintain their population by natural increase. They gladly opened their gates to the rural poor, so long as it was understood they must fend for themselves.

✛

Until the eleventh century *cities* functioned mainly as administrative centers. The county, a Roman political unit preserved by medieval rulers, was ruled by the count from a castle in his major *civitas* (city). Towns were but a shadow of what they had been in late Roman times, for social upheavals and barbarian invasions had repeatedly devastated urban life between roughly 250 and 850. As ecclesiastical rulers of dioceses that often perpetuated the boundaries of Roman administrative units, bishops too occupied fortified urban centers; within the boundaries of the Holy Roman Empire, they often ruled their cities as prince-bishops. Counts and bishops governed with the help of a sparsely documented local elite. Some of these "better sort of people" (in Latin, *meliores*) were merchants grown prosperous in local or even long-distance trade; others were lesser nobles who settled in town without cutting their ties to the rural economy. Between about 1050 and 1150, earlier in Italy than elsewhere, the better sort of people set up town governments of their own, the so-called *communes,* relegating the count or the bishop to the background. The cities of northern and central Italy were generally larger than those north of the Alps, and their communes were stronger, often asserting economic and military control of the entire county; communes in Germany and the Low Countries were fortunate to master more than a mile or two of territory beyond their city walls.

The commune was a sworn association of male citizens. In Italy and southern France, citizen assemblies elected a two-man team of consuls each year. In Castile, annual town meetings in which women as well as men participated (this was unusual) chose officials whose titles reflected centuries of Muslim rule. In Germany and the Low Countries and northern France, councils of aldermen chose their own successors, permitting members of the same families to rotate in and out of office. After about 1100, new towns were usually chartered as cities by a local ruler and endowed from the outset with the kind of communal government now familiar in older cities. The ruling elite were often known as "magnates" in Italy. Elsewhere they were simply "the families," but historians have dubbed them *patricians.* They governed some cities north of the Alps for roughly two hundred years, others for many centuries more.

Even before the communes were organized, grievances that the "better sort of people" lodged against their rulers hinted at a commercial awakening in Italy. The Crusades (1096–1293) encouraged maritime cities like Venice and Genoa to tap into the caravan trade bringing silks and spices from faraway Asia to various eastern Mediterranean ports. Deposit banking got its start in the thirteenth century, stimulated by the papacy's need for a means to transfer funds. Meanwhile, new instruments of credit facilitated payments in distant markets, and Italian bankers gained privileged access to commodities like England's wool exports through large loans to rulers. The availability of high-quality English wool fueled the manufacture of top-grade woolens, especially in Florence, which now competed in European markets with England's other customers, the woolen manufacturers of Ghent and Bruges in Flanders. By the 1270s merchant firms in Venice and Genoa had agents moving back and forth along the "silk road" to the fabled capital of China's Yuan (Mongol) emperors. Italy's "commercial revolution" drew migrants to cities in need of workers and stimulated trade elsewhere, as in the south German cities of Augsburg and Nuremberg. From around 1300, when Venetian and Genoese galleys began plowing the waters of the Atlantic, Bruges, in Flanders, became a clearinghouse where merchants trading with Italy could settle accounts. This in turn prompted the Hanseatic League, based in Baltic cities like Lübeck and Gdansk (Danzig), to make Bruges its obligatory trading station for the Low Countries. Europe's major trade routes were beginning to form an integrated network.

The Hanseatic League (in German, Hanse) was an unusual variation on the *merchant guilds* that began to appear around 1150. In large Italian cities some family firms had the resources to deal on nearly equal terms with Europe's crowned heads. Smaller firms, the great majority, found security in banding together with other merchants of the same town. The German word *hanse* originally meant an association of merchants from one city traveling together for their own safety. By about 1300, the word had come to refer to a super-federation aimed at protecting the collective interests of north German towns with merchant guilds. In the sophisticated economies of large Italian cities like Florence, there were several so-called greater guilds, including one each for goldsmiths, bankers, and silk manufacturers and two for woolen manufacturers.

Merchant guilds traded in the precious commodity of legal privileges. In a society in which nobles and clergy were set apart by privileges, like exemption from most forms of taxation, merchants demanded privileges of their own, like freedom from tolls or exclusive rights in the trade of certain commodities. Where cities were ruled by a prince, the simplest strategy was to make a financial offer the prince could not refuse; for example, the count of Holland was persuaded to mandate (1289) that goods moving up- and downriver had to be off-loaded for sale at Dordrecht, a privilege that Dordrecht fiercely defended against rival towns (sometimes by force of arms) for four centuries. In Italy, where there was no accepted authority to referee bitter economic rivalries, towns took whatever they could get with citizen militias or (after about 1350) mercenary armies. For example, Florence realized a long-term ambition by conquering Pisa in 1406: Pisa, at the mouth of the Arno, had for centuries obstructed the ocean-bound trade of its upstream rival. The whole purpose of the Hanseatic League, focused on exclusive trading stations like Bruges, was to keep traffic in and out of the Baltic in the friendly hands of member cities. But the Hanse had its own internal conflicts: Gdansk, angered by Lübeck's insistence on off-loading for its own markets all merchandise headed from the Baltic to the North Sea, helped open the Baltic to non-Hanseatic intruders from Amsterdam and other ports in the province of Holland.

The fact that towns went to war for their trading interests may look unsurprising to a twentieth-century reader, but it has few demonstrable historical precedents. The mercantile interest had never previously had so much influence with town governments as in medieval Europe. In ancient times, Athens dominated the sea but did not employ naval power to advance its trade. Venice and Genoa, in their contest for domination of the eastern Mediterranean, made economic warfare an art to be emulated by great powers of the future.

Yet the fact that merchant guilds were effective pressure groups does not mean merchants controlled the town governments. Where merchants as a group did gain power, they often did so in alliance with *craft guilds* formed by skilled artisans who prospered from the revival of trade. These self-governing and self-regulating associations of tradesmen emerged earliest in northern Italy, south Germany, and the Low Countries. In some places, guilds were preceded by an era of town-government regulations forcing practitioners of the same craft to live in the same neighborhood, so that city overseers could better supervise the quality of production. Guilds sometimes formed in the teeth of repressive legislation enacted by magistrates and their wealthy constituents to thwart the formation of such associations, especially for industrial production, like the manufacture of woolen cloth. In France, where craft guilds formed relatively late, often in the fourteenth century, they were promoted by the crown, which was happy to sell certificates confirming the status of master craftsmen. Like the merchant guilds, fully developed craft guilds demanded privileges of their own; in particular, no one not a member of the guild was allowed to practice the trade within the limits of the city's jurisdiction. Craft and merchant guilds eyed one another suspiciously, especially in cloth towns, but they also had reasons to join forces against the ruling patrician families.

In northern and central Italy, the guilds' principal grievance was the arrogant behavior of the magnates, combined with the violence of their endemic clan feuds. Merchants and craftsmen together formed (in the 1200s) a new sworn association based on guild membership, usually called the *popolo* ("people"). When the *popolo* assumed control of the commune, magnates were excluded from public office, and governance was in the hands of boards of guild members, chosen by lot to avoid factionalism. But the new regime fell victim to the same clan feuding that bedeviled the old, and by about 1300 most towns had accepted the rule of a city-lord who claimed to keep the factions in check. Florence was the only major city that preserved the guild-based regime of the *popolo* for as long as a century and a half, from 1289 to 1434. Here, the recurring tension was between the craft guilds and the greater guilds.

North of the Alps, patrician rule was harder to displace. In north Germany, southern France, and most of the northern Low Countries (including Holland), the traditional ruling elites either did not allow craft guilds to form at all or thwarted their efforts to gain a voice in the governance of the city. Armed uprisings by guildsmen often made the difference in south Germany and in the southern Low Countries. In south Germany, the patrician-dominated city council was renamed the small council, with some seats now reserved for guild members, especially the merchants; on important matters, the small council had to convene a large council representing the craft guilds. In the southern Low Countries, including Flanders and Brabant, the patrician council often became one chamber in a multicameral urban legislature, with separate chambers for the merchants and for a variously defined association of craft guilds. Such arrangements were not as egalitarian as they may seem, for wealthy guild members—craftsmen or merchants—had common interests and influence far beyond their numbers. Friction between the guilds and the patricians was a lingering issue in south Germany, but not in Flanders and Brabant, where the real battles were among the guilds. Late medieval Europe's bitterest urban civil wars pitted Ghent's weavers, small-scale entrepreneurs, against the fullers, their wage-earning employees.

Most towns were hard-hit by the depopulation of the post–Black Death era, and the scale of economic activity declined proportionately. Connections between Italy and China along the silk road broke off, and bankers were more wary of the risky business of lending to princes. A relative lack of customers for luxury goods pinched the luxury woolen industries of Flanders and Florence alike; new beginnings had to be made in products with wider appeal, like lighter woolens and fustian (a combination of linen and cotton). Master craftsmen sought security for their families by making it difficult for anyone but their own sons and sons-in-law to become full members, thus converting the hitherto fluid relationship between journeymen and masters into a fixed hierarchy that generated new social tensions.

The trading economy that revived with the slow growth of population after 1450 had new centers of gravity. Portuguese voyages of exploration down the African coast reached a long-sought goal when Vasco da Gama, having rounded the Cape of Good Hope, sailed on to Calicut in southwest India (1498). Portugal now had direct access to the spices and silks of the East, cutting out the "Moorish" (Muslim) enemies of Christendom—not to mention their Venetian trading partners. Captains of Portugal's "State of India" did in the Indian Ocean as Venice had done in the eastern Mediterranean: choke points controlling key straits were conquered and fortified, forcing local merchants to respect the rules laid down by Portuguese warships. This strategy was not completely successful, and the mainly Muslim merchant skippers of the Indian Ocean increasingly found the means of moving their merchandise, some of which found its way to the Mediterranean ports where Venice had outposts. During the first half of the sixteenth century, however, the bulk of Asian silks and spices reaching Europe went through Lisbon to the Low Countries for distribution. The entrepôt the Portuguese chose was not Bruges but Antwerp (Brabant), which had been gaining ground by trading with central and south German merchants not welcome in Bruges, since their towns were not members of the Hanseatic League. Augsburg and Nuremberg in particular were seeking outlets for the copper and silver that came from a technology-based revival of the mining industry in regions like Saxony, Tirol, and Slovakia. The demand in Antwerp for copper and for bronze (an alloy of copper and tin) increased dramatically because of the overseas requirements of Portugal's maritime empire: copper was one of the few commodities Europeans could trade advantageously in India, reducing the need for sending out silver to buy spices. Armbands and other bronze artifacts were prized trade goods in West Africa, where the Portuguese had begun the long and dismal history of Europe's African slave trade.

If Bruges had been the nodal point of a European trading network, Antwerp was the nodal point for an incipient world network. The possibilities of these multiple connections are illustrated in the careers of Augsburg's Jakob Fugger (d. 1525) and Antwerp's Erasmus Schets (d. 1544). The Fuggers began as fustian-weavers in the late fourteenth century. A hundred years later they were trading with Venice and making loans to rulers, like the Habsburg archduke of Tirol. Jakob Fugger parlayed his partnership with a key mining engineer and the Habsburg mineral rights he gained as collateral for his loans into a dominant position in the mining industry in Tirol, later extended to Slovakia by the firm's next generation. To satisfy Portugal's demands, huge quantities of Fugger copper were carted over the Carpathian mountains, shipped down Poland's Vistula River to the Baltic, thence to Amsterdam and along the Low Countries' inland waterway system to Antwerp.

Erasmus Schets married into a family that owned a mine for calamine, a key mineral in the new copper-smelting technology. As a young man he traded from Lisbon, shipping bronze armbands to West Africa, and formed connections with men bound for a new country that Portugal's mariners had accidentally hit upon to catch a better wind as they arced west across the south Atlantic toward the Cape of Good Hope—the land known as Brazil. Brazil's first sugar mill was set up by one of Schets's agents. Back in Antwerp, Schets bid against agents of the Fuggers for the three-year monopoly contract to distribute Portugal's spice cargo. If Jakob Fugger had provided a good part of the huge loan Charles V needed to bribe the empire's electoral princes in 1519, Erasmus Schets and the agents of Jakob's nephew Anton Fugger (d. 1560) sometimes competed for the honor of financing Charles's wars. These men combined great wealth and access to power to a degree not hitherto seen in Europe. This was precisely why small-scale merchants and ordinary guildsmen harbored the darkest suspicions about what such "great purses" were up to.

Firms like the Schets and the Fuggers were in fact the leading edge of a merchant capitalism that was transforming the economy in ways profoundly threatening to the small-scale enterprise characteristic of the guilds. In Tirol, later in Slovakia, miners who had been independent operators became, under Fugger control, wage-earning employees, and not by choice. All over sixteenth-century Europe, investors found among the surplus population of the countryside a willing pool of cheap labor for new rural industries. The bans on rural brewing or clothmaking that towns sometimes secured from their princes were not very effective. In some places urban guildsmen who were now being undersold vented their fury on the competition, like the men of Chemnitz in Saxony, who marched out to smash the linen looms of a nearby village (1522). But the economic logic that supported a displacement of low-skill enterprise to the countryside was inexorable. Even within urban guilds the traditional safeguards against having a few rich men monopolize the trade were crumbling. Masters who could afford to do so ignored regulations about how much capital equipment or how many workers a single shop might have. Small-scale brewers in Delft (Holland) complained of such practices to the magistrates, as did furriers in Strasbourg. But the magistrates were friends and partners of the men of wealth. In Strasbourg, for example, rich members of the craft guilds were often members of the social club formed around the merchant guild, Strasbourg's wealthiest guild.

Though their livelihood might be imperiled, guildsmen were still the solid citizens of Europe's proud cities. Like tenant farmers in the countryside, the urban "common man" had people to look down on. Guildsmen were always burghers (citizens) of the town. People who were not born in the town or who could not afford the substantial fee for purchasing rights

Figure 12.5. Rembrandt's "Beggars receiving alms at the door of a house." Rembrandt van Rijn (1606–1669), 1648. *Rijksmuseum, Amsterdam.*

of citizenship were classed as "inhabitants"—the journeymen who often wandered from town to town in quest of advancement and especially those who had neither a skill nor steady work. Guildsmen viewed such people as riff-raff, but they were simply the *urban poor* (fig. 12.5), transplanted from the countryside. In rare cases the urban poor resorted to arms to seize a place for themselves in the social pecking order, like the woolcarders of Florence, who for a time (1378–1382) gained for unskilled workers in the wool industry the right to form guilds and play a role in city government. Mostly they strove to do as others like them had been doing for centuries, to find a niche where hard work might lead to the respectability of guild membership and town citizenship. But around 1500 such newcomers were more numerous than before, and they found fewer possibilities for advancement. They could take to the roads, swelling the ranks of the vagabonds that towns increasingly complained about during these years, or they could stay put, somehow making do on seasonal employment and the occasional handout. Thus at a time when a few families scaled the heights of wealth, in cities across Europe a larger proportion of inhabitants than ever before, ranging from 30 to 50 percent, were classed as too poor to pay taxes. This era of growing social polarization was also the era of the Reformation.

Secular clergy and members of religious orders were a microcosm of Europe's social divisions. Chantry priests barely eked out a living; pastors lived comfortably. Members of cathedral chapters enjoyed a living standard like that of the noble families from which most of them came. There were convents whose modest entrance fees met the needs of guild families seeking an honorable place for a surplus daughter, others that demanded not only a rich dowry but sixteen quarters of nobility as well. By and large, however, tensions among the men and women of the church came not so much from differences in family background as from corporate self-interest. Monasteries and convents were corporations; so were cathedral chapters and parish churches. How were the competing claims of such bodies to be sorted out? For example, how was the bishop to share authority with his cathedral chapter in governing the diocese? And what rights did the bishop have over convents and monasteries that claimed to have papal exemption from his jurisdiction? Escalation to the level of armed combat was unusual in such matters, but not unknown. The bishop of Brixen (Tirol), at odds with his chapter, ruled that local shepherds be allowed to lease a mountain pasture. The owner, an allegedly exempt convent of noble ladies, said no. The chapter sided with the convent, and so did the archduke of Tirol, who raised troops and drove the bishop from his diocese.

Franciscan and Dominican friars saw themselves as showing up the ill-disciplined parish clergy by their good example of how to preach the gospel to urban layfolk. But parish priests resented competition from the churches of the friars, and some resented even more the friars' claims to moral superiority; if a priest's own parishioners did not mind his having a "second-class wife," what right did self-righteous friars have to thunder from their pulpits against "fornicating" priests? Franciscans and Dominicans were not the best of friends either. The two orders' principal theologians had disagreed over the question of Mary's Immaculate Conception: Had the Blessed Mother of Jesus conceived without the stain of original sin? In later generations each order denounced the other for heresy on this point. Finally, within the different orders, there were bitter fights about how strictly the founder's rules were to be applied, especially among the Franciscans. Most of St. Francis of Assisi's spiritual descendants believed the one-paragraph directive he had left behind needed amplification, but not the Spiritual Franciscans of the late thirteenth century, the Observant Franciscans of the fifteenth century, or the Capuchins of the sixteenth and seventeenth centuries, all of whom insisted that the deliberate simplicity of the original rule was necessary to guard against corruption by wealth and physical comfort. The clergy and religious of the pre-Reformation era were not a solid body marching to the same tune, but a loose collection of corporate cells, each marching to a music of its own. In this way too they resembled the larger society from which they sprang.

Despite all their differences, clergy and religious were set apart by their enjoyment of common privileges, in some cases dating back to Roman times. Townsfolk paid a sales tax for the wine or beer they purchased; priests and religious houses did not. In the countryside, landholders and their tenants were taxed for the land they farmed; pastors and monasteries were not. When lay persons accused of a felony stood trial before a town court, death sentences were common for crimes like theft (not to mention murder). Clerics and religious could only be tried before the bishops' courts, which had no right to sentence anyone to death and were known for their leniency. Moreover, these church courts also had jurisdiction over lay people in matrimonial disputes and in cases involving wills and other statements attested by oath.

During the later Middle Ages there is evidence for a growing resentment of clerical exemptions from rules binding ordinary people, partly because of the growing sense of solidarity (see below) in lay communities. Why should a thieving or murderous priest get off with a few years of confinement, instead of being strung up by the town executioner, like a proper felon? Or what right had the local Dominicans to disregard an ordinance requiring all edifices upriver from where the town got its drinking water to cease discharging their sewage into the river? Why should the Franciscans be allowed to pay no excise tax on beer sold in their tavern, meaning that honest tavernkeepers had to charge more? Why did church courts punish good Christian folk for falling behind on debts to "Jewish usurers" or the tithes they owed rich priests who bought these church incomes as an investment? And why must dairymen in the Cologne region suffer the monopoly for making a local cheese that the prince-archbishop had granted the nuns of a poor convent, under pain of excommunication?

This rising tide of anticlericalism is surely related to the Protestant Reformation that followed. Yet the depth and intensity of anticlerical sentiment varied greatly from place to place. For both England and France, scholars disagree about how widespread it was and whether it did or did not prepare the ground for Protestantism. In rural south Germany and Switzerland, sharp differences between one locality and another may reflect the history of relations between important monasteries and the peasantry. To take the two extremes of the debate, the sources for late medieval and sixteenth-century Germany are rife with a global critique of the clergy that is almost entirely lacking in contemporary sources for Castile. Was this because the reforms imposed on the clergy in Castile by Queen Isabella and Cardinal Cisneros had made a difference? Or because the mere presence of the Inquisition discouraged Castilians from adverse comment about their priests? Or was Germany rather than Castile the outlier, possibly because the empire's prince-bishops and prince-abbots wielded authority in a heavy-handed way that was not permitted to bishops and abbots in lands governed by strong rulers? And how important was this apparent difference in starting point for the differing outcomes, a Germany more than half Protestant, and a Castile more solidly Catholic? There are no agreed-on answers to these questions. All we can say is that the good local histories of the Protestant and Catholic Reformations are those that take into account the previous history of relations between clergy and laity.

COMMUNITY

The affection that binds members of a family together (or ought to) provides the underlying metaphor for all the other ideals of community to be discussed here. Marriage was thus viewed as the foundation stone of the larger society. Ancient Germanic law treated marriage as a contract between the two families. By contrast, the canon law of the Catholic Church treated marriage as a contract between the two parties, to which the free consent of both—including the young bride—was essential. As this view prevailed over time, "betrothal," which had meant an exchange of gifts between the families, came to mean a ceremony involving the parties. From at least the twelfth century, the church also viewed marriage as a sacrament, a ritual by which God imparted his grace in a special way. Sacraments had to have ministers but in this case the ministers were the couple themselves. Parental consent was encouraged, and so was the blessing of a priest and publicizing the marriage through the so-called banns, read aloud in church, but neither was necessary for a canonically valid marriage. Because matrimony was a sacrament, the bond between husband and wife could not be broken. Church courts recognized various grounds for separation from bed and board, including impotence and infidelity, but no one was free to remarry, not even the injured party. They also claimed

jurisdiction over cases involving someone (always a man) who was alleged to have promised marriage but did not keep his word. Town courts
took it upon themselves to punish adultery, a serious matter, especially if
it was the wife who violated the obligation of marital fidelity.

From the standpoint of the Protestant Reformers, the Catholic understanding of marriage had two glaring weaknesses. First, on the basis of St.
Paul's injunction that "it is better to marry than to burn" (with sexual desire), the church always viewed the married state as less worthy in the
sight of God than the life of those who renounced their sexuality in the
service of God. But since in their view such renunciation was neither en-
joined by Christ in the gospels nor possible for sinful human beings, the
Reformers eliminated monastic life as a choice for Christians. It was thus
of profound significance that the Reformers themselves—erstwhile celibate clerics—took wives themselves, as in Martin Luther's marriage to
Katherine von Bora, a former nun (1526). Not monks and nuns, but the
pastor and his wife were to be the models for Christian life. At the same
time, because baptism and the Eucharist were the only sacraments insti-
tuted by Christ, marriage was a purely human bond, and could for certain reasons be dissolved. Luther recognized three grounds for divorce
with the right of remarriage (impotence, infidelity, refusal of sexual congress), and Zwingli added others, including abandonment. In lands
where the old episcopal courts were abolished, new "marriage courts"
were created, combining the jurisdiction over marital issues formerly exercised by episcopal courts and town courts.

The second great failing of Catholic teaching was that its heavy emphasis on consent by the parties led to what were called clandestine marriages:
couples forbidden to marry by their parents could present them with a fait
accompli. By the sixteenth century, marriages of this kind were a sore point
among propertied families all over Europe. Fathers were increasingly anxious lest a daughter's foolishness give some no-account adventurer a claim
on the family patrimony. The Council of Trent (1563) addressed these concerns by requiring a church ceremony and the presence of witnesses (if not
consent of the parents) as conditions for a valid marriage. The same concerns were addressed earlier and more fully in Protestant lands. As in
Basel (1533), the new marriage courts required both parental consent and
the blessing of a clergyman as conditions for a valid marriage. In general,
Protestant tribunals stressed publicity more than consent as a condition for
the validity of marriages, and they also interpreted a husband's responsibilities more broadly, to include material support as well as sexual fidelity.
Preachers were as vigorous as their Catholic rivals in denouncing as sinful
all forms of sexual contact except for vaginal intercourse, but they did not
call on couples to refrain from sexual relations during Lent. The common

thread of novelty seems to be that marriage in the Protestant view was more consistently seen as a social institution. Couples were not just individuals answerable to God for their vows to each other, they were the cells that made up the larger body of the Christian community.

As cells in the larger Christian body, families were also to be nurseries of piety. Father and mother were to be the teachers of their children (fig. 12.6), but it was the father's role that was stressed by preachers of all persuasions. This emphasis on male authority in religious conceptions of the family during the Reformation era was echoed in many other spheres of life, from the guild workshop (as noted above) to treatises on morals written for the educated, in which virtue was often identified with control of the emotions. Emotionalism was seen as a characteristically feminine weakness (this devaluation of the emotions, rooted more in ancient Greek and Roman thought than in the bible, was promoted by the humanist revival of classical texts). It seems, then, that women were increasingly confined to a domestic sphere, where their proper submission to a husband's authority was increasingly emphasized by teachers of religion and morality.

Figure 12.6. A godly household in Flanders. Anthonius Claeissins, "A Family Saying Grace before a Meal," ca. 1585. *The Shakespeare Birthplace Trust, Stratford-upon-Avon, England.*

How did married women react, particularly in terms of their religious choices? Scholars are divided. On the one hand, there is no doubt that Protestant doctrine elevated the spiritual dignity of the married state, and many women responded, especially in the early years of the Reformation; women of the lower orders were often to the fore in anticlerical riots, and women of aristocratic families were very often the first to draw new meaning from scripture, converting their influential husbands to the new teachings. On the other hand, since family devotion was now to be concentrated on the reading of scripture, there was no longer room for the small devotional chores of a Catholic wife and mother, like gathering the curative herbs that were to be blessed by the priest, or making sure that each member of the family had the right color candle to bring to church on Candlemas day (February 2). Gone too, for Protestant women, were the many female saints of the Catholic cult, and the countless local shrines devoted to the Virgin Mary. Conversely, among Catholic reformers, the Jesuits in particular promoted selected local shrines; there were also new female saints to whom one could pray, including the founders of new orders for women that took a more active role in life outside the cloister (see chapter 14). If women were a factor in the spread of Protestant ideas, it seems they were even more of a factor in the subsequent revival of Catholicism.

The *parish* system was distinctive to Christendom, east and west. No other great religion covered the ground with an unbroken network of cells of activity, each precisely bounded and centered on its house of worship. In this the early medieval church imitated the ancient empire, whose writ ran to the remotest valley. In some areas rural parishes were not well developed until the ninth or tenth century. In later times new parishes formed as towns grew too big for one main church, and villages lobbied successfully for a parish of their own. It was thus a work of many centuries to create the landscape one still sees in many parts of rural Europe, where a visitor standing on a knoll can often make out village church spires in each of the four cardinal directions.

The parish was a grouping of believers, defined not by social status or personal affinity, but solely by geography. This promiscuous unity was subject to a process of fissuring by which the actual multiplicity of society reasserted itself. Noble landholders could keep private chaplains, so as not to have to worship with their peasants. Country people in the far corners of a parish preferred wayside chapels where a priest might come a few times each month. In the towns, the parish mass said at the main altar in the chancel competed for attention with the many private masses said in side chapels, often by chantry priests. Literate folk set themselves apart at mass by reading the prayer books that were common from the fourteenth century. Others among the devout regularly attended mass at a Franciscan or Dominican church or at a chapel built around a local shrine, rather than in the parish where they lived. The wealthy donated stained glass windows adorned by their family coats of arms; guilds provided windows featuring their patron saints. Pews, an invention of the fifteenth century, allowed people of quality to reserve spaces for themselves toward the front of the nave, where they would not be disturbed by the idle chatter of lesser folk or the beggars who commonly tugged at the sleeves of churchgoers, demanding alms. Parishes also spawned confraternities, at least a few in country churches, dozens in a large city parish. There were also age-specific groups, as in rural England, where contributions, to keep candles burning before the altar, were raised by young men yoked to a plow (threatening to plow up the gardens of noncontributors) and young women who organized dances.

Was there a shared sense of purpose, beneath the buzz of separate activities, despite social distinctions that were as visible inside the church as outside it? Certainly the priest's elevation of the consecrated host was a solemn moment for all, as noted in an earlier chapter. Though most people did not receive communion more than once a year, it was a custom on Sundays to pass around the *pax,* a small wooden or silver plate with an image of the crucified Christ, to be kissed by all as a symbol of their unity. It was also considered one of the priest's principal duties to reconcile those among his parishioners who had become enemies. God's blessing for the parish was invoked in vernacular prayers during the Latin mass and also in the Rogation Day processions in which many parishioners followed the priest in his vestments as he made a circuit of the parish boundaries.

The parish's collective will was expressed in another way through a system of governance that appeared in most areas during the thirteenth century. The pastor was expected to use his income to maintain his part of the church, the chancel, but upkeep of the nave now fell to the parishioners. Churchwardens, chosen by the local landowner or sometimes elected by the parishioners, spent as needed the income from portions of the church's endowment set aside for their use; they also provided church furnishings, including statues, mural paintings, chalices, and altar cloths. Other respected parishioners oversaw the relief of the parish poor. In France from the thirteenth century, so-called Tables of the Holy Spirit distributed bread to the needy from the church porch on stated days. In the Low Countries, somewhat later, parish officials had regular days and routes for bringing food to "the poor living at home." It was not unknown for a large urban parish to maintain a school for children, a hospital for the sick, and homes for elderly men and women. Some scholars have been impressed by the apparent capacity of late medieval parishes to build a sense of solidarity among their members. Others warn against judging on the basis of the kind of documentation that survives, mainly telling what should happen rather than what actually did happen. If we think in terms of the standard by which people measured themselves (whether they lived up to it or not), there seems less room for argument. Parishioners saw it as their responsibility, not just the priest's, to make their small bit of society a community.

Village is an aggregate name for many different kinds of cultivator settlements, the earliest of which trace back to the agricultural revolution of the fifth millennium B.C. Villages across the world vary enormously in size. In medieval Europe they could have two thousand people or more, larger than some agglomerations officially recognized as towns, or less than a hundred, no larger than the small, unorganized settlements known as hamlets. Villagers had regular ways of cooperating among themselves even during the centuries of serfdom. Even though they were subject to the criminal jurisdiction of the lord's bailiff, serfs often had a court of their own for minor altercations inside the hedge or the fence that marked the village boundary. If a landlord chose to convert his demesne land to leaseholds for his serfs, the serfs took on the task of deciding which crops to plant where, formerly handled by the lord's estate manager. At some point, as early as the twelfth century in western Europe, villages secured recognition as organized bodies that may, for the sake of simplicity, be described as communities (*gemeinde* in German, *commune* in French and Italian). In more developed rural communities of the fourteenth century or later, villagers held an annual assembly that approved regulations to govern village life and elected members of a village council or nominated them for approval by the lord's bailiff, who usually presided at council meetings. As in urban communities, villagers were expected to renounce their feuds with one another in order to participate in the assembly; henceforth the village council, not family patriarchs, would be arbitrators of justice.

By the fifteenth century, villages functioned as corporate entities at law, for example in contracting debts. Since village councils were able to levy small taxes, these receipts were used as collateral for loans, to build a grain mill, repair a dike, or even to surround the village with a brick or stone defensive wall, as many rural communities did in Germany and France. The village often had a history and a siting quite separate from that of the parish church that served its people, but where the agrarian and the ecclesiastical communities overlapped, the village council might gain the authority to appoint the churchwardens, or borrow money to make repairs that could not be paid for from the church's endowed income, like rebuilding the roof after a fire. The church itself became the village hall, for the annual meeting and other purposes. In Switzerland and south Germany, village governments petitioned church and territorial authorities for the right to name their own pastors, as villages in a few areas already did. As towns did, some villages found the means to purchase land from local nobles or fund utilities like mills and baking ovens. By the era of the Reformation, larger villages had enough business to require a full-time secretary and a full-time legal adviser.

The way villagers lived their lives is never documented as well as it is for many towns, where fat volumes of council proceedings permit scholars to trace the history of quarrels great and small. Villagers placed a high value on being "neighborly"; tenant farmers greeted one another as "neighbor," as a sign of their essential equality (fig. 12.7). But rural neighbors, like urban guildsmen, were becoming less and less equal. After about 1450, some peasant proprietors and some tenant farmers were able to profit from the rising demand for grain by expanding their holdings significantly. These "village roosters" (to use the French term), often literate, took a lively interest in the

Figure 12.7. View of a village. Pieter Bruegel the Elder (ca. 1525–1569), "A Village and Its Fields," from Max Friedlaender, Pieter Bruegel (Berlin: Propylaen, 1922), p. 91. *Courtesy of University Libraries, University of Minnesota, Minneapolis.*

wider world, sometimes in new ideas for religious reform. Small-scale tenant farmers were being squeezed down into the ranks of the hired hands, who had never been addressed as "neighbor," not even in the bygone days of rough equality among tenant farmers. For the pre-Reformation era, it seems likely that villagers sensed a growing disparity between the "neighborliness" everyone theoretically owed one another and the reality of division between the haves and the have-nots. Some local studies based on the period after 1600 find villages seething with conflict.

Superficially, Europe's *cities* were never more unified as communities than in the hundred years or so before the Reformation. In many parts of Europe, larger towns built wider circuits of walls during the fourteenth or fifteenth centuries, enclosing settlements outside the old wall within high and seemingly impregnable fortifications. To give defenders a free field of fire, settlement outside the new walls was discouraged; the separation between town and countryside was, however, not quite so stark as it appears to be on the many engravings and bird's-eye views of cities that begin to be common around 1500 (fig. 12.8). The walls were often manned by guildsmen, whose training in "shooting guilds" gave them civic importance even in towns where they did not have a voice in local government. Scholars recounted glorious urban histories, like the one that boasted (1517) of Toulouse's first charter as a city in 439, older than the French monarchy itself. It was not that the kingdom did not matter, but it mattered less; for townsmen of this period, as one French scholar has said, "foreigners" began at the city gates.

Meanwhile, town governments enacted into law the principle that the community was responsible for the well-being of all its people, inhabitants as well as citizens. Parish institutions like schools, hospitals, and homes for the elderly were taken over by the magistrates for better oversight and supported if need be from city revenues. Charitable institutions founded by private bequests were sometimes treated in the same way, though many continued to be governed as provided for by the founder, like the Fuggerei, a veritable city for the poor of Ausgburg built by Jakob Fugger (1519). Since the city was answerable to God for how burghers behaved, magistrates mandated civil penalties for blasphemy, banned styles of clothing deemed suggestive, and forced prostitutes to ply their trade only in the less respectable parts of town. In this official urban morality, sins against God's law and sins against the social order seen as willed by God were not clearly distinguished. Sumptuary laws, which helped preserve the visible boundaries between status groups, were justified as a means of preventing folk from wasting their substance on frivolity.

Figure 12.8. Section from a bird's-eye view of Amsterdam (1544). This section of Cornelis Anthoniszoon's view of Amsterdam (1544) shows the Old Church ("Oude Kerk"), one of the city's two parish churches, and Vegetable Street ("Warmoes Straat"), a fashionable are where merchants from the Baltic held the openair grain exchange. *Amsterdam Historical Museum.*

The church too was subject to regulation. Taking note of how much property was already in the hands of tax-free monasteries and convents, magistrates prohibited further alienation of land for religious purposes; they took over administration of the properties of religious houses, especially those marked by scandal, and applied every pressure they could to secure the removal of unworthy men from pastorates and other church positions. For many people, these long-term efforts to make a city one community under God found their logical conclusion in Reformation-era laws forcing clergy to become citizens, subject to the same laws as everyone else.

At the same time, however, new opportunities were steadily prying wealthy burghers loose from their social moorings in the urban collective. Florentine statesmen of the early fifteenth century no longer thought of themselves as representatives of their guilds, but as members of an elite naturally fitted to govern. Even before he came to power in Florence, Cosimo de Medici (r. 1434–1464) built a palace such as no private citizen had ever built, rather as Jakob Fugger did in Augsburg a few generations later. Families like the Medici and the Fuggers also set the fashion for building rural villas for summer recreation. In Siena, near Florence, wealthy testators left fewer and fewer bequests for the urban poor, but more and more for private chapels to glorify the family name. North of the Alps, town magistrates were coming to have more in common with their brothers and cousins in princely service than with their fellow burghers. In the Low Countries, and in many German and Italian states, demands by rulers for higher subsidies to fight their wars did not seem so unreasonable to magistrates who had learned to profit from cooperation with the prince by providing credit at favorable rates or participating in revenue-raising state monopolies. In France the king's imperious need for money allowed ambitious merchants, bankers, and lawyers to climb into the ranks of the nobility, merely by purchasing one of the many royal offices put up for sale after about 1520. Elsewhere, rich dowries for impecunious nobles enabled burgher families to form connections among the lords of the land. In south Germany urban statesmen saw themselves as the equals of the nobility; they too demanded to be addressed as "lords" by their subjects, that is, by their fellow townsmen. In the Low Countries, magistrates who served as deputies to the provincial states were now styled "high mightinesses."

If the ruling elite understood the "community" as a corporate body, all of whose members were bound by the decisions of its rulers (themselves), the "common man" understood the "community" as the whole body of citizens, whose interests were often disregarded by the magistrates in their all-too-friendly negotiations with princes. Thus resistance to higher taxation came from the guildsmen, whose loyalty was to the town itself and who felt the pinch of urban excise taxes more keenly than their social betters did. The guild had always been the common man's last line of defense, but now rich guildsmen were setting the rules at naught (see above) to become richer still. Hence the common man's growing alienation from the ruling institutions of the town was loud enough to be heard, so much so that magistrates used it to their advantage in negotiations with higher powers. In the Low Countries, Charles V's officials listened with sympathy when spokesmen for the towns, pressed as to why they refused to authorize higher subsidies, blamed the fact that "the common man" (*de gemene man*) demanded taxes be kept as they were. When magistrates of south German towns were pressed by Charles's officials in Germany as to why they tolerated a "gospel" contrary to the teachings of the church, they had an equally plausible reply: "the common man" (*der gemeine Mann*) demanded it.

The "common man" in south Germany's towns did in fact take a special interest in gospel doctrine, but so did people from many levels of society. Appeals for a "reformation of the community" were heard from village councils, from wealthy town magistrates, and from officials and clergymen who sought to make a whole territory a "community," as defined in the religious confession (Catholic or Protestant) espoused by their prince. Can such grand schemes for changing the selfish ways of ordinary people possibly have succeeded? The stream of complaints by official visitors, who found little or no change in the ingrained and not very edifying habits of rural folk in particular, gives ample reason for skepticism. Nonetheless, the next two chapters will argue that generations of preaching and indoctrination eventually did bring about a different kind of society, if not the true community devout Christians longed for. Pre-Christian magical beliefs about the world gradually lost their grip, even as the witchcraft craze that had begun in the fifteenth century reached a crescendo during the century from about 1550 to 1650. Children more commonly learned how to read, so they could read their catechism lessons. Adults seemed more willing to heed the injunctions of their pastors, even in matters of sexual behavior. The rich were more apt to take some responsibility for the poor, if only as a matter of their own self-esteem. Finally, dissident religious groups, fired by their own preaching and indoctrination, gave the lie to the age-old Christian belief that only the orthodox could lead good lives. All but the last of these changes reflected in some way the aims of the reformers. For the future character of European society, however, this last change was the most important of all.

Society and Community

The German and Swiss Reformation

This chapter explores the connections between social tensions, group solidarities, and confessional identity, from the beginnings of the German and Swiss Reformation to about 1600. Discussion of the social background of religious choice focuses on the "common man" in general and the cities in particular. Next, there are the blueprints for a true Christian community crafted by preachers of the Lutheran and Zwinglian Reformations: To what extent did they adjust their presentation of the gospel message to the special wishes of the groups where they found most support? Finally, there is the question of results: To what extent were these fond hopes for a more Christian society realized?

THE COMMON MAN

The German and Swiss Reformation was a communal movement. Lay people embraced the new doctrine not only because of its promise of individual salvation, but also because it seemed to point the way to a true community, under God. In the towns, better documented than the countryside, the strongest support for the new teachings came from the guilds, the natural home of the "common man" who so closely identified his well-being with that of the community. The communal character of the Protestant message is already implied by the pulpits from which the urban Reformation was so often proclaimed. Some preachers of the new gospel were members of religious orders, but more often they were secular clergy. A surprising number occupied one particular niche in the parish hierarchy: they were holders of the endowed preacherships created by civic-minded benefactors, starting in the early fifteenth century. Since pastors and vicars often did not preach, it had become customary for preaching friars, like the Franciscans, to make a regular circuit of parishes within reach of their monasteries. Parish preacherships were an alternative to mendicant sermons. The endowments required preaching in the language of the people and sometimes called for "the pure gospel." In the early sixteenth century, theology graduates who had studied the biblical languages usually did not have the family connections needed for high positions in the church, as pastor of an important parish or a member of a cathedral chapter. But their humanist theological training gave them impressive qualifications as exponents of "the pure gospel." Huldrych Zwingli, "People's Preacher" at Zurich's main parish from 1519, was only one of many humanist clerics who used his endowed pulpit to launch a Protestant movement. In fact, during the 1520s church authorities in Swiss and south German cities had trouble finding suitable preachership candidates who were not "tainted" by Reformation doctrine. The preacherships thus became, in one scholar's phrase, a "bridge" between the communal religion of the fifteenth century and the Reformation of the sixteenth.

That ordinary people interpreted Protestant teaching according to communal values can be shown from the outpouring of vernacular-language pamphlets during the early years of the German Reformation. The educated few wrote most of these pamphlets, including some that claim to speak for "Farmer Jack" (in German, *Karsthans*) But scholars have sorted out the ones that seem to have been penned by men or women of relatively little learning, just as they have been able to detect, in rural petitions drafted by village pastors, the ideas of the peasants themselves. In these documents the "common man" of the 1520s left a record of his thoughts not matched in any previous time, and not found again until the nineteenth century. The predominant theme was the gospel: The priests taught mere human opinion, but no one could be saved without the pure gospel.

What did the gospel mean? There were echoes of Luther's "by faith alone," but more commonly the gospel was the rule by which Christians live. This view resembled Zwingli's belief that the gospel was a kind of law, except that the emphasis of the pamphlets and the petitions on "love of neighbor" was closer to the good-works Catholicism of the late Middle Ages. Christians were saved by being neighbors to one another—in other words, by building a true community. The demand that everyone be on the same footing before God shows the wide appeal of Luther's "priesthood of all believers," but it also reflects communal values. In one scholar's findings, only the pamphlets written by artisans expressed fears about the Christian community breaking up into "sects" instead of maintaining its unity. This may have been one of the reasons why artisan pamphlets and peasant petitions alike were harshly critical of monasticism, which might be seen as splitting Christians into rival factions. No monasteries or convents were needed, only one priest for each parish, chosen by the civil community. Likewise, baptism and communion were the only sacraments needed; noble pamphleteers envisioned alternative forms of the sacrament of confession, but artisans wanted it abolished altogether. Thus the popular understanding of the Reformation was a blend of three elements: the teachings of Luther and Zwingli; the ideal of the community; and the life experience of working men and women who saw themselves as the backbone of "neighborliness."

The Reformation movement was communal also in the sense that it was usually the common burghers who demanded its implementation. Members of the urban elites, inherently suspicious of all novelties, were doubly cautious about religion: They rightly saw any change as an implied threat to social stability, and their own kinsmen often had high posts in the local church hierarchy. Their hesitation about accepting the new ideas gave citizens stronger reasons for distrusting the magistrates. As noted in the last chapter, "community" seemed to many people of the middling sort to be breaking down: What had the magistrates done to prevent the rich and successful from growing ever more powerful, while hard-working guildsmen struggled to stay in place? Were they now going to stand in the way of the gospel as well? In almost every city where the Reformation triumphed, it was because popular opinion centered in the guilds pressured reluctant magistrates to dismantle the Catholic religious establishment step by step: First clergy were instructed to preach "according to the gospel," then some churches were opened to Protestant worship and some monasteries were closed.

In some towns support for the new doctrines seems to have varied according to socioeconomic rank: the less wealthy guilds harbored the most ardent Protestants, while the magistrates preferred to change as little as possible—for them, Lutheranism was better than Zwinglianism. Constance and Zwickau are exceptions that prove the rule of popular support for the Protestant cause. In Constance, a city whose patrician magistrates actively supported the Reformation, the less wealthy guilds showed clear signs of loyalty to Catholicism. In Zwickau, a Saxon mining town, patrician magistrates, frightened by the radical doctrines of Thomas Müntzer and his disciples, sought as an antidote a preacher who had the blessing of their Lutheran prince. At least initially, however, guildsmen showed no interest in the religion chosen by their patrician magistrates. On Easter in 1524, only twenty people received communion according to the Lutheran rite.

In these and other cases, religious disagreements often followed preexisting lines of division between magistrates and burghers. But there was also a second pattern of preexisting conflict, pitting cities as corporate bodies against their princely rulers, and conflicts of this sort also found a religious expression. Territorial princes had been demanding higher taxes to subsidize their wars; they were also weaning members of the burgher elite away from their urban loyalties by offering them posts in the territorial administration. Cities ruled by the princes had to accommodate their rulers, but they endeavored to do so without giving up their hard-won rights of self-rule. Even the fully self-governing Swiss cantons and the empire's free imperial cities felt pressures from above. If most Swiss cantons allied with France in its wars against Charles V, one reason was that the Habsburg dynasty was the traditional enemy of Swiss liberties. By contrast, the free cities of south Germany formed close connections with the Habsburgs under Maximilian I (d. 1519), because the growing power of the territorial princes threatened their independence as well as the emperor's authority.

These time-honored political strategies ran into a brick wall as soon as social tensions within the cities were further stirred up by Reformation preaching. Of the sixty-five free imperial cities important enough to send representatives to the imperial diets, only a dozen remained Catholic all through the sixteenth century, despite all the influence Charles V and his agents in Germany could bring to bear. Even as the magistrates took steps to appease the common man's demand for the gospel, they knew they were alienating the emperor, who measured his friends according to their orthodoxy. The imperial cities that became Protestant included most of the empire's commercial centers, with the interesting exception of Cologne, which had a city council that kept clerical privileges well under control and a staunchly orthodox university whose theology professors were well integrated into the city's churches. In the many territorial cities with Catholic rulers, magistrates had to choose between preserving the goodwill of the prince and making concessions to the growing evangelical movement among their burghers.

The outcome of this three-way struggle depended in good part on local political alignments. In cities governed by politically aggressive prince-bishops the transition from Catholicism to Lutheranism seems to have been almost seamless. The prince-archbishop of Bremen, preoccupied for more than a decade by his efforts to conquer new territory, suddenly found himself confronted (1522) by magistrates and burghers united behind a new Lutheran preacher. In Magdeburg, whose prince-archbishop was a notorious collector of bishoprics, the story was much the same. But most episcopal cities remained Catholic. There were often Lutheran movements among the burghers, especially among the more prominent members of the craft guilds, but they were not able to withstand the civil power wielded for confessional aims by strong-minded prince-bishops in the latter part of the sixteenth century.

Among the secular princes, Henry of Brunswick-Wolfenbüttel (r. 1514–1542) was if anything a more determined defender of Catholicism than William IV of Bavaria (r. 1514–1550). But William's key advisers were laymen and natives of the duchy; the steps they took to curtail the privileges of the clergy probably helped keep Bavaria's towns Catholic. Henry's advisers were either clerics or laymen from other territories; their attempts to use control of religious policy as a means of advancing ducal authority helped provoke Lutheran movements led by the magistrates of his cities, first in Brunswick, then in Goslar, whose appeal to the Schmalkaldic League led to Henry's expulsion from his territory. Here too there are exceptions that prove the rule. The few secular princes who eagerly embraced the Reformation at an early date sometimes faced Catholic opposition movements in their towns. In Brunswick-Lüneburg, Lüneburg's salt-master patricians saw Duke Ernest's Reformation as a ploy by which the ruler meant to gain control of the city's vital salt trade. Their loyalty to Catholicism was shared by guilds active in the salt industry but not by other craft guilds, which had their quarrels with the patricians and whose members found the duke's Lutheranism more to their liking.

The urban Reformation usually culminated in the abolition of Catholic worship throughout the territory controlled by the city. This was a grave matter, all the more so in episcopal cities, where mass was prohibited also in the cathedral of the city's prince-bishop. The magistrates preferred not to assume all responsibility for such decisions. In south Germany and Protestant Switzerland, where the guilds had a formal voice in town government, guilds were consulted on this key issue through the large council, most of whose members were chosen by the guilds. In some towns the guilds were not content with traditional rules of consultation. In Basel, the victory of the Reformation put in place (for a time) new voting rules giving the guilds more authority and the patricians less.

In north Germany, where exclusively patrician town councils still ruled much as they had done for centuries, the community in a wider sense often played a role in the final triumph of the Reformation, even if craft guilds as such did not. Lübeck is instructive, because this great maritime city's patrician regime was resolutely Catholic. The magistrates were troubled that some members of the merchants' guild, just below the patricians in Lübeck's social hierarchy, were known "Martinians." Their strength was displayed in the "song war" of December 1529: A group of men and women singing Luther's hymns, joined by others as they processed along a main street, peaceably occupied one of the city's parish churches. But this was not the decisive event. What tipped the scales was the fact that Lübeck had debts contracted by raising money to help Gustavus Vasa gain the throne in Sweden (chapter 10), and could not pay off its debts without new taxes; the patrician government was not able to impose new levies without summoning an assembly of the community. The committee of burghers chosen to draft needed fiscal legislation insisted in its report, also in December 1529, that there would be no new taxes without new preachers. The city council had no choice; Lübeck too became Lutheran.

What of the urban poor, and their view of the new doctrines? The short answer is that we know too little. There are no pamphlets specifically traceable to journeymen, and it would be unusual to find unskilled workers who even knew how to read, much less write. The angry crowds that often stormed and sacked urban monasteries during the 1520s certainly included lesser folk, and journeymen and day laborers are also found among men and women arrested for individual acts of desecration directed against statues and other symbols of Catholic belief. Yet later evidence from the Low Countries suggests that support for the new doctrines did not come from the lowest levels of society. According to religious censuses conducted in towns recaptured for Spain by Parma in the 1580s, Calvinists were most often found among the middling sort of folk, including members of the craft guilds, but both the rich and the poor were mainly Catholic.

Münster offers one final variant on the ways guild members attempted to shape their city's religious life. Following the conquest of the Anabaptist kingdom (1535), Münster's prince-bishop prohibited all forms of Protestant worship and attempted to govern his depopulated capital city through an appointed council. Pressed by the imperial diet, he agreed to restore Münster's rights of self-government (1541), but only partially. Restoration of the rights of the craft guilds came only in 1553, when the prince-bishop needed funds for war. Tensions now developed between the traditional communal aspirations of the city and the prince-bishop's growing bureaucracy, for whom Münster was simply the capital of a sizable territory. By the 1580s these two visions of Münster's place in the world found expression in two different forms of Catholicism. On one side were members of the new Jesuit order, authorized by the prince-bishop to convert his cathedral school into a university. From other parts of Germany, even from other countries, Jesuit teachers promoted High German, the common literary language, rather than the local dialect of Low German. For lawyers and other officials of the prince-bishop's territorial administration, often members of the Jesuit sodality, the Jesuit fathers were agents of a needed transformation, bringing Münster into step with the universal culture of Catholic reform. But for guild members to whom High German was a foreign language, the Jesuits were foreign priests. The burgher assembly dominated by the guilds first attempted to prevent the Jesuits from taking up residence in the city and then barred them from teaching in city schools. The assembly also took up the cause of Protestant burghers, who could not bury their dead in church cemeteries, because the prince-bishop (backed by the Jesuits) had forbidden it. Members of the assembly noted pointedly that they did not tolerate Protestant worship in the churches, but their Catholicism was not good enough for the prince-bishop, whose forceful intervention (1612) ended the participation of the guilds in political decision making. In their losing struggle, Münster's guilds were late witnesses to the belief that a city's religious life must be controlled by its own people. In earlier decades this communal ideal more often found a Protestant form of expression. Where the Reformation was not made by the princes, it was made by the common man.

TRUE COMMUNITY

Those who wrote and preached on behalf of the Reformation knew their audience. Vernacular-language publications appealed in a hundred different ways to the common man's anticlericalism. The broadside—an illustrated printed sheet—catered to public curiosity about lurid or dramatic events, like a battle, or the burning of a witch (fig. 13.1). Protestant broadsides might depict a grotesque carnival procession, with fat priests, lecherous monks, and sleek cardinals led by the devil himself. Luther's scatological rhetoric set the tone for this kind of propaganda: since the papacy was the Antichrist, the worst imaginable perversion of the gospel, no human language could be filthy enough to describe it. But hatred of the clergy was good only for tearing down the old order. When the elector of Saxony authorized the first visitation of rural parishes, visitors were taken aback to find peasants who knew the pope was the Antichrist but had never heard of justification by faith. Luther appealed to the elector of Saxony to take control of the church. The prince, in his view, could be a "bishop in case of need" to remove unsuitable clergy and to apply church wealth to the training and support of new pastors. But did the preaching of true doctrine imply a new and truer form of Christian community? Some have argued that Luther's insistence on the total depravity of human nature due to original sin limited his interest in any project for the moral betterment of society. The idea that scripture is a guide for Christian living comes instead from Zwingli, himself a burgher and familiar with how the "common man" felt about Christians working out their salvation as members of a community. This view makes too sharp a distinction between the free cities of Switzerland and south Germany and the territorial cities of the north, and between the Zwinglian and Lutheran Reformations. Lutheran preachers, no less than Zwinglians, envisioned a community of men, women, and children living more truly according to God's law. These blueprints were the theological counterparts of the common man's

Figure 13.1. The burning of witches. Contemporary broadside describing the burning of witches at Denerburg in the Harz Mountains, 1555. *Germanisches Museum, Nuremberg.*

sense of the gospel. The following pages touch on four specific measures of a more Christian society: the reform of worship, religious indoctrination, poor relief, and the campaign against witchcraft.

Worship. The pre-Reformation parish church was a place where one had access to the power of the holy. It was already a protection against evil to dip one's finger in the holy water fount and make the sign of the cross upon entering church. People took small containers of the holy water blessed by the priest, or palm fronds blessed by the priest on Palm Sunday, to guard their homes against the power of the devil. Most of all, the priest had power to offer the sacrifice of the mass. For Catholics, the mass was a representation of the sacrifice by which Christ had offered Himself on the cross to atone for the sins of humankind. Reverence for the miracle of transubstantiation did not prevent people from walking about or carrying on conversations in church, but the moment when the priest raised the wheaten host and the chalice of wine for the adoration of all was the high point of Sunday worship.

For Lutherans, the church was a place to hear God's Word. For rituals marking the stages of human life, Luther's German-language texts simplified the Catholic order of worship, so as to bring out the Word more clearly. Engaged couples were to have their unions blessed by a clergyman, not just in front of the church, but before the altar, so they might hear God's commands to married folk in texts that grew more elaborate as the sixteenth century progressed. In the baptismal rite, the exorcisms—prayers calling on God to free the person about to be baptized from the power of the devil—were reduced in number, but not eliminated. Luther believed in the reality of the devil's power in human life, but he wanted Christians to trust solely in God to ward off the Evil One.

The mass required more serious alteration. To speak of it as a sacrifice offered by the priest was an "abomination" to Luther, a derogation from the honor due to God alone and a blasphemous corollary to the false Catholic belief than human works could be holy in the sight of God. Yet since God's Word did indeed assure believers of the comfort of Christ's presence in the sacrament of the altar, Luther's German mass retained most of the prayers and gestures from the Latin rite, purging only what related to the idea of sacrifice. He even kept the custom of lifting up for all to see the bread in which the Lord's body was present; to avoid the suggestion that this miraculous testimony of God's favor depended on the clergyman's recital of Jesus's words at the Last Supper, Luther transferred the elevation to a different part of the mass. Without explicitly acknowledging that ordinary believers grasped the meaning of religion most easily through symbolic actions, the Lutheran Reformation allowed people to carry forward into the new order much that was comfortable and familiar

from Catholic practice. But the medieval custom of having the priest celebrate mass with his back to the people was altogether unacceptable. In
Lutheran lands, altar tables were set in front of the high altar, so the minister could face the people and speak to them, in their own tongue, the
Word of God's promise.

To Zwingli, Reformed worship demanded more thoroughgoing change.
If Luther found prayers, gestures, and church furnishings acceptable if they
did not contradict scripture, Zwingli found them unacceptable if they were
not prescribed by scripture. Image-covered walls were to be whitewashed;
statues of all kinds, even crucifixes, were "idols" to be removed and destroyed. Luther composed hymns of great beauty, and the long tradition of
Christian organ music reached its greatest heights among Lutheran com-
poser-organists, including Johann Sebastian Bach (1665–1750). Zwingli,
though himself a lover of music, found in scripture no justification for congregational singing, except for the Psalms; since scripture did not mention
organs, they too had to be removed. Luther is reputed to have helped pop-
ularize the Christmas tree in family celebrations, but for Zwingli there was
no Christmas: scripture commands believers to make holy the Lord's day,
only the Lord's day. Baptism did not free the recipient's soul from the power
of the devil; it simply incorporated him or her into the body of believers,
much as the Jews of old did by circumcising male infants as a sign of their
covenant with God. Instead of rushing newborns to church lest they die
without the grace of baptism, parents should pick a suitable date for having
their infants baptized as part of the Sunday service. To avoid superstition,
the traditional parish baptismal font, silently tolerated by Luther, must be
replaced by a simple basin, and the "magical" exorcism prayers (as Martin
Bucer of Strasbourg described them) must be eliminated altogether. Without explicitly identifying the spoken word as the only medium through
which faith could validly be expressed, the Zwinglian Reformation required worshipers to cast off utterly a deep-rooted religious culture of symbols, gestures, and songs. The Sunday service was built around scripture
and the sermon. Since bread and wine were blessed only on days set aside
for communion, there was no need for a fixed table at the front of the church,
much less an altar (a word that connoted sacrifice). The pulpit, as in Zurich,
could thus claim the place of honor in the chancel, the better to show that
one came to church only to hear God's Word (fig. 13.2).

Indoctrination has become an evil word in an age mindful of totalitarian
attempts at thought control. It was not so in the era of the Reformation. The
fundamental Protestant charge against the Catholic Church was a failure of
indoctrination, from top to bottom. Despite universities scattered across
Europe, Latin schools in the towns, and vernacular-language schools in not
a few villages, the faithful did not know the doctrine needful for salvation,

Figure 13.2. Preaching from a wooden pulpit in Zurich. Though it represents a scene from the mid-fifteenth century, this drawing gives an idea of how Zurich's Reformers had makeshift pulpits built in front of the high altar, to focus attention on God's Word: from Christoph Silberisen, Schweizer Chronik, as reproduced in Walter Muschg, E. A. Gessler, Die Schweizer Bilderchroniken des 15en/16en Jahrhunderts (Zurich: Atlantis, 1941), no. 198. *Courtesy of University Libraries, University of Minnesota, Minneapolis.*

because they had been wrongly taught by their priests. The new Protestant liturgy, in both its Lutheran and Zwinglian versions, was part of a grand program of Christian indoctrination. Luther led the way by reforming Wittenberg's theology curriculum, setting aside the scholastic authors, and requiring study of the biblical languages as well as the church fathers. The theology faculty now began forming earnest young men willing to preach the gospel wherever they were needed; with their wives and children, these new pastors would also be models for a sober and righteous evangelical household. One might even say that indoctrination began within the pastor's family (fig. 13.3). Luther urged towns that did not already have Latin schools to establish them, for the preparation of pastors and territorial officials. Philip of Hesse's church ordinance of 1526 created a new Protestant university at Marburg and called for establishment of schools of the appropriate level in every village and town. Elector John of Saxony issued a similar decree in 1528, the same year that visitors made their first full circuit of rural parishes. The visitors found many long-time pastors or vicars paying only lip service to the new doctrines, to keep their jobs. Many among the faithful were seduced by the ranting of radical preachers or grasped little about the Reformation beyond Luther's denunciation of the papacy, as noted above. The few recent theology graduates who had taken

Figure 13.3. A Mennonite pastor and his wife in the Dutch Republic. Rembrandt van Rijn, "Pastor Ansloo and His Wife," 1641. *Bildarchiv Preussischer Kulturbesitz/ Art Resource, NY.*

rural churches complained bitterly that church incomes rightfully theirs had either been appropriated by others or were painfully inadequate to support a wife and family. Revenues set aside for starting new schools were also insufficient, at least according to village officials. Territorial officials now grasped for the first time how much of a struggle it would be to find the resources for pastors with families and for new schools.

Luther had cherished the belief that scripture itself should be the content of basic Christian education. Now, having seen from the visitors' reports how "the gospel" could be interpreted by ordinary folk in wildly differing ways, he concluded that children must have the essential teachings of scripture presented to them in handbook form, for memorization, the usual method of learning. In 1529 he penned a *Large Catechism* for the instruction of preachers and a *Small Catechism* whose language was simple enough to be conveyed directly to children. Luther followed the format of well-known fifteenth-century catechisms, but, as he did in revising the liturgy, he gave them a new direction by highlighting key doctrines. The *Small Catechism* in particular quickly became the basis of instruction in Lutheran primary schools. While princely officials worked to ease out the old pastors and find a decent living for their successors, the new pastors

pressed villagers to erect schools and carefully checked the doctrinal orthodoxy of teachers. The story was much the same in Reformed areas.
Zwingli's *Short Introduction to the Christian Religion* (1523) may be compared to Luther's *Large Catechism;* others in Zurich or Strasbourg wrote catechisms for the young. Pastors trained at Zurich's theological academy
cultivated a sense of solidarity perhaps not found among Lutheran clergy,
owing to continuation of the regular meetings or colloquies begun by
Zwingli. All over Protestant Germany, university-educated pastors gradually filled the pulpits, and schools were established where none had existed before. But did rural folk let their children attend these schools? And
did children who had the precepts of evangelical doctrine drummed into
their heads grow into adults knowledgeable about religion and devout in
their faith? Answers to these questions must for the moment be deferred.

   Poor relief illustrates the connection Reformers drew between correct
doctrine and building true community. In Germany as in Europe generally, the misery of the urban poor made the gap between social reality and
Christian ideals painfully evident. The resources of privately endowed
and parish institutions like hospitals and homes for the elderly, even if
taken under the supervision of the city council, could not keep pace with
the needs of a growing indigent population. Sermons, especially those of
the mendicant friars, exalted the poor for their detachment from worldly
comforts, while excoriating the rich for grasping after still more wealth
and for shirking their duty, before God, to be charitable to the less fortunate. But did the friars by their praise of poverty obscure the real wretched-
ness of indigence? And did they by their own begging encourage others to
look for handouts rather than looking for work? This was also the era of a
nascent capitalist ethos hostile to that of the friars. Lorenzo Valla (d. 1457),
a famous Italian humanist, condemned the Franciscans as useless drones
buzzing at their prayers; for the merchants whose quest for riches created
work for their fellow citizens he had words of praise.

   Juan Luis Vives (1492–1540) complained bitterly of the files of filthy and
ulcerous beggars importuning respectable burghers from both sides of the
church door on Sunday mornings. Vives, a Spanish humanist living in
Bruges, penned an influential treatise, *On the Subvention of the Poor* (1526).
Poverty such as was now to be seen in Bruges, he warned, was a breeding
ground for an insurrection against the rich. For their own good and that of
the city, magistrates must consolidate the funds of all existing private and
parish charities to provide relief for those duly enrolled as deserving poor,
that is, genuinely unable to work. Others must be made to work for their
upkeep or be expelled from the city; begging must be banned altogether,
and strangers sent back to their own cities. A few months earlier, the nearby
cloth town of Ypres had incorporated many of the same ideas into a statute

for the poor, later revised (1531) to include added points suggested by Vives. The 1531 Ypres poor law was endorsed by the theology faculty in Paris, a bastion of Catholic orthodoxy, and later by Emperor Charles V. But other theologians, especially among the mendicant orders, condemned legislation of this kind as an assault on traditional Catholic beliefs about the holy state of poverty; in their view, caring for the poor was the responsibility of the church, not of civil society. Reflecting this conflict of values within the Catholic world, many towns that had enacted poor laws revised them to permit begging by the friars and to recognize the autonomy of church-sponsored charitable organizations such as confraternities.

Luther and the Reformers came to similar conclusions about helping the poor, without any of the hesitations one finds in Catholic writers like Vives. According to the new theology, giving to the poor was not a "good work" meritorious in the sight of God, nor was there any basis for the claim (by members of religious orders) that all who freely chose a life of poverty lived a more perfect Christian life. The Wittenberg town council's "Ordinance of the Common Chest," issued after consultation with Luther (1522), expelled the mendicant orders, prohibited begging, and mandated weekly collections in the churches for a civic fund for the poor. The following year Luther helped draft a common chest ordinance for nearby Leisnig, in which the civic fund was to be replenished from confiscated church properties and an annual tax for relief of the poor. Leisnig's magistrates resisted both of these provisions but eventually gave in to pressure from Saxony's territorial government. The idea spread quickly, for example to Nuremberg and Strasbourg, even before these towns formally adopted Protestant worship.

The fact that similar institutions were created at about the same time in Catholic as well as Protestant territories indicates that poor-law reform was more a social than a religious process. The prohibition of begging, conspicuously including the friars, points to a specifically antimendicant strain in urban anticlericalism. Certainly the "common man" was pleased to see action at last taken against the "sturdy beggars" whose piteous pleas were well-crafted to deceive honest folk. There may also have been, as some have argued, an element of calculation on the part of large-scale employers, who benefited from having laborers they needed only occasionally supported by the city the rest of the time. Yet there also had to be religiously sound reasons for changing a system based on religious conceptions of the poor as favored by God and of the Christian duty of charity. Whether Catholics who saw charity as a work pleasing to God donated more or less than Protestants who saw it as something expected of believers is not possible to say. The more important difference lies in the fact that Protestant poor relief was less ambiguous than its Catholic coun-

Figure 13.4. Amsterdam's workhouse. The rasping of wood at which inmates were frequently employed gave the institution its Dutch name (Rasphuis): the Amsterdam Workhouse ca. 1614, from Joannes Pontanus, Beschrijvinge van Amsterdam, p. 133. *Courtesy of University Libraries, University of Minnesota, Minneapolis.*

terpart in shifting responsibility for the poor from the church to the state. Protestant town governments often accommodated separate systems of church poor relief, especially where it was organized by Calvinist diaconates. But it was the magistrates who made the key decisions and launched major new initiatives, like the civic workhouses where the working poor were confined, the better to instill proper discipline. Amsterdam's was the first in 1596 (fig. 13.4). This was an important step in the process by which the town itself, not the semipublic religious bodies to which citizens belonged, assumed the main burden of making society a community.

The campaign against witchcraft. Hexing is an age-old practice found all over the world. In ancient Roman law, witchcraft (*maleficium*, literally, an evil deed) was a crime punishable by death. In the early Middle Ages folk beliefs about the casting of spells were not seen by church officials as a diabolical threat. One document advises priests that women who say they have flown through the night air by the power of "Diana" (Roman goddess of the moon) are to be treated as deluded—God does not grant evil spirits control over nature. But the great scholastic theologians opened the door to a dark future by entertaining the possibility that God could allow Satan to compass the "evil deeds" traditionally attributed to witches. By the fourteenth century, inquisitors warned of heretical groups consorting with the devil, and the fifteenth century saw the first witchcraft panics: accusations snowballed as persons charged with doing "evil deeds" by the power of the devil named others in hopes of exculpating themselves. Two German Dominican friars gave witchcraft belief its classic formulation in a 1486 manual for prosecutors. A witch, usually a woman, was one who consigned her soul to the devil in return for powers to fly through the night and cause evil deeds at will; witches gathered in "covens" of thirteen for obscene rites, sometimes including intercourse with the devil.

Although the two Dominicans had trouble selling this new theory of witchcraft to some church officials, the great European witch hunt was by now well underway. Between 1450 and 1750, between 100,000 and 200,000 people, the majority of whom were women, were tried for the crime of witchcraft, mainly by secular courts; tens of thousands were executed. Among the multiple explanations of how the craze got started, two are worth mentioning here because they tie the rise of witchcraft belief to beliefs about the community, albeit in different ways. One scholar argues that people no longer willing to be charitable to older female neighbors projected their own sense of guilt on these women by accusing them of witchcraft. The person most likely to be accused of witchcraft was in fact a poor older woman living alone—as in "Little Red Riding Hood." Another scholar sees witchcraft belief as rooted in fears that the community has become polluted, contaminated as if physically by the intrusion from without of a frightful evil.

Regional variation across Europe was enormous. Seventy-five percent of all the trials took place within the boundaries of the Holy Roman Empire. In England, few people were executed, because England's common law, unlike the continent's Roman law tradition, did not permit the use of torture to obtain confessions for capital crimes. Spain had few trials for witchcraft, because the Spanish Inquisition held on this point to a prescholastic theology that denied the devil any agency in the world. The wave of trials ended soonest in the Dutch Republic (1590s) and continued longest in parts of eastern Europe. Some have contended that the idea of witchcraft lost credibility as the scientific view of the world slowly took hold, but the legal profession's standards of proof and due process seem to have been more pertinent; after a certain point in time, high courts (as in France and Denmark) routinely overturned all convictions for witchcraft in lower courts. Conversely, the courts of small, autonomous territories in the empire, not subject to any appellate jurisdiction, pursued the hunt for witches well into the seventeenth century and often had the highest rates of execution for those convicted.

The Reformation did not initiate the campaign against witches, and may in some ways have retarded it. For all his belief in the reality of the devil's power, Luther, like the inquisitors in Spain, rejected the whole idea that God would allow the devil to do "evil deeds" in the physical world. During the early decades of the Reformation, from 1520 to 1560, the number of known witchcraft trials across Europe dropped somewhat. But it rose again after 1560 and peaked in the period from about 1580 to 1650, which was also the period of the most intense religious conflicts, especially between armies pledged to causes Catholic or Calvinist. It seems that proponents of the rival visions of reform competed with one another in their zeal to cleanse the world of witchcraft, perhaps more so in Catholic and Calvinist than in Lutheran territories. In parts of the Holy Roman Empire where territories have been studied comparatively, Lutheran lands had fewer trials and lower rates of execution than Catholic lands. Calvin's Geneva burned remarkably few witches, but smaller Calvinist territories had some of the highest rates for trials and executions, comparable to those of small Catholic territories.

Comparative studies of social standing suggest that the accused were relatively poor and isolated, while their accusers were somewhat better off and more likely to play leadership roles in the local community. In the end it was the accusers, even more than the theologians or the trial judges, who drove the baleful engines of prosecution forward. Especially in a climate of religious reform, people of goodwill had to take the Bible's words to heart: "Thou shalt not suffer a witch to live" (Exod. 22:18).

GODLY COMMUNITIES?

We may conclude that the German and Swiss Reformation was communal also in its blueprint for a more Christian life. The Protestant reform of worship aimed at centering the Sunday gathering of the people on God's Word, to the relative or (for Zwingli) total exclusion of all possible distractions. The reform of instruction, top to bottom, sought to harness existing forms of schooling to the dissemination of the Word. Protestant poor relief made the civil community responsible for achieving this vital dimension of moral community, just as Protestant marriage set each couple more clearly in its place as a living cell of the body social. Witchcraft trials may seem a jarring exception to this focus on community, but they were not. Like all things human, the ideal of community had its dark dimension. The flip side of solidarity with one's neighbors was a suspicion of everything "foreign" and a downright loathing for anything by which the community might be polluted. For sixteenth-century Christians, a town or village was polluted—rendered liable to God's wrath—by its toleration of false worship, even more by its toleration of devilish witchcraft. Hence many of those who clamored for the gospel clamored also for the exclusion of popish idolatry from all houses of worship within the city walls.

Hence too, in many towns and villages, the same middling sort of folk who embraced ideas of reform might also come forward to accuse others (often outsiders in the town or village) of commerce with the devil—it was their Christian duty. Thus for those accepted as members, the community could be a wonderful source of strength; for those extruded from the charmed circle, it could be a nightmare.

Success or failure. Did better preaching and better indoctrination make for better Christians? The Reformers were soon disabused of the idea that the pure Word of God would by itself work wonders among the faithful. Accordingly, the Reformation became a campaign to use all appropriate means to bring the people to that standard of righteous living that the Catholic Church in its long history had so manifestly failed to achieve. Reform of the clergy was the first task. Properly trained preachers graduated in increasing numbers from universities that had become Protestant or new ones created to advance the reform. If only a fraction of the Catholic parish clergy at the beginning of the sixteenth century had attended universities, by the end of the century all but a fraction of the Protestant clergy had degrees. Regular meetings, like the synods established by Zwingli in Zurich, created an esprit de corps among the clergy, abetted by the fact that Protestant clergy were over time increasingly likely to be the sons of clergymen. By around 1600 the Catholic Church too was filling its pulpits with a better class of men, in some cases graduates of the seminaries mandated for each diocese; the order priests set a new standard of learning and decorum for Germany's Catholic clergy, among whom the rule of celibacy was more and more strictly enforced. One way or another, the clergy was becoming an elite corps, conscious of its mission to elevate the ignorant laity to a higher moral and spiritual plane.

Paradoxically, however, this process of professionalization, the proud achievement of religious reformers and territorial governments working together, probably made it more difficult to reach the larger goal of changing Christian society for the better. The new ministers and priests were too educated to have any sympathy for the mind-set of ordinary folk and too conscious of their dignity to consort with parishioners at the local tavern. They had much more to say than their medieval predecessors, but would people listen?

Zealous Protestant pastors had in fact many errant sheep. Some had never come to church anyway, not even when threatened with excommunication by the Catholic Church. Others rejoiced in the overthrow of priestly authority but scorned the new clergy's pleas for attendance or showed up for Sunday services occasionally, giving nary a hint of inner engagement. Still others clung stubbornly to some radical doctrine or resorted in time of illness to the nearest Catholic shrine. By the second half of the sixteenth century, reform-minded clergy of all major confessions were agreed on two essential points: the people needed to be disciplined and no real progress could be made unless those who scoffed at God's truth were cowed by the power of the state.

Within this framework of consensus there were many different ideas about how to get people to take Christian teaching to heart. In Bullinger's Zurich, all coercive authority rested with the Christian magistrates. Anabaptists and other spreaders of false teaching were punished without pity, and Sunday church attendance was ensured by the simple device of levying large fines for noncompliance. Strasbourg's magistrates claimed the same authority but were not nearly so zealous; this was why Martin Bucer tried various means of instilling virtue in the people, including the formation in each parish of circles of the devout meant to serve as a leaven for the whole. As Strasbourg gravitated toward a Lutheran rather than a Reformed orientation in its theology, the city's religious leaders remained at odds with the magistrates, but they had different means for forming a Christian conscience among believers, such as individual confession of sins to the pastor. Yet church leaders in the nearby Lutheran duchy of Württemberg had more confidence in the duke's church council—made up of theologians and civil officials—than in the parish clergy: the church order of 1559 vested the key power of excommunication in the church council. Similarly, most of the twenty-odd German territories that became Calvinist put in place a state-centered approach to the control of morals, rather than the parish-centered consistory of Calvin's Geneva.

In Catholic Germany the old tradition of clerical independence of the state was deeply compromised by rulers like the dukes of Bavaria, who merely kept Rome informed as they governed the church through a church council, more or less as their Protestant peers did. Rulers all over Germany backed the clergy in bringing the wayward to heel: Marriages had to be blessed by the clergy in order to be lawful, teachers had to have their religious orthodoxy certified, and nonconformists were subject to expulsion. By the seventeenth century, civil officials were requiring persons moving to a new place to have their good character attested to by the clergyman of their former residence—a usage appropriated by immigrants to the United States in more recent times (fig. 13.5). Historians now use the term "confessionalization" to describe this collaboration of state power and clerical authority to achieve a reformation of morals. But subjects are never so pliable as rulers want them to be, least of all in matters of the mind and heart. The heavy hand of the state, like the professionalization of the clergy, may actually have made it more difficult to elicit the inner consent of the people to the process of reform.

Figure 13.5. An immigrant woman's character reference. "I know Katherine Horkan of Carralacky parish, Kilmovee, to be a sober, industrious and religious per[son], not yet married." (Signed) Rev. Ian O'Hara, p[arish] p[riest], 4 March 1882. Katherine Horkan, a secondary school languages teacher in the west of Ireland and a seamstress in Iowa, was the author's maternal grandmother.

Roughly speaking, scholars have judged the urban Reformation a success in changing the minds of the people and the rural Reformation a failure. Strasbourg's transition from a Reformed to a Lutheran version of Protestantism was dictated by the magistrates' grasp of political imperatives: the Lutheran Schmalkaldic League afforded protection against a Catholic emperor, the small alliance of Reformed cities based on Zurich did not. Once the change was made, however, popular opinion proved decisive in the city's adoption (1591) of the Formula of Concord, despite the magistrates' preference for a measure of ambiguity in confessional matters. Calvinist Emden was the capital of the county of East Friesland. When Emden became the rule of an ambitious Lutheran count, its preacher and a city council chosen by the people blocked his attempt to impose Lutheranism (1595–1599). In Lemgo, capital of the county of Lippe, magistrates who bowed to the count's demand for Calvinist preaching were overthrown in a popular uprising (1609) that kept the city Lutheran. In 1614 Brandenburg's Elector Johann Sigismund (r. 1608–1619) announced his conversion to Calvinism. But when a would-be Calvinist pastor mounted the pulpit of Berlin's cathedral, "the common mob . . . shouted curses and blasphemies, and ran out" (1614). With crowds throwing stones at Calvinist preachers in Berlin and other cities, the elector backed off: The dynasty would be Calvinist; Brandenburg remained Lutheran. This kind of popular support for a specific creed does not necessarily mean that people have changed in their heart of hearts. It does indicate, however, that the people have become "confessionalized": This creed, and no other, was now henceforth a part of their identity.

We should also be wary of assuming that preachers had simply implanted their ideas in the minds of listeners. People paid little heed to the novel idea that engaged couples should refrain from sexual relations. They saw no good reason to curtail the merriment of their festivals. Even in Zurich, dedicated to the proposition that the Word alone sufficed for man's spiritual needs, they practiced obscure rituals, like digging up the bones of ancestors to recite the traditional prayers for the dead. The Reformation took hold only through a process of appropriation, by which the people made it their religion, not just that of the preachers.

For evaluating the success of the Reformation in rural Germany, scholars depend on the reports of officially sanctioned clerical "visitors" who made regular circuits. Visitors followed printed forms with questions for the pastor and his parishioners, so that answers can be compared over time. Country people were no doubt intimidated by these prying, citified strangers, but not enough to give the right answers. Even if taught their catechism as youngsters, they were seldom able to recite the Apostles Creed or the Ten Commandments, and they had only the vaguest ideas about how sinners were saved from damnation. Pastors complained again and again about the many who jumped up to leave as soon as the sermon began, or stayed away from church altogether, and about village officials who silently obstructed the mandates of godly princes for a reformation of festivals and other popular customs. There seems little difference between the visitors' reports from Lutheran and Calvinist territories or between Catholic and Protestant territories. Rulers who applied the full force of their authority could achieve some results—people did generally go to church where they were fined for nonattendance—but compulsion does not make for inner conviction. Yet the picture is not uniformly bleak. In some rural districts that have been studied, there is evidence that people attended Sunday services regularly, worried less than their ancestors did about evil spells or other threats from the realm of magic, and used the disciplinary procedures of the new church to resolve conflicts among themselves. In one corner of Catholic Germany where no ruler had the power to impose either Protestantism or a Tridentine form of Catholicism, the process of appropriation is a bit clearer: by the eighteenth century, villagers attended Sunday mass more regularly, but they still preferred the pastors they knew—never mind whether or not these priests had concubines—to austere and learned Jesuits representing an alien faith. Rural folk whose religious identity had once been decided by princely fiat eventually did create for themselves a religious culture based on the new beliefs, but only over a very long period of time.

The principle that separates the relative success of urban Reformations from the painfully slow acceptance of new religious ideas in the country-side was grasped by the great Muslim historian Ibn Khaldun (d. 1395): "One cannot expect [prophets] to work the wonder of achieving superiority without group feeling." Ibn Khaldun was referring to the Prophet Muhammad and the "group feeling" of Arab tribes. But one can apply his reasoning to the civic solidarity that powered the urban Reformation and made it difficult for princes to reverse a religious choice once accepted by townsfolk. In this sense, too, the Reformation in its most successful form was a communal movement.

14 Society and Community

Reformations across Europe

Calvinism and Tridentine Catholicism were the two forms of Christianity that competed most aggressively for the allegiance of early modern Europeans (chapter 7). Most of the leaders willing to use war as a means of achieving religious objectives were found among militant Calvinists or militant Catholics (chapter 9). This chapter focuses on the fact that Calvinism and Tridentine Catholicism were also conspicuous in their zeal for the reformation of morals, albeit in very different ways. As in chapter 13, the discussion here will consider the social basis of each movement, its vision of a more Christian community, and its successes and failures as measured against this objective. Like German Lutheranism, Calvinism and Tridentine Catholicism were able to engender a sense of confessional identity strong enough to enable both faiths to withstand the pressures of minority existence in societies dominated by other creeds. The Catholic preachers who tried to convert Huguenot La Rochelle after its conquest by Richelieu (1628) did not have much success; neither did Calvinist ministers the Dutch Republic sent into northern Brabant (also in 1628) after conquering a territory that by then had two generations of Counter-Reformation preaching. Thus if the various Reformations changed European society through the creation of better disciplined communities of believers, they changed it even more by making such communities strong enough to survive in a religiously hostile climate. The time when religious pluralism would be accepted as a positive good lies beyond the chronological limits of this book. But it will be appropriate to end our survey of the Calvinist and Catholic Reformations with a brief look at a few urban societies where political circumstances made pluralism a fact of life.

CALVINISM

The *social basis* of Calvinism was to be found in the towns. Calvin's creed held few charms for peasants. In west Flanders, where the new textile industry was centered, the towns had many Calvinists, but surrounding villages had none. In France, Nîmes and La Rochelle, Calvinist for generations, bought grain from and had vineyards worked by Catholic peasants. The rural areas of France or Flanders where Calvinism had success—marked by cottage industry and unusually high rates of literacy—are exceptions that prove the rule.

If Lutheranism readily identified with movements for local control, Calvinism had a special appeal for those with broader horizons. Calvin himself welcomed to Geneva the refugees of many nationalities, and he and his successor, Theodore Beza, kept up a voluminous exchange with correspondents from most corners of Europe. Leaders of the movement knew what it was to choose exile for their beliefs. While in exile, in Geneva, London, or Emden, they rubbed shoulders with coreligionists from distant lands. Calvinism's ability to rise above the limits of a local outlook seems to have been one of the sources of its appeal for the twenty or so German princes (starting with Count Palatine) who converted Lutheran territories to Calvinism between about 1560 and 1620. This so-called second Reformation was backed by bureaucrats who grew beyond identification with their native towns by serving the prince. For these reformations from above, parochial loyalties were merely obstacles to be overcome. Something similar can be seen in the French-Pyrenean principality of Béarn, where a Huguenot military victory (1569) permitted Jeanne d'Albret (d. 1572), lady of the ruling house, to impose Calvinist reforms that the largely Catholic estates of her land had hitherto resisted.

Calvinism's international flavor may also help to explain its appeal for Europe's cosmopolitan nobility, from Scotland to Transylvania, and from southwestern France to Lithuania. In France, it is estimated that around 1560 some 10 percent of the population were Calvinist but 50 percent of the nobles were. It was rare in Protestant churches elsewhere, but not in France, for clergymen to come from noble families. Scotland's Reformation was largely made by the nobles, Poland's almost entirely so. Nobles were prominent also in early stages of the protest movement against Philip II's repressive religious policy in the Netherlands, though not in the Dutch Reformed Church after 1572. In Hungary, Calvinism, backed by many of the kingdom's great magnate families, became the majority religion not just in Transylvania but also in the largely Magyar-speaking central region ruled by the Turkish Sultan after 1541. Politics had something to do with these choices. In France, clients of the Bourbon family often followed their chieftain's religious lead. Scotland's Protestant nobles were linked to the pro-English faction; Hungary's and Poland's magnates shared an anti-German feeling directed against the Catholic Habsburgs. But Reformed religion was also a matter of conscience, certainly for literate and strong-minded noblewomen who converted their male kinfolk. At the next level down in the order of status, there were certainly devout Calvinist families among the well-to-do, but merchants involved in long-distance trade were on the whole no more likely than their neighbors to turn to Calvinism. There were few Protestants among leading families in Europe's great banking centers—Antwerp, Lyon, Genoa, and Augsburg. Antwerp's merchant community was prominent among local Calvinists in 1566–1567, when it seemed that Catholicism in the Low Countries was about to collapse, but underrepresented in earlier years, when churches "under the cross" faced persecution. In Lyon, wealthy businessmen who rallied to the Reformation were mostly émigrés, like the master printers; the native elite remained largely Catholic.

Guildsmen were the backbone of urban Protestantism in France and the Low Countries, though with some distinctions that may not apply for Lutheran Germany. In the 1550s, Calvinism had a powerful appeal for "proletarian" guild workers in the new textile industries of west Flanders, but none at all for those protected by well-established guild regulations in the centers of traditional woolen production, like Ghent. In Antwerp at roughly the same time, guildsmen were disproportionate in number among those persecuted for their Protestant beliefs. In Utrecht of the 1580s, orthodox Calvinism had its strongest support from the guilds, including craftsmen with shops along the city's main canal. La Rochelle, where Calvinism was quickly embraced by the wine merchant and vineyard owner elite, was perhaps an exception for France, rather like Constance in Germany. Elsewhere, guildsmen were the most reliable Calvinist constituency, even though often outnumbered, as in Dijon, by guildsmen who remained Catholic. Those most likely to hearken to the new doctrines came from the high end of the scale of craft skills, where literacy was common or even required: in Lyon, printers, goldsmiths and jewelers, and silkworkers; in Rouen, bonnet-makers; in Antwerp, diamond-cutters and silversmiths, and, in the textile industry, braid- and trimmings-makers. Many of these highly specialized craftsmen were outsiders seeking opportunity in centers like Antwerp and Rouen, where, as in Lyon, they found in underground Calvinist communities a haven for newcomers frozen out of established parish hierarchies. Urban Calvinism in France and the Low Countries was, it seems, a religion not of the common man in general, but of the discriminating common man, able to read scripture in the vernacular and conscious that his superior skill was not matched by superior status.

There may also have been a Calvinism of the unskilled. The spread of Reformed Protestantism was punctuated by iconoclasm, a venting of anticlerical fury stoked by incendiary preaching. In many cases, this violence was attributed by contemporaries to the lower orders of urban society. Statements of this kind may be taken with a grain of salt, but are not implausible. In La Rochelle, where Calvinist magistrates sought to keep passions under control, some 300 people from the poorer quarters broke away from a huge outdoor communion service to smash each of the city's churches, threatening death to the mayor who bade them cease (1562). During the previous year, actions of this kind, including killings of priests, comparable to the murders of Huguenots in Catholic riots, were especially common in the region around Agen, between Bordeaux and Toulouse. The preacher whose sermons lay behind some of these incidents was dismissed from his post; in La Rochelle, preachers and consistory alike rebuked all who presumed to destroy churches without the consent of the magistrates. In the turbulent early years of the Dutch Revolt, most preachers and consistories denounced those responsible for attacks on Catholic churches and priests. Calvin had set the tone by rebuking his erstwhile colleague in Geneva, Guillaume Farel, for resorting to violent methods. Preachers who followed Calvin's lead could not altogether prevent violence against the "idolatrous" Catholic worship their sermons so roundly condemned. But their conscientious effort to keep pure religion from being contaminated by mob passions was surely a part of Calvinism's appeal to Europe's aristocracy.

True community. Proponents of Germany's "Second Reformation" distinguished between Luther's reformation of the individual conscience and the reformation of society promised by Geneva's example. Reminders of the Catholic belief that divine grace can work through material objects were tolerated under Lutheran regimes but not in the new Calvinist order. There must be no altars, no baptismal fonts, no statues, no paintings. Likewise, the common folk must renounce long-held beliefs against which Lutheran preachers had campaigned (or so it was thought) with insufficient zeal. Unlike popish priests, the ministers of God's Word claimed no spiritual power that could touch people's daily lives. There was no need to bless crops or fishermen's boats, for all things were in the Lord's keeping. There was no sacrament of the dying, only pious laymen deputed to attend upon the dying and read from scripture. There was no holy water to take home for warding off evil spirits, no fronds or branches blessed by the priest on Palm Sunday: the only religious object a Christian home needed was the Bible.

The same demands were made on the inhabitants of territories influenced by Zwingli's teachings, but Zurich had no consistory to impose them on church members. The lay elders who served with pastors on Geneva's consistory were cut from the same cloth as members of the city council—both were chosen in the same annual elections. After 1555 the two groups collaborated closely: those excommunicated by the consistory were exiled by the council.

Larger territories that adopted Calvinism recognized a distinction, not found in Geneva, between members of the church, eligible to participate in the Lord's Supper, and those who merely attended services. To become a member, one met with the pastor (bringing two character witnesses) and swore to uphold the church's confession of faith and submit to its discipline. Names of prospective members were read aloud to the congregation, in case anyone had something unsavory to report that would bar admission. In churches ruled by consistories, members might also be visited in their homes by one or more elders just prior to a celebration of the Lord's Supper. There could be probing questions about beating one's wife, gambling parties, or the sudden bursts of anger that so often led to unseemly violence. Elders knew what to ask because dutiful church folk kept them informed: The husband's visit to the brothel had been noticed, and the respectable merchant's wife had been heard by many when she shouted insults on the open street like a fishwife. The reason for this scrutiny was to keep the Lord's Supper unstained by the pollution of sin, or even public rumor of sin. A Dutch tax-farmer charged with malfeasance convinced his elders he was not guilty, but he was nonetheless excommunicated from the church because he could not prove his innocence beyond all doubt. Members declaring bankruptcy might be excommunicated automatically, on the assumption that only spendthrifts and wastrels were unable to maintain their credit among honest folk.

Some cities were able to approximate the identity between church membership and membership in the civil community for which Geneva was the model. In Emden, a Reformed church built by a Polish refugee preacher and scholar took hold among the people over two generations and successfully resisted a change of religion ordered by its Lutheran prince. The Calvinist movement in Nîmes started among teachers at the Latin school, drew inspiration from conversions among local mendicant friars, and gained the allegiance of most magistrates by about 1561; adhesion of the populace was signaled by a riot in which about 100 Catholic notables were massacred (1567). In later years, among some 12,000 there were at most 400 Catholics, mostly of the lower orders. But in La Rochelle, where houses of Reformed worship were established only in the central wards where the elite lived, the consistory was openly mocked by a self-styled "carnival king," and it was nearly two generations before the new beliefs took hold among artisans.

Changing the outlook and behavior of an entire kingdom, like Scotland, was even more difficult. Calvinist preachers in the Gaelic-speaking Highlands were forced to accommodate local culture: No one confused the locally prized gift of "second sight" with damnable witchcraft, and the Reformed liturgy included a blessing for fishermen's boats. In Béarn, Jeanne d'Albret's determination to impose Calvinism on a "rude and ignorant" populace brought a warning from her leading preacher, Pierre Viret (d. 1571): "A small flock of sheep and lambs is better than a large flock that has more wolves and pigs than sheep and lambs."

The Dutch Reformed Church opted for a solution similar to what Viret had proposed. Civil authorities tolerated no other form of public worship, but church membership was voluntary, not constrained. In cities where magistrates put their weight behind it, the church came to embrace most of the population; in cities where they consistently fought against it, the church claimed only a fraction of the citizenry. For the republic as a whole the choice for selective membership had consequences. On one hand, not much could be done to reform public morals. Visiting English Puritans were shocked to find that in a professedly Calvinist country dancing and theatrical shows flourished in the towns, and peasants worked as needed in their fields on Sundays. On the other hand, it was all the more urgent for believers who freely gave their allegiance to the church to form a truly Christian community, a miniature Geneva shining its light among the ungodly.

Broadly speaking, then, Calvinist ministers worked in one of two kinds of setting. Where the work of pastors was sustained by a shared sense of community, whether on a civic basis (as in Geneva, Emden, or Nîmes), or on a voluntary church basis (as in the Dutch Republic), they preached to willing and enthusiastic congregations. As in solidly Lutheran German cities like Strasbourg, preachers and congregants together developed a strong sense of confessional identity. But where the Reformed religion had little popular support, as in Béarn or the Scottish Highlands, it was an uphill battle to make godly folk of the indifferent, just as it was for rural pastors in German territories that had become Lutheran by princely fiat. But can Calvinists can be distinguished from Lutherans or Catholics in their behavior? Did consistories really make a difference?

Success or failure. Examination of court records before and after the Reformation bears out the Calvinist claim that the men and women of Reformed Geneva were less quarrelsome, more sober in their habits, and

FOEMINA HONESTA GENEVENSIS.

Figure 14.1. "A Virtuous Woman of Geneva." "Foemina Honesta Genevensis" from H. Weigel, *Habitus Praecipuorum Populorm* (Nuremberg, 1577). *Bibliothèque Publique et Universitaire de Genève, Geneva.*

more honest in acquitting public responsibilities than their Catholic forebears had been (fig. 14.1). What were the secrets of this transformation? Calvin's followers attributed great things to the cumulative influence of his preaching over the years. No doubt they exaggerated his impact. But the Calvinist sermon, featuring an hour or more of detailed scriptural exegesis with some "punishing of the papacy" sprinkled in, gripped the minds of early modern folk in ways that are difficult to fathom in a media-saturated age. The behind-the-scenes work of Geneva's consistory, locked up for centuries under the indecipherable handwriting of official secretaries, is just now beginning to be better understood. The tribunal's aim was to reconcile sinners to the church; excommunication, the extreme sanction, was seldom employed. The typical person summoned might be a young bachelor cited for fisticuffs, a married man who treated his wife harshly, or an old woman overheard mumbling her Our Father in popish Latin instead of proper French. Forms of behavior control associated with later English Puritanism were of less concern than offenses against the family unit or the public peace. Being a good Christian meant being a good spouse and a good citizen. This focus on community building appears also in other urban churches that tried to copy Geneva's success.

Emden's church leaders campaigned against inebriation for generations, but to no avail; consistory records corroborate the gossip of nearby towns—Emdeners carried a deserved reputation for drunkenness into the eighteenth century. There was, however, a slow but perceptible decline in the number of citations for out-of-wedlock pregnancies, physical violence, and the kind of verbal abuse that led to fights. Young women who conceived apart from marriage were being shamed, and men as well as women were developing stronger inhibitions against violence. At Nîmes, the consistory made headway in curbing prostitution and in protecting the virtue of servant girls living in households headed by older men. Festivals and merrymaking could not be curbed, despite such dramatic actions as the smashing of violins and carnival masks by repentant church members. Banned in Nîmes, dances were still held in surrounding Catholic villages. In an age when combative notions of a gentleman's honor were spreading from Italy into France, the church's great success lay in inducing many of its male members to lay aside the quarrels that so often led to duels. As in Emden, the consistory strove to preserve the family unit and the public peace.

In Scotland and the Netherlands, discipline was exercised by church councils at the parish level rather than by citywide consistories. Most people cited before Scottish church tribunals during the first fifty years of the Reformation era were accused of sexual offenses like adultery or fornication. This focus on the more obvious sins suggests a church not yet strong enough to attack other sources of public disorder in a society known for its protracted feuds. In the university town of St. Andrews, the church council, strongly backed by the magistrates, could boast of a sharp and fairly rapid decline in the number of sexual cases considered, especially for fornication. The Scots *kirk* employed a method that may help explain this success: Confessed fornicators had to sit for three successive Sundays on a "stool of repentance" and hear themselves denounced from the pulpit by the minister.

By comparison with St. Andrews (about 4,000 people), Amsterdam was a metropolis, rising from around 40,000 souls in 1580 to around 200,000 in 1650. Despite this difference in scale, Amsterdam's church councils resembled similar bodies elsewhere both in their priorities and in their successes and failures. In a city where most people were not Reformed, the councils had to abandon the usual Calvinist prohibitions against dancing and theatergoing. But over time the church instilled in its members new standards of sexual conduct: By the late seventeenth century, the relative numbers for persons cited for fornication were dwindling. In the shaming of unwed mothers, records indicate that parish elders and the "neighborhood folk" who kept them informed shared the same values. The councils gave great attention to fights and shouting matches, expending much time and effort to induce contending parties to give each other "the hand of friendship." That they had some success in changing the way people reacted to insults is indicated by the many members who, if slandered by a neighbor, seemed content with the satisfaction they received by having a church council publicly certify their good reputation.

In sum, while popular amusements were relatively immune to ecclesiastical censure, it seems that people who accepted the discipline of the church learned over time to moderate their sexual urges and to contain their angry impulses. If seventeenth-century Europeans were indeed becoming more civil in their behavior—less prone to random sexual adventures and spontaneous outbursts of violence—religion was certainly not the only reason, but it is a part of the explanation, perhaps especially so in strongly Calvinist church communities like those just discussed. Presuming that Calvinism could and did reach into the human psyche to discipline the instincts, scholars have speculated about the historical significance of this inner transformation. One view is that Calvinism prepared the way for capitalism, in part by training its followers to curb their spendthrift appetites, the better to accumulate capital. But merchant capitalism of a Jacob Fugger or an Erasmus Schets (chapter 12) was a well-established fact of life before the Reformation began. Also, the relative economic ranking of European regions of Catholic and Protestant background looks very different now than it did nearly a century ago, when this theory was propounded by a German sociologist, Max Weber. Another view is that Reformed Protestantism's repression of aggression had the effect of turning it inward, creating a potentially destructive self-scrutiny, as is suggested by Zurich's rising suicide rate during the late sixteenth century. Even if this argument is correct, however, it need not apply to the Calvinist form of church discipline, in which members discussed their spiritual lives with pastors or elders, a psychological safety valve comparable in some ways to the Catholic practice of confession. Could a Calvinist "reformation" of the instincts have produced a conscience that was finely honed, without being self-punishing? This is a fascinating question, but consideration of diaries and other materials that might yield answers would take us too far afield. The surest conclusion is one that leads back to the social dimension of religion to which this section of the book is devoted: Calvinist consistories worked hard to build a Christian community among their members, and they clearly had some degree of success.

CATHOLICISM

The Catholic and Protestant Reformations had many of the same objectives. Germany's new Protestant universities were matched by new Catholic foundations, and the seminaries slowly put in place by Catholic bishops bear comparison with the theological academies of cities like Geneva and Nîmes. When educated clergy of any denomination took a country parish, they carefully avoided tavern drinking and other indecorous pastimes; they were not to be members of the community, but beacons of instruction, standing above it. The *classes* in which Calvinist preachers met regularly provided fellowship for these lonely professionals, and revived rural deaneries did the same for Catholic pastors. To catechize the people, the basic points of true religion (different for each confession) were boiled down to simple statements, to be repeated in sermons for adults and drilled into the heads of schoolchildren. For children not attending school there were weekly catechism classes. As in Protestant lands, however, Catholic young people were not eager to devote Sunday afternoons to religious enlightenment. This was an area in which civil governments might intervene. In some German Calvinist territories, parents were fined for not sending their children to catechism classes. In Spain, people of the centrally located diocese of Cuenca learned their catechism well, as determined by questioning persons held in prison by the local inquisition. Yet in the diocese of Ourense in remote Galicia, a region with its own language and culture, not even monetary fines induced parents to send children to catechism classes. In staunchly Catholic Lille, the magistrates organized Sunday religious instruction at sites throughout the city. Elsewhere in the Spanish Netherlands, the idea of monetary "attendance prizes" was bruited about, but neither parish boards nor village councils wanted to put up the money; complaints from clergy eventually induced the government to issue the needed instructions—village councils fell into line, and children started coming.

Yet there was a fundamental difference. Much as they yearned for a purer Catholicism, Catholic reformers could not condemn as Protestants did the religion bequeathed to them by earlier ages. Rather than attacking the tyranny of the clergy, they accepted the structure of the church hierarchy as fundamentally sound. Rather than castigating ordinary believers for their superstition, they sought in the religious culture of the people valid elements on which to build. This conservative stance frames the distinctive features of Catholic reform: its social dimensions reflected the contrast between pre- and post-Tridentine Catholicism; its vision of a more Christian society depended on rebuilding the church hierarchy; and its successes and failures were measured by attempts to modify rather than replace the religious culture of the people.

Social basis. As noted above, in France neither peasants nor members of the more traditional urban guilds (e.g., butchers and bakers) showed much interest in Calvinism. In Lyon, most people who were not newcomers seemed to find contentment in customary arrangements that ensured a place in the city's civic and religious hierarchy for each guild and each confraternity. People who change their religion may be presumed to have reasons for doing so, but those who persist in the same belief could be acting from inertia more than conviction. When Catholicism in France seemed to be threatened by the Protestant Henry of Bourbon's emergence as heir apparent to the throne, guildsmen in towns all over France, especially in the north, rallied to the militant program of the Catholic League. In the Low Countries, however, people of presumably Catholic sympathies stood passively by as ruffians hired by fanatical Calvinist ministers looted churches and smashed the symbols of their belief. One weakly governed area in Germany suggests what kind of religion ordinary Catholics might choose for themselves when the moral authority of seminary-educated priests was not backed by the coercive power of the state. Seventeenth-century villagers attended Sunday mass more regularly, but they balked at changing the way they kept their festivals and refused to discriminate against the occasional fellow villager who happened to be of the wrong persuasion. They eventually did accept Catholicism as an identity that separated them from the Lutherans and Calvinists of nearby villages, but this "confessionalization" of the people was not complete until the eighteenth century.

Tridentine Catholicism had a more sharply defined social profile. The Protestant Reformation rejected the idea that men and women could be holy—there was no such thing as sainthood. The Catholic Reformation, especially through its many new religious orders, resembled the great ascetic movements of the past in demanding a heroic renunciation of self. The call to holiness is never answered by large numbers, but many of the men and women who now did respond came from the upper levels of society. Teresa of Avila (1515–1582) was the daughter of a New Christian cloth merchant who had purchased a title of nobility. Joining a convent in 1535, she began around 1555 to have the intense spiritual experiences, including seeing visions, that brought her a sense of personal union with God and a determination to work for the reform of her Carmelite order. Facing down opposition, she founded a new branch of the order, based on strict poverty and strict enclosure; its spread beyond Spain was aided by the growing fame of her spiritual writings. Ignatius Loyola, founder of the Jesuits, was a nobleman. Two of his early companions in Paris had been shepherds in Savoy, but another was Francis Xavier (d. 1552), the Spanish nobleman Ignatius sent as a missionary to Portugal's outposts in India.

In the generation after the end of the Religious Wars (1598), France witnessed an extraordinary surge of religious energy. Barbe Acarie (1566–1618), widow of an ardent Catholic Leaguer connected with the Paris Sixteen, sought to live a quiet life of prayer, but reports of her ecstatic experience brought men and women eager for her guidance. Inspired by a vision of Teresa of Avila, she founded the first French house of the reformed Carmelites. Francis de Sales (1567–1622), son of a noble family in Savoy, was a popular spiritual writer whose earnest but noncontentious preaching won many converts in the diocese of Geneva, of which he was titular bishop. With Jeanne Françoise de Chantal, the widowed daughter of a leading royal judge in Burgundy, he founded the order of the Visitation, whose members, though later compelled by church authorities to live in convents and dress as nuns, initially wore lay clothes as they went two by two visiting the sick and poor. Jacqueline Arnaud (1591–1661) joined the convent of Port-Royal (outside Paris) at eleven and became its abbess at thirteen, thanks to the influence of her father, a leading magistrate of the Parlement of Paris. Long restive in a life she had not chosen, she experienced a conversion through the Lenten sermons of a Capuchin friar and pushed through a reform of convent discipline that initially shocked her family. Soon the convent was not big enough for those demanding admission. The new Port Royal (1626), built in the suburbs of Paris, became a focal point for devout lay men and women, like the male "solitaries" who abandoned promising careers, gave away the proceeds of their property, and started a school for poor children. Pierre Bérulle (d. 1629), son of another member of the Paris Parlement, was influenced by Madame Acarie, who came to stay with his family when her husband was sent into exile (1594). He founded the French branch of an Italian order, the Oratory of Divine Love, which under his guidance opened secondary schools and taught in many of the new diocesan seminaries. Vincent de Paul (1581–1660), an immensely popular preacher who was born of a peasant family, founded an order of priests, the Congregation of the Mis-

Figure 14.2. St. Vincent de Paul and the Daughters of Charity. Anonymous, "St. Vincent de Paul and the Daughters of Charity," ca. 1740. *Musée de l'Assistance Publique-Hôpitaux de Paris.* © *François Marin—AP-HP.*

sion, to preach "missions" (see below) in rural areas. The networked confraternities he created to distribute food and clothing to the poor were known as "Charities." He encouraged Louise de Marillac (d. 1660), a niece of Cardinal Richelieu's political rival, to found an order of nuns, the Daughters of Charity, to coordinate and extend the work of the "Charities" (fig. 14.2).

Vincent de Paul was not the only Counter-Reformation saint to come from humble people. The peasant-born John of the Cross (1542–1591), one of the great poets of mystical experience, was inspired by a meeting with Teresa of Avila to extend her Carmelite reform to the male branch of the order. Philip Neri (1515–1595), from a poor family in Florence, gathered a group of followers in Rome and in effect refounded the Oratory of Divine Love as an order of priests, later established in France by Bérulle. But the prominent background of the others mentioned here is not the only indication that Reform Catholicism depended on people of wealth and position. Jesuit secondary schools mainly attracted the sons of noble and wealthy burgher families. These "colleges" were the main recruiting ground for the society, which had over 8,500 members by 1600, and also for the Jesuit-guided lay confraternities known as sodalities. Members were encouraged to pray according to the rules of Ignatius's *Spiritual Exercises*. Jesuits initially formed sodalities among the top students at colleges, priests holding important positions in a diocese, or leading members of lay society. Jesuit spirituality was not restricted to any one level of society, but there was a conscious strategy of working through those who set the tone for others. In northeastern Italy, noble sodality members accompanied Jesuit fathers in preaching missions to the countryside, to show the peasants an example of devotion.

The status group solidarity of Europe's noble families was growing stronger during the sixteenth and seventeenth centuries. All churches had to accommodate this trend, for example, by reserving front pews for the better sort of people, who paid a rental fee. But Protestant reformers insisted on the unity of the worshiping community: There must be no privileges of rank, no special groups meeting to pray apart from the rest. To prevent members of a large congregation from forming divisive attachments to individual preachers, Dutch churches made a practice of not announcing who would be preaching at which Sunday service. By contrast, Catholic reform capitalized on the popularity of preachers like Vincent de Paul, encouraged the formation of special groups like confraternities, and gave existing divisions of society the sanction of religious approval. All across Catholic Europe nobles sought to form confraternities or sodalities of their own, breaking the tradition that these religious associations were to be a meeting ground for all respectable people. With the blessing of the clergy, they did so, and merchants and artisans soon followed their example. In far-off Mexico, where confraternities initially included Indian converts, Spaniards demanded associations of their own in which to practice good works, and so did Indians (fig. 14.3). In a native society brought low by conquest and ravaged by European diseases, Indian confraternities became cells for rebuilding. This affirmation of existing social and even ethnic distinctions has parallels in other aspects of Catholic reform.

True community. The Protestant Reformation drastically simplified the church hierarchy. Once Luther undercut the whole idea of a sacramental priesthood, Lutheran clergy married and became citizens subject to local

Figure 14.3. The corporal works of mercy among the Incas of Peru. "A Good Work of Mercy" (Burying the Dead), from the work of an Inca scholar, Felipe Guaman Poma de Ayala (flourished 1613), El Primer Coronica I Buen Gobierno, p. 613, facsimile manuscript with an introduction by Richard Petschmann (Paris, 1936). *Courtesy of University Libraries, University of Minnesota, Minneapolis.*

taxes. In Calvinist lands clergy also shared the dignity of the ministry with lay elders. After the closing of monasteries and the repudiation of the papal and (in most areas) episcopal authority, what remained was a tiny band of ministers more or less equal in rank. Before the Reformation, the diocese of Geneva had a prince-bishop, 110 parishes, and 53 monasteries; by 1546, this structure was replaced by a mere 31 Reformed pastors.

By contrast, the Catholic vision of reform reinforced the distinctive spiritual authority of the priesthood at every level. In Rome, new committees of cardinals known as congregations worked to make the papacy's supremacy effective. The Congregation of the Inquisition (1542) claimed supervision over heresy trials in church tribunals. For more than sixty years this claim was rejected by Venice, where magistrates were accustomed to giving orders to inquisitors and other local church officials. With help from Spanish Milan, the papacy finally went to war and forced the republic to submit (1605–1608). There were also papal commissions for special topics, like correction of the calendar inherited from ancient Rome, based on a year of 365 days. In 1582 Pope Gregory XIII promulgated a reform that required dropping eleven days that year in order to make human dating match celestial time. But Italy's greatest scientist, the Florentine Galileo Galilei (d. 1642), ran afoul of the Roman inquisition when he insisted on describing the heliocentric theory as a fact, rather than a mere hypothesis. Meanwhile, papal nuncios traversed Europe pressing rulers to cooperate with Catholic reform, and overseas missions were placed under the authority of a new Congregation for the Propagation of the Faith (1622).

The Council of Trent gave bishops greater powers to supervise all aspects of religious life. Zealous prelates like Milan's Archbishop Carlo Borromeo (r. 1565–1584), later canonized as a saint, set an example by visiting even the remotest parishes and holding regular synods to instill higher standards among his priests. At the parish level, the seminary-trained clergy who took over in most places during the course of the seventeenth century were generally faithful to the church's rule of celibacy. New-style priests were instructed to take under their watchful supervision any new confraternities, as well as traditional lay bodies hitherto bereft of clerical oversight. No one was to have any doubt that spiritual authority lay in the pastor's hands.

The pastor wielded his authority over the faithful most clearly in the sacrament of penance, in keeping with the obligation of all Catholics to confess their sins to a priest at least once a year at Easter time. From the fifteenth century the proper relationship between confessor and penitent was symbolized in new church furnishings: a chair for the priest and a prie-dieu (kneeler) for the lay person. This arrangement allowed the priest to lay his hands on the head of the penitent, in token of the words of absolution he pronounced; but it was not proof against the scandals that arose when priests used their powers of absolution to demand sexual favors of female penitents. Sixteenth-century Italian churchmen thus developed the confessional, a large wooden box with a chair for the priest; a kneeler for the penitent; and a screen between them, to prevent physical contact between them. For good measure, the doors on both sides were to be kept open during confession. Parish priests were to issue certificates to those who made their Easter confession, and keep registers of parishioners who had confessed, and those who had not. Zealous Catholic governments joined in by requiring subjects to show their confession certificates on various occasions. Milan's Carlo Borromeo demanded that his priests use the power of the confessional for the moral betterment of society, by refusing absolution to those who would not absent themselves from what were considered occasions of sin, like the traditional dances at which young men and women became acquainted; the result was an impasse, for while people in Milan refused to give up this "most ancient custom of the country" Borromeo remained inflexible. Other reform-minded bishops saw the sacrament of penance more as a means of educating the faithful than as an instrument of social control. But Borromeo's intemperate zeal indicates that some ways of attempting to change people's behavior were even more intrusive than Geneva's consistory.

Counter-Reformation Catholicism, like the church of medieval centuries, was also energized by order priests not subject to episcopal authority. Every sphere of church activity was marked not just by a plurality of jurisdictions, but by multiple understandings of the devout person's role in Christian society. The Confraternities of Christian Doctrine, formed under the influence of Bologna's reforming bishop, had pastors send trained laymen into the streets to round up children as best they could for catechism classes. The Capuchin fathers were a branch of the broad Franciscan movement, based on an imitation of Jesus's life as described in the Gospels. If Jesus prayed and fasted forty days in the desert, preachers too must break off for long periods of prayer and solitude. If Jesus had come to preach the gospel to the poor, Capuchins must seek out the poorest quarters wherever they established themselves. Capuchin-founded confraternities took a special interest in the poor, and, as the friars themselves did, they embraced the traditional ascetic practice of disciplining the sinful flesh. Like flagellants of old, hooded confraternity members processed through the streets on solemn occasions, scourging one another. In the Jesuit sodalities such corporal discipline, if deemed necessary by one's father confessor, was to be practiced in moderation and never in public.

These differing approaches were often complementary, as with the "missions" to rural areas poorly served by the existing parish structure. Members of orders active in Catholic Europe's overseas missions sometimes expressed the belief that people of the continent's remote corners needed Christianizing as much as the heathen of Asia or the Americas. Often chosen for their oratorical skills, mission priests traveled two by two—Jesuits, Capuchins, or members of St. Vincent de Paul's Congregation of the Mission. Following the example of late medieval circuit preachers, they

preached for several weeks in a given parish, striving to instruct the ignorant and rouse devotion.

But the mere existence of many different models of the Christian life,
each supported by its own order or other institutions, also meant that controversy was inevitable. One example may suffice. From about 1550, the
strongly orthodox theology faculty at Louvain (near Brussels) developed
a serious interest in the writings of St. Augustine, in order to refute
Luther's claim to stand in the Augustinian tradition. In the early seventeenth century Louvain's Augustinian theology spread to France through
graduates like the abbot of Saint-Cyran, an influential theologian and a
champion of the Port-Royal movement. More important, Augustine's
dour views on human nature fitted the life experience of a new generation
of urban-born and seminary-trained pastors, confronting surly rural folk
who seemed to think about religion no more often than they thought about
bathing, that is, once a week. Hence the *Augustinus* (1638), a posthumously
published exposition of Augustine's theology by a bishop and Louvain
graduate named Cornelis Jansen, found an audience in France as well as
the Spanish Netherlands. But Jesuit defenders of human free will pounced
on the book for espousing a doctrine of predestination hardly distinguish-
able from Calvin's heresies. In turn, Saint-Cyran and others linked to the
austere convent of Port-Royal denounced the Jesuits as purveyors of an
easy morality suitable to their friends among the high and mighty. Cardinal Richelieu, angered by criticisms of his war policy among the Port-
Royal circle, had already given Saint-Cyran a taste of prison. This heavy-
handed act of state, coupled with reactions to Jansen's book, touched off a
long and many-sided struggle over "Jansenism" in Catholic Europe.

Every church of this era had its unseemly internal quarrels. But in the
Catholic Church squabbles of this kind were an inevitable consequence of
the fact of plural ministries. Just as Tridentine Catholicism accepted and
built on existing social divisions, it also accepted and built on a pluralism
of religious perspectives not unlike that of the late Middle Ages. Paradox-
ical as it may seem, Europe's most clerical form of Christianity was also the
one most characterized by multiple and often conflicting centers of wide-
ranging initiative.

Success or failure. The reformed Catholicism of the late sixteenth and seventeenth centuries has not left records comparable to the consistory books
of Geneva and other Calvinist centers, through which one can track, over
time, the moral failings of which church members are accused. There was
of course a distinctively Catholic form of church discipline—the sacra-

ment of penance—but scholars have only begun to raise questions of the sort that have engaged students of the consistory records: If the priests hearing confessions were better trained, and more zealous in their inquiries, and if church and state joined in ensuring that Catholics made their Easter confession, what difference did it make in people's lives, or in the formation of a more sensitive conscience? Some scholars, impressed by the intrusive character of the Counter-Reformation penitential regime, have doubted whether external pressures of this sort can have had a lasting effect. Others have argued that, over time, those who submitted to norms imposed in the sacrament by the priest "appropriated them inwardly, as habits of conscience." In other words, it seems that a process noticeable among the devout in the late Middle Ages was broadened and deepened by the Catholic as well as by the Protestant Reformation. Whether one calls this long-term process "guiltification" or "conscience formation" is a matter of opinion.

In terms of public worship, Catholic reform sought to correct rather than to eradicate traditional belief. Instead of eliminating the cult of saints, church authorities pruned the liturgical calendar of saints' days added in recent centuries, and created instead feast days for holy men and women of the early Christian centuries whose lives were well documented. In pre-Reformation Europe, the understood way of professing that a given town or village stood under God's judgment was through a procession in which all participated. In time of plague, citizens of Renaissance Florence processed to a nearby village to bring back and carry around the city a reputedly miracle-working statue of the Virgin Mary. In Paris, when a locally revered statue was decapitated by Protestant iconoclasts (1528), King Francis I organized a procession of penitence in which the citizens joined. Each guild, each parish, each confraternity had its assigned place, making the order of march a walking model of urban society. This habit of collective religious display found little scope in Protestant Europe, but Counter-Reformation clerics saw it as needing only pruning here and guidance there. Priests were instructed to take the lead of processions they had not led before. Processions associated with rural festivals were to be made truly religious by inducing villagers to abandon boisterous habits (like shooting off their weapons) and march quietly behind the eucharist carried aloft by their priest. Like Venice's magistrates, who carefully refashioned the republic's great civic processions during the same era, Catholic reformers believed ideas could be conveyed by ritual, not just by words.

Many Protestant preachers (if not always their people) accepted Calvin's dictum that the age of miracles was long past. The healing shrines at which country people sought cures for their ailments were blasphemous at best

and more likely clerical frauds —if not outright sorcery practiced by devilish priests. Even in strongly Catholic lands like Bavaria, visits to wonder-
working shrines tapered off during the middle decades of the sixteenth
century, no doubt as an echo of Protestant critique. From the latter part of
the century, however, pilgrimages to some shrines revived and even sur-
passed earlier levels. Counter-Reformation priests examined the history of
these shrines and the documentation for the relics of the saints they contained. Some local cults they rejected as spurious; others they promoted
through their sermons and by writing learned treatises and popular pamphlets. The age of miracles was not over, and people could prove it for
themselves by bringing their humble petitions to approved shrines of
Catholic saints.

People feared the devil as much as they hoped for miracles. In the later
sixteenth century, the upsurge in witchcraft trials was paralleled by a dramatic increase in cases of alleged demonic possession, in which the minions of hell were believed to have forcibly taken over the body of an innocent person. The classic indicators of possession—people speaking in
unaccustomed voices or languages and racked by convulsions or showing
unbelievable strength—were observed and carefully described not just
among Christians of this era, but also among Jews. Since ancient times, the
Catholic Church had employed exorcism to deal with such phenomena.
Most dioceses had rules requiring examination of the person or persons involved to determine whether the symptoms could be explained by natural
means. If not, a priest with a reputation for probity was chosen for the
solemn ritual in which the possessing demon was abjured, in the name of
Christ, to depart from the victim. Most Protestant theologians accepted the
possibility of demonic possession and believed that "dispossession" was
possible through prayer and fasting; Luther himself attempted a dispossession late in his life. Some later writers, citing Calvin's belief about miracles, argued that the age of possession and dispossession was also past.
But all Protestant writers condemned Catholic exorcism as fraudulent, and
this made the church's traditional rite, like miracle-working shrines, a test
of Catholicism's credibility. In 1570 Peter Canisius, the celebrated Jesuit
preacher, caused a sensation by expelling several demons from a young
noblewoman in a publicly announced ceremony held in Augsburg's cathedral. The devil's power was real, but no match for the power of Christ, mediated by the rites of the church.

What was the relationship between the Catholicism of the elite and that
of the lowly? Scholars working on French history have found a gradual
withdrawal of elites from participation in what had hitherto been a common culture, extending to beliefs as well as amusements. One may distin-
guish between the refined preoccupations of better-educated people—

including Catholic Reform—and what may now be termed popular culture and popular religion. But for some scholars working on Spain the only meaningful distinction is that each locality had beliefs and practices not current elsewhere. Between high personages and the humble Spanish believers there was no real difference. When either Charles V or Philip II met a priest bearing the eucharist through the streets to a sick person, he knelt on the spot, heedless of the puddle at his feet.

One may envision a spectrum of attitudes whose range was not necessarily the same for all Catholic lands. At one end, devout Catholics shared the beliefs of common folk but always saw room for improvement: not every alleged case of demonic possession was genuine, nor was every shrine to be maintained. At the other end, those who shared the skeptical temper of an Erasmus might wonder whether miracles were worked at any shrine or any person was truly possessed by the devil, without rejecting the possibility that such things could occur. Just as post-Reformation Catholicism had room for the social solidarity of rival status groups and for competing centers of clerical initiative, it also had room for different levels of belief.

As a communal movement, the Reformation in its Lutheran and Calvinist forms struggled to overcome this confusing multiplicity, ultimately medieval in origin: All Christians were to profess the same gospel truth, submerging their differences in a unified community. This was a noble dream, but it collided with the natural human tendency to form associations based on interests and affinities of various kinds. Post-Reformation Catholicism, precisely because of its backward-looking rootedness in medieval multiplicity, may have been better adapted to a European society that was, after the Reformation as before, characterized by a nearly endless multitude of corporate bodies, each ready and willing to defend its lawful turf against all comers. Yet Protestantism as a whole was multiform in a different way: There were different ways of being Protestant, and members of rival churches usually did not wholly regard one another with quite the same hostility that Catholics and Protestants did. This opening toward a tacit acceptance of diversity of creeds was lacking in Catholicism, which remained medieval also in its more determined repression of dissenters. French Protestants had more freedoms than Dutch Catholics in the first half of the seventeenth century, but not in the second. Catholics in England and Scandinavia had a less difficult life than Protestants in the Spanish Netherlands or Austria, not to mention Spain. What neither Protestants nor Catholics of this era could accept was the idea that civil society was best not founded on a specific creed. Where different faiths were practiced, the dominant party viewed this state of affairs as something to be overcome through a combination of patience, proselytizing, and social pressure. There were, however, places where people of different denominations lived together long enough to begin to think of religious division as permanent, if not desirable—places like Augsburg and Colmar in Germany, Haarlem in the Netherlands, and the tiny walled town of Layrac in France. These were the places that pointed to a new conception of society.

DE FACTO RELIGIOUS PLURALISM

Augsburg grew from around 20,000 people in 1500 to around 40,000 in 1600. On the eve of the Reformation, the guilds controlled five-sixths of the seats on the small council responsible for daily concerns and all seats on the large council convened for major decisions. Zwinglianism predominated among the craft guilds, Lutheranism among the so-called greater guilds, whose members took the lead in city politics, and Catholicism among patrician banking families like the Fuggers. The large council voted by a sizable majority for a Zwinglian Reformation (1534). But with a watchful eye on the Catholic princely territories that surrounded it, Augsburg did not prohibit Catholic worship altogether until a year after it had joined the Schmalkaldic League in 1536. In 1548, residing for several weeks in the Fuggers' great mansion, Charles V personally imposed the hated Interim on the city for which it was named and also decreed new electoral rules to strip the guilds of power: Patricians henceforth had three-fourths of the small council seats, commoners only one-fourth. The new patrician government, mainly Catholic, then replaced the guilds with trade associations headed by council-appointed leaders. The 1555 Peace of Augsburg recognized only Lutheranism and Catholicism as lawful in the empire, which induced Augsburg's Zwinglian majority to choose Lutheranism. But it also provided that in filling lesser city offices a one-for-one parity must be observed among the two denominations. The Catholic minority's control of the small council was balanced by the predominance of Lutheranism among middling-to-rich tradesmen who made Augsburg thrive. Catholics had more churches, but in some of them Protestants retained control of the pulpit and the nave, leaving only the sanctuary to Catholics.

Within these parameters imposed from above the two communities groped their way toward a new sense of urban citizenship. The city's Latin school was founded (1552) by Protestant humanists who kept doctrinal disputes in the background; Catholic pupils were welcome, even after the Jesuits founded a school of their own (1579). After 1555 the mostly Catholic small council appointed mainly Lutheran "alms lords" to administer the unified (1522) civic charity that controlled the city hospital and many other activities; contributions came from the wealthy, especially the Fuggers. When an influx of starving poor from the countryside prompted Augsburg to open Germany's first orphanage (1572), the "orphan-father" and most of his small clients were Lutheran, but Catholic children were raised in the religion of their parents. The military vicissitudes of the Thirty Years' War encouraged first one party, then the other, to reach for exclusive control of the city. But the 1648 peace restored a balance here as in the empire at large, and it was not disrupted when each confession created an orphanage and a hospital of its own. It was by now understood that the two communities still made up one urban society, even if they created separate institutions to replace the common civic institutions of old.

Colmar too was a free imperial city, but had only about 7,000 inhabitants, and its economy was based on trade in wine and other agricultural products up and down the Rhine, to Basel or Strasbourg. Influenced by ties to Reformed Basel and Lutheran Württemberg, Colmar's merchants and tradesmen might have introduced a Reformation earlier, save for contrary pressure from another neighbor, the Alsatian territory ruled by the Habsburg dynasty. In 1575 the magistrates, having gained approval from the city's ten guilds, decreed that Colmar, as an imperial city, had a "right of Reformation" under the terms of the 1555 Peace of Augsburg. This right did not include compelling everyone to attend Protestant services, or even disturbing existing arrangements at the city's one parish church or its religious houses. Indeed, the Protestant preacher appointed to a vacant chapel had to promise to avoid public disputes with Catholics, or quarrels with other Protestants. The magistrates preferred to blur distinctions between Lutheran and Reformed teaching, but rising tensions between the two parties in the empire forced a choice in favor of Swiss Reformed doctrine, as professed in Basel (1589). The one sense in which Colmar became publicly Protestant was that public spaces were cleansed of shrines, statues, and all other traces of the Catholic past. Confessional allegiance reflected the contacts people had in their daily lives. Protestants (more numerous and wealthier) were especially strong among guilds with trading connections to Basel or Strasbourg; the Catholic minority was concentrated among agricultural guilds whose dealings were with the mainly Catholic villages of Colmar's hinterland. Within the city, what both sides wanted was civic peace, even amid the vicissitudes of the Thirty Years' War. In 1628, Emperor Ferdinand II installed a garrison in the city and decreed that Protestants would have six months to convert to Catholicism, or sell their goods and move elsewhere. But the new Catholic magistrates were not happy to see Protestant fellow burghers depart, and would not take steps that might cause a further depopulation; for example, they ignored the emperor's instructions for punishing Protestant youth who refused to attend Catholic catechism classes. In 1632 Gustavus Adolph, backed by his army, restored Protestant worship in Colmar, but insisted that only Lutheran preachers be appointed. This was the biconfessional settlement that persisted into the future, even after King Louis XIV decreed that all of Alsace was now part of France (1683). In 1649, when a Catholic bishop visited Colmar for confirmation, he complimented the Lutheran chief magistrate for preserving the religious peace and bade him continue his good work. Colmar, like Ausgburg, tamed the demons of religious strife through an arrangement in which, as a recent scholar has said, the two "confessional groups became one more corporate subset within the body politic."

Layrac had about 1,100 people in 1600, most of them Huguenot. Its four annually elected consuls and the "sworn men" who advised them were solidly Huguenot by 1580, when Layrac expelled its Benedictine monks and abolished Catholic worship. After the Edict of Nantes in 1598, Huguenot consuls, though grumbling that there were no two Catholics of appropriate wealth and status, were forced to make their college biconfessional. Following a revolt against the crown in which many of southern France's Huguenot towns joined (1620–1622), royal orders excluded Huguenots from the consulate. Yet the principle of parity was still observed; the Huguenot schoolmaster received a larger share of city funding because he had more pupils. When a new Catholic pastor (armed with a doctorate in theology) and those who joined his new confraternity pressed for a more zealously Catholic policy, most Catholic magistrates stood with Protestant colleagues in resisting. They opposed his attempts to increase the level of the tithe and refused to bar Protestant burials in the city cemetery. Beginning in 1644 Huguenots were readmitted to the consulate, despite the objections of militant Catholics. This small victory for a common civility reflects a common sociability; Layrac's leading families shared in business dealings, civic processions, and (despite the fulminations of the Huguenot pastor) carnival festivities. Even more, it reflects the fact that it was the job of urban magistrates in France to help siphon off a certain amount of wealth through taxation, for fighting the king's wars. In a town like Layrac this was not possible without Huguenot cooperation. Layrac's confessional coexistence ended only when troops backing Louis XIV's Revocation of the Edict of Nantes (1685) forced its Huguenots into exile.

Haarlem made its definitive choice for the Dutch Revolt in 1578. The initial agreement with the rebel States of Holland called for freedom of worship in the city, but violent disruption of Catholic services by fanatical garrison troops (including the killing of a priest) led to a Calvinist takeover of Haarlem's parish church. A new agreement of 1581 provided for freedom of conscience but allowed none but Reformed worship, "to avoid confusion." Meanwhile, a stream of mainly Protestant émigrés from the southern Netherlands was already flowing in, helping Haarlem to grow from around 15,000 people (1564) to around 40,000 (1622). The Flemish linen workers who now revived the local industry were often Anabaptist, or, as the Dutch now said, Baptist minded. Baptist-minded congregations frequently split over disputes as to how strictly church rules for "shunning" sinners were to be applied, but they claimed as many as one-seventh of Haarlem's inhabitants. In the relaxed climate of the Twelve Years' Truce with Spain (1609–1622) they built an unmarked meeting house (1616), later divided in two to accommodate a schism among the members. Haarlem's Lutherans, mainly German immigrants, built their unmarked house of worship at about the same time. Other refugees from the south, including cloth workers, formed the backbone of Haarlem's Reformed congregation; there were 400 adult members in 1580, 4,000 in 1617, or about one-fifth of the population.

The old religion was kept alive in the city and in the prosperous and still Catholic villages near Haarlem by priests of the Holland Mission, chartered by Rome in 1592. Illegal "assemblies" were frequently broken up by the sheriff so long as it seemed that Catholicism meant loyalty to Spain. But the allegiance of most Catholics to the republic (and bribes to the sheriff) led officials to look the other way after about 1600. Informal communities of religious women taught catechism classes, tended the sick, and knocked on doors to give the time and place for Sunday mass. By 1625 Haarlem's Catholics were said to have eighteen "hidden churches," usually in the upper stories of large houses.

A sense of confessional identity was taking hold, apparently among all of Haarlem's denominations; workers sought employers of the same faith, and employers did the same for employees. At the same time, many Haarlemmers seem to have been content to profess no particular religion. Though some churches gained over time, notably the Calvinists and to a lesser extent the Catholics, the existence of many options apparently left room for some people to choose none. Meanwhile, magistrates, Protestant but not necessarily Calvinist in sympathy, kept alive the idea of a civic culture not tied to confession. Haarlem's Latin school and its unified system of poor relief were under their control so that efforts in these areas by confessional bodies were at most supplementary. If Haarlem's relative toleration did not extend to non-Christians, it was because the Portuguese Jewish congregation whom magistrates encouraged to settle here (1605) received a better offer from nearby Amsterdam (fig. 14.4).

Seventeenth-century Haarlem approximated the religious pluralism of later centuries in fact, if not in theory. Few individuals espoused the principle that civil society should not be built on confessional foundations, but in

Figure 14.4. Interior of Amsterdam's Portuguese Jewish synagogue. Emmanuel de Witte, "The Portuguese Synagogue in Amsterdam," 1680. *Rijksmuseum, Amsterdam.*

practice this was a civil society whose confessional foundations were kept in the background. Rather than attempting to permeate civil society, as in the past, religion had come to play the role of enabling believers to form within the larger society smaller communities according to their own liking. This resolution of the ancient tension between community and society was an outcome no reformer had foreseen or desired. It came about because of an unpredictable coalescence of religious fervor with political ambitions and social reality. In Haarlem as elsewhere, this was the combination of circumstances that reshaped society in the era of Europe's Reformations.

15 | Conclusion

Europe's Reformations in Global Perspective

The era of the Reformation was also the era in which Europe reached out to the rest of the world, not only with merchants and gunboats, but also with missionaries. In the period covered by this book the missionaries were mainly Catholic, not Protestant. The Catholic nations of Iberia established overseas colonies well before the Protestant English and Dutch did; also Calvinist theology of the time had hesitations about carrying the gospel to pagans. The English were at first uncertain whether North American Indians were worth converting, while the Dutch in what is now Indonesia reasoned that if these heathen had not become Christians after so many centuries, it must be God's will. If, by contrast, members of the new Catholic religious orders were eager to make converts abroad, it was partly because they saw in mission lands a spiritual harvest to offset the souls lost to Protestant heresy in Europe. In effect, the Counter-Reformation exported to Asia and the Americas both the dynamism of the new forms of spirituality and the disagreements that divided them.

A second reason for missionary enthusiasm among Catholics was that they sought and found imagined homologies between their own beliefs and those of Asian and American peoples. One of many strands in Portugal's push toward the Indian Ocean was the hope of finding legendary Christian peoples said to dwell on the far side of the hostile Muslim world. In the wake of Hernan Cortés's conquest of the Aztec empire for Spain (1522), Franciscan friars identified the unexpectedly civilized Mexicans with the so-called Lost Tribes of ancient Israel, whose return to true religion would betoken Christ's return to earth to establish his everlasting kingdom. Inspired by Renaissance humanist conceptions of a universal human nature, both Franciscan and Jesuit missionaries sought at various times to build Indian utopias, where the generous qualities of America's native peoples, secluded from European greed, could flourish under the guidance of faith. In China, as in Europe, Jesuits sought to win the minds and hearts of those who set the tone for others. Permitted to reside at the emperor's court in Beijing, they lived and dressed as scholar-officials (fig. 15.1). They studied Chinese literature, looking for points of contact between Confucian and Christian teaching, and concluded that the concept of "Heaven" (T'ien), so venerated in the Chinese classics, could properly be translated as "God." They slowly made converts among the empire's bureaucratic elite. Was it a problem if Chinese Christians made obeisance to the emperor as Son of Heaven, as court ritual required? No, reasoned the Jesuit fathers: This was a civil ceremony, not an act of worship. But Franciscans aimed, in China as in Europe, at bringing the gospel to the poor. They dressed in their European habits, sought out the common people neglected by the Jesuits, and violated Chinese law by preaching their alien doctrine in the public streets. Frequently imprisoned for their pains, as Jesuits seldom were, they denounced the Jesuits for allowing their converts to participate in idolatrous court ceremonies and demanded action from Rome.

It is easy at a distance of centuries to see how the missionaries were wrong in the comparisons they made between European and Asian or American beliefs. For example, modern authorities believe that by translating "Heaven" as "God," Jesuit scholars confused the impersonal force of Chinese tradition with the personal deity of biblical faith. But they were not wrong in looking for analogies. Contrary to the common saying, history does not repeat itself. Historical understanding demands that ideas be grasped in a context that is unique to a given period and region, a concatenation of circumstances that in the vast span of human time occurs only once. This means (I would argue) that although historians may borrow from sociology or economics, history itself is not a social science. To a historian, the historical event or process is of interest in itself, not as a case study useful for validating or disproving some conceptual model of human behavior in general. Yet the uniqueness of a given historical situation does not preclude comparison to others that are somewhat similar.

Indeed, for European historians in particular, a growing awareness of Europe's connectedness to the rest of the world—in the past as well as at present—requires that we give some thought to how a particular process unfolding in Europe may compare with or relate to the histories of other areas of the globe. In the case of Europe's Reformations, the religious concerns that this book has discussed may be seen to bear some resemblance to the concerns that have animated reform movements in other traditions. For this concluding reflection on the global context of Europe's Reformations, I have chosen reform movements that show some analogies with distinctive features of the Protestant Reformation as discussed here: (a) the

Figure 15.1. A German Jesuit, Adam Schall, at the imperial court in Beijing.
Schall in his mandarin garb as court astronomer and President of the Board of
Rites, responsible for determining the astrologically auspicious dates for Confu-
cian court ceremonies: from Athanasius Kircher, S.J., E Societatis Jesu China Mon-
umentis Illustrata (Amsterdam, 1667), among the illustrations following p. 112.
Courtesy of University Libraries, University of Minnesota, Minneapolis.

Neo-Confucian recovery of the Confucian scripture, (b) the Wahhabiya purification of worship in eighteenth-century Arabia, (c) the holy community of Hasidic Judaism in eighteenth-century Poland-Lithuania, and (d) the Iconoclast purification of worship in the seventh- and eighth-century Byzantine Empire.

The Neo-Confucian recovery of the Confucian scripture. China stands out from every other region of the globe because of its cohesion through the millennia as a political entity. Starting around 1500 B.C. with the Shang Dynasty, China has been ruled for most of the past thirty-five centuries by imperial dynasties that followed one another either directly or, in some cases, after a period of "warring states" lasting a century or two. The emperor was styled "Son of Heaven," meaning that his rule enjoyed celestial approval and that he was responsible for correct observance of the traditional rituals by which China maintained a proper relationship with the higher powers of the cosmos. From 221 B.C. until 1939, when the last emperor of the last dynasty was deposed by Japanese invaders, emperors were assisted in governing their vast realm not by a military aristocracy, as was common in Latin Christendom, but by civilian officials who prided themselves in their learning. Emperors of the T'ang Dynasty (618–907) inaugurated a system, revived in later centuries, in which entry to the ranks of officialdom was based on competitive examinations that required a polished literary style and a command of the Chinese classics.

By common consent, the greatest of the classical authors was the sage known in Western languages as Confucius (551–479 B.C.), who lived during one of the warring-states periods. Among his many interests, Confucius was a moralist, framing ethical precepts to guide the private life of a thinking man; for the public good, these same precepts were all the more necessary should one be called upon to serve the state as an official. His thought also had a religious dimension, since duties to Heaven counted among the obligations whose fulfillment was the measure of a man's true worth. But by the time the examination system took root, poetry was getting more attention from scholars than the ethical teachings of Confucius and his disciples—"the Way," as adepts called it.

Also, other doctrines now competed for allegiance. Buddhism, having come by way of Central Asia in the sixth century A.D., soon sprouted monasteries for men and for women all over China, propagating the ideal of withdrawal from the worldly occupations for purposes of interior self-cultivation. T'aoism, building on traditional Chinese beliefs about communication with the world of spirits, offered yet another set of precepts for cultivating the soul within. The reformulation of the Way that historians describe as Neo-Confucianism focused on the element of self-cultivation in Confucius's thought, so as to satisfy the taste for "rectification of the mind and heart" without abandoning the traditional Confucian emphasis on duties to the ruler and to society.

The scholar-official Ch'eng-i (d. 1107) credited his brother Ch'eng-hao (d. 1085) with a momentous discovery: By diligent study of Confucius's writings, he was able to "pick up the threads of what had not been transmitted for a thousand years" and "illumine the Way" by clearing away "overgrowth and weeds" obstructing the correct path. One might compare this sense of the recovery of lost meaning to the feeling of European scholars and theologians who, for the first time in many centuries, pored over scripture in its original languages. Ch'eng-hao had rediscovered what he saw as the neglected moral core of Confucian teaching, contained especially in a treatise called *The Great Learning*. "Rectification of mind and heart" meant rigorous control of selfish desires and vigilance against the corrupting influence of false doctrines (such as Buddhism and T'aoism, according to Ch'eng). This interior renewal was the sole basis for a renewal of human society. Hence it was the scholar-official's highest duty to lecture the emperor on the truth of the Way, at the risk of losing his position. Chu-Hsi (d. 1200), who codified the ideas of the Ch'eng brothers in his *Commentary on the Great Learning*, was arrested as a spreader of false doctrine.

Later generations would see things differently, after China was incorporated into the vast Yuan or Mongol Empire founded by Genghis Khan (d. 1227). Genghis's grandson Khubilai Khan (d. 1294) was impressed by the teachings of Neo-Confucian masters brought from south China to his capital in Beijing, so much so that he established an Imperial College devoted to the study of Confucius's writings as interpreted by Chu-Hsi and the Ch'eng brothers. Starting in 1313, this curriculum, somewhat simplified to make it accessible to officials of Mongol as well as Chinese origin, became the basis for a revived system of competitive examinations. Under the Yuan emperors and the subsequent Ming Dynasty (1368–1644), scholar-officials inspired by the example of Chu-Hsi held public lectures to impart the Way to the emperor's subjects. The Yuan Dynasty needed a unifying belief system to bridge differences between Mongol conquerors and the Han or ethnic Chinese population. Neo-Confucianism had many attractive features, including the linkage it made between personal integrity and service to the empire. Thus the once-despised doctrine of a few dissident scholars became, by stages, the favored religion of a great empire.

The Wahhabiya purification of worship. Within a century of the Prophet Muhammad's death (632), Islam spread with astonishing rapidity, to the Pyrenees mountains of northern Spain in the west and the Himalayas in the east. The new creed was uncompromising in its worship of Allah, the one and only God, and straightforward in its demands. Having once made their formal profession of faith, Muslims were to pray five times a day, fast during the month of Ramadan, give alms, and make a pilgrimage to Mecca, the ancient holy city of Arabia, whose capture by the Prophet had marked Islam's first great triumph. Mosques served as gathering places for daily prayer, often with a sermon by the prayer leader on Friday, the Muslim holy day.

Upon Muhammad's death, his followers had chosen a caliph ("successor") who succeeded to the prophet's authority in both spiritual and temporal matters. After the death of the third caliph (656), a dispute and soon a war broke out between the Umayyad kinsmen of the late caliph and the partisans of Ali Ibn Abi Talib, cousin and son-in-law of the Prophet. Ali reigned for a time as caliph, only to be assassinated in 661. The Umayyad claimant now succeeded to the caliphate; his descendants ruled from Damascus until 750, followed by the Abbasid caliphs, who funded a new capital at Baghdad and held sway until 1258. The majority of believers, known as Sunni (followers of tradition), accepted the legitimacy of the Umayyad and Abbasid caliphs. But Ali's followers, the Shi'ites, insisted that only a kinsman of the Prophet could be the Imam, his legitimate successor. Over the generations Shi'ites disagreed about Ali's line of descent, but the most common view was that the last lawful Imam, of the twelfth generation from Ali, was "hidden away" in 874, to return one day to claim his rightful place. Shi'ites of this persuasion would not have a kingdom of their own until Iran's Safavid shahs (1504–1724) made Shi'ism the state religion of Iran.

For both Sunnis and Shi'ites, God's Word as revealed to Muhammad in the Koran included a comprehensive code for living. Some religious scholars devoted themselves to the study of the Koran itself or to the authentication of the *hadith* ("traditions"), collections of sayings attributed to the Prophet and his companions. Among Shi'ites there were also collections of sayings attributed to the Imams, Ali's lawful heirs. Others turned to Arabic translations of the writings of Plato and Aristotle, seeking to reconcile the revealed truth of the Koran with the pagan wisdom of ancient philosophy, a pattern to be followed by certain Jewish thinkers as well as by scholastic writers of the Christian Middle Ages. Still others built up a body of legal opinions by which the teachings of the Koran and the *hadith* could be applied to disputes arising in daily life. In time, Sunni legal scholars organized themselves into several distinctive schools of thought; one school, the Hanbalis, differed from the others by its reluctance to take *hadith* or previous legal opinions into account; if at all possible, only the Koran itself should be counted as authoritative—an idea not the same as Luther's *sola scriptura*, but not entirely different either.

Some among the faithful were not satisfied by external observances, for the Koran also described how the soul could experience ecstatic union

Figure 15.2. A Sufi preacher. Madjalis al-'Ushshah (a sixteenth-century Persian artist), "A Sufi Preaching." *Bodleian Library, Oxford, MS Ouseley Add. 24, fol. 55 v.*

with God. Teachers called Sufis developed regimens of prayer aimed at enabling devout Muslims to achieve this exalted state (fig. 15.2). Religious brotherhoods grew up around magnetic Sufi leaders, who often designated successors to carry on after their deaths. For devotees, the tomb of the holy founder became the shrine of a saint, a site for pilgrimage, and a source for stories of miraculous cures, much like the tombs of martyr-saints in early Christianity. Thus by the tenth or eleventh century, Islam had developed a rich religious culture, in which many of the faithful who gathered for Friday prayer at the town's chief mosque might sort themselves out for the rest of the week into smaller groups pursuing interests that were distinct and even conflicting.

For some, however, this great variety of practice and belief betokened a lamentable departure from the Prophet's austere simplicity. Taqi al-Din Ibn Taymiya (d. 1328), a Sunni legal scholar of the above-mentioned Hanbali school, was so rigorous in his condemnation of the tomb-cults of Sufi saints that he would not countenance any special honor being paid to the memory of the Prophet: No man, only Allah, deserved the worship of the faithful. Owing to his denunciation of popular local cults, Ibn Taymiya spent much of his adult life in the prisons of Cairo and Damascus. But later scholars preserved and continued to discuss his writings. At a school in Medina, not far from Mecca, Ibn Taymiya's works were read and recopied by Muhammad Ibn Abdul Wahhab (1703–1791).

Ibn Abdul Wahhab, a Hanbali scholar like his father, began preaching in public shortly after his father's death in 1740. Like Ibn Taymiya, he denounced all the elements of the tomb-cults of Sufi saints: kissing the tombstone or other acts of reverence, leaving candles or other gifts, and praying for the saint's intercession with God. Like Ahmad Ibn Hanbal (d. 855), founder of the Hanbali school, he told of how the Prophet himself had prayed, "O God, make not my grave into an idol that is worshiped." On the basis of travels through Arabia, Ibn Abdul Wahhab was familiar with the practice of the Islamic religion, and he did not like what he saw. If Zwingli and Calvin believed that the veneration of saints among Catholics was a continuation of ancient polytheism, Ibn Abdul Wahhab believed that superstitious practices among Muslims of his day represented a recrudescence of the ancient paganism of pre-Islamic times. He and his followers described themselves by a term meaning "those who confess that God is one," while referring to their enemies as "cupola people," an allusion to the domed mausoleums of Sufi tombs.

His attacks on usurers as oppressors of Islam earned respect among common people, if not the rich, but he made enemies by denouncing religious scholars who opposed him as "pagans." By 1744, Medina had become unsafe, but he found refuge with a warrior chieftain, Muhammad Ibn Sa'ud. The two men made a pact: Inhabitants of the lands to be conquered by Ibn Sa'ud would be required to practice the pure form of Islam preached by Ibn Abdul Wahhab. Wherever the armies of Ibn Sa'ud succeeded, his Wahhabi followers in their zeal for pure worship leveled the Sufi mausoleums that had dotted the landscape of Arabia for many centuries. Like the Calvinist Reformation in certain princely territories, such as the Palatinate, Ibn Abdul Wahhab's austere and uncompromising monotheism only became the norm for all believers when it was backed by the power of the state.

By 1804, the Sa'udis, having taken Mecca and Medina, were masters of all Arabia. But the Ottoman Turkish sultan in Istanbul, whose empire included the Arabian Peninsula, sponsored a counterattack. For over a century the Sa'udis had to be content with something like their former status. Meanwhile, Wahhabi doctrine carried by wandering preachers took root in various parts of the Islamic world, notably in West Africa. During the First World War Sa'udi ambitions were rekindled by Britain's need for an ally against the Turks. When the house of Sa'ud entered Mecca in triumph for a second time (1924), the Wahhabi version of Islam became the state religion of what has since been known as Saudi Arabia.

Shi'ite legal scholarship flourished in Safavid Iran, and also in the holy cities of Najaf and Karbala in Iraq, normally an Ottoman province, but sometimes under Safavid rule. Independent-minded religious scholars rejected the shah's claim to be the Imam's representative on earth. Teachers of the Akhbari or "traditionalist" school, based in Najaf and Karbala, bore some resemblance to the Sunni Hanbali school in focusing on the sacred texts: Authoritative sources for legal decisions were to be sought only in the Quran, or the sayings attributed to the Prophet and to the Imams—certainly not from rational interpretation (*ijtihad*). By contrast, teachers of the rival *Usuli* or "principles of law" school, based at Qom (Iran) attached great importance to rational interpretation, and they also insisted that a faithful Muslim must find a learned "interpreter of the law" to serve as his "source of inspiration" in matters of practical ethics. Some even contended (though this was not the dominant view) that it was the religious scholars themselves who were the Imam's true representatives on earth. Over the generations the two schools fought a see-saw battle of argument and political influence. Though Usuli jurists had strong ties to the court in early Safavid times, Akhbari scholars dominated the schools of Najaf and Karbala in the eighteenth century, especially after the final collapse of Safavid rule in Iran. But the rulers of Iran's Qajar dynasty (1779–1925) favored the Usuli school, and during the nineteenth century its teachings gained sway not just in Iran but also in Najaf, where Shayka Murtada Ansari (d. 1864) was the first teacher to be recognized as the supreme source of interpretative authority—a position currently held by Ayatolloh Ali al-Sistani.

The holy community of Hasidic Judaism. Among Christians and Muslims, Jews were a readily identifiable and despised minority. In bad times their settlements were assaulted by angry mobs, and even in good times they were subject to a regimen of restrictions imposed by the ruler. Mob violence was more frequent in Muslim lands, but the restrictions were more severe in Christian countries. As people do when living in a hostile environment, Jews protected themselves with a panoply of community institutions. Even fairly small communities had a synagogue (house of prayer) with a cantor to lead the congregation in song and a rabbi learned in the Hebrew Bible. Larger communities boasted schools for organized study of the scriptures and of the Talmud, a vast compilation of commentary on scripture and application of its teachings to daily life, and governing councils made up of prosperous men and leading religious scholars.

In the Muslim kingdoms of Spain, where the Jewish population had been large and influential since Roman times, scholars had the luxury of branching out. Some pored over Arabic translations of pagan philosophers like Plato and Aristotle, seeking, as Muslim and Christian scholars did, to reconcile the truth of faith with the conclusions of human reason. Others delved into a collection of Hebrew writings known as the Kabbalah, purporting to show how the holy words of scripture could be made to disclose hidden truths about the nature of the world, to heal the sick, or to enable the soul to rise to an experience of union with God. As has been recounted earlier (chapter 7), Jewish life in Iberia was first diminished by the conversion of the New Christians, then brought to an end by the expulsion of Jews from the peninsula's kingdoms, starting with Castile in 1492. The refugees, from Iberia, known in Hebrew as "Sephardim" (the westerners), proved that communities having a high degree of complex organization could be scattered by a sudden blow, but not extinguished. They rebuilt their lives in Muslim North Africa; in Italy, where restrictions on Jews were generally less severe than in other Christian lands; and especially in the Ottoman Turkish Empire. Down to the twentieth century, a form of Spanish known as Ladino was still spoken among descendants of Sephardic Jewish exiles in cities like Saloniki (modern Greece) and Izmir (modern Turkey).

This sequence of persecution and rebuilding is found also in the history of the Ashkenazic ("eastern") Jews of Poland-Lithuania. Poland's kings had welcomed the refugees who, after the persecutions of the fourteenth century, looked eastward for a new home. Poland's major cities—taking a cue from craft guilds that feared competition—enacted laws that prevented Jews from settling within their walls. But the kingdom was dominated by its nobles, great and small, who were busy planting new villages and eager to have estate managers, craftsmen to supply their peasants with goods, and more peasants to till virgin soil. Thus Jewish settlements took root in royal or aristocratic lands in Poland-Lithuania, a process that accelerated during the sixteenth century as neighboring Bohemia expelled its Jews.

The Jewish population of Poland-Lithuania is estimated at 30,000 in 1500, 450,000 in 1648 (about 4.5 percent of the population), and 350,000 in 1660, after a terrible slaughter of Jews during the Cossack-led rebellion that brought western Ukraine under the rule of Moscow. Though Jews came from many lands, as far away as Spain, they spoke Yiddish ("Jewish"), a German dialect influenced by Hebrew. As the Catholic Reformation took root in Poland, from the late sixteenth century, the church demanded stricter enforcement of traditional restrictions against Jews. But Poland's rulers protected Jewish subjects, as is indicated by their firm stand against the hoariest of anti-Semitic legends, the "blood libel" that had Jews sacrificing Christian children in secret rites.

Though the threat of persecution was always present, Jewish communities had room to breathe. A community's governing council (*kahal*) was often controlled by managers of noble estates, and the rabbi often owed his appointment to the local noble (bribes were not unknown). Estate managers and religious scholars joined in lending at high rates to poor peasants, Jewish as well as non-Jewish. But as in contemporary Christian cities, where the growing wealth of elite families set them more and more apart from their fellow burghers, the prosperity of a few took a heavy toll on the traditional sense of solidarity within the Jewish community. *Kahal* leaders took to wearing gentile (non-Jewish) clothes; they threatened poor Jews with expulsion from their lands for nonpayment of debt and haled them before Christian courts to make good their threats.

Such practices were condemned in sermons by synagogue preachers who came from poor families themselves. Unlike the rabbis and the Talmudic scholars, these poorly paid men, wandering from one community to another, often drew their inspiration from writings based on the Kabbalah. Their message was that the spiritual and moral renewal of a sinful and unjust world depended on achieving the blessed state of union with God and that this in turn was only possible for the man who renounced gentile ways and lived as a devout (Hasid), Law-observing Jew in every detail of his life. In some communities, circles of the devout (Hasidim) formed around a charismatic leader, often a preacher, known to his followers as a *zaddik*, a just man.

Such was the wandering preacher known as the Baal (Healer) Shem Tov (1700–1760), whose name implies that he practiced a form of faith healing. He urged listeners to "set the world aright" through prayer and devotion. Rural Jews understood that his call for "ransoming Jewish captives" meant freeing Jewish peasants from back rents owed to Jewish estate managers. The Hasidim who rallied to his teaching were few in number at the time of the Baal Shem Tov's death, but their numbers grew under the men recognized as his successors, Dov Baer (d. 1772) and Rabbi Nachman of Bratislav (d. 1810), a grandson of the Baal Shem Tov.

The Hasidim came to be characterized not merely by their punctilious observance of the Law and their study of the Kabbalah, but also by ecstatic and tearful prayer as a sign of joy in the Lord, and by the use of the folktale as a medium for religious instruction. These practices were denounced in a celebrated pronouncement by the leading religious scholar of the important city of Vilnius (Lithuania) but to little avail, since the traditional religious elite had already lost the allegiance of many Jews. By the early nineteenth century, what had begun as a dissident movement among the less fortunate was well on its way to embracing the majority of Eastern Europe's Jewish population.

The Iconoclast purification of worship. For early Christians, religious images had dangerous associations with contemporary paganism. In Greek and Roman worship, deities were believed to be present in and acting through their images, especially statues. Thus, as one fifth-century bishop of Sardinia put it, once images were held up to the veneration of Christians, "pagan customs do the rest." The objects of devotion for Christians of the fourth and fifth centuries were the relics of martyr-saints and images of the cross on which Christ the Redeemer had been crucified; both were carried in processions calling on God to ward off evil; both were believed to have miracle-working powers.

Only in the sixth century did the religious panel paintings known as icons (images) begin to be produced in the Byzantine or East Roman Empire, especially in certain important monasteries. Paintings on the interior walls of churches date from the same era, as do the splendid religious mosaics of a style that would become known in the West as Byzantine. Icons were soon receiving the same cult worship previously bestowed on the cross and on relics of the saints—they were carried in procession in times of danger, and stories circulated about icons that had delivered a city from Muslim or pagan invaders or cured the sick.

It is not unlikely that some Christians were alarmed by this departure from tradition, but signs of such a reaction are hard to detect in the scattered sources available for the seventh century. It is possible, but not certain, that a few bishops of Asia Minor were censured by the patriarch of Constantinople for having ordered the removal of images from their churches early in the eighth century. On the whole, it seems that the iconoclastic (image-breaking) reform of Christian worship was promoted from the top down, by a series of emperors: Leo III (717–741), his son Constantine V (741–775), and Leo V (813–820).

Leo III apparently took a great earthquake centered on the Aegean island of Thera (726) as a sign of God's wrath, directed against idolatrous icon worship. After some preliminary moves against images in the capital city, he decreed that wall paintings be covered and icons be removed from all the churches of the empire. Some of his advisers seem to have recommended casting out only the images of the saints, not those of Christ the Savior or Mary, the Mother of God, but the emperor made no such distinction: all the images must go. What support there was for these measures came from members of the parish or secular clergy, while monastic writers took the lead in opposing them. As if recognizing the relative novelty of icon worship, Leo III at the same time actively promoted devotion to the relics of the saints, and especially to fragments of the True Cross on which the Savior had hung.

Leo's son Constantine V continued his father's policies, convening bishops of the Byzantine world in 754 in a council that proclaimed that the only true image of Christ was to be found in the consecrated bread and wine of the eucharist and the only true image of the saints in their virtues. Constantinople's patriarch opposed this proclamation, but Constantine had him deposed and replaced by a more pliant successor. Beginning in 760, leading monks who continued to oppose the reform of worship were imprisoned or forced into exile. But when Constantine's son and successor died after a short reign (780), the Byzantine world learned that his wife the Empress Irene, now ruling in the name of their young son, was an "icondule," or devotee of images. She convened a council of bishops to revoke the iconoclastic decrees (786–787) and was not deterred when the first session of her council was broken up by soldiers from the imperial guard, who apparently identified the iconoclastic faith of Leo III and Constantine V with the military successes of that era, sorely missed in Irene's age. Despite signs of opposition from secular clergy and even from some monasteries, the campaign to restore the icons to the churches gained momentum under Irene and in the years immediately following her death (802). There was a temporary reversal under Leo V, who convened in 815 a synod of bishops that reinstated the iconoclastic decrees of 754. By this time, however, image worship was a subject for intense debate among the faithful, not easily controlled by imperial or ecclesiastical decrees. Popular admiration for the monasteries that were centers of the cult of icons began to make a difference, as did the arguments of icondule writers who maintained that if God Himself had become incarnate in the man Jesus, there was nothing inherently problematic about icons or other material objects being a vehicle or instrument for divine power. At a council of bishops meeting in 843, the iconoclastic decrees of 754 were again set aside, this time for good.

✟

These sketches may suffice to suggest how reform movements in quite different traditions can resemble one another. The Ch'eng brothers' rediscovery of the essential meaning of the Confucian Way, lost from sight for "a thousand years," bears comparison with Luther's rediscovery of the meaning of the gospel, lost from sight, as he believed, since the days of the early church. Both Ibn Abdul Wahhab and Byzantium's iconoclast emperors sought to purify the worship of the faithful by eliminating false accretions, as did the Protestant Reformers, especially Zwingli and Calvin, who altogether banned the religious veneration of images or other material objects. The weeping and joyful singing of Hasidic congregations represents a different spiritual impulse, comparable to Islam's Sufi brotherhoods rather than to the austere simplicity of Calvinist Christianity or Wahhabiya Islam. But the Hasidic movement also bears a resemblance to the community-based character of urban Protestantism: in Christian Germany as in Jewish Poland-Lithuania, the middling sort of people who embraced the new doctrine were to some extent also rebelling against the overweening authority of their social betters. The position of the Catholic clergy in medieval Europe had no real counterpart in the Jewish or Islamic traditions, but both the Wahhabiya and the Hasidic movements represent a withdrawal of allegiance from religious elites that is not wholly unlike Christian anticlericalism. Finally, the triumph of Neo-Confucianism in China and of the Wahhabis in Arabia, like the temporary triumph of iconoclasm in the Byzantine Empire, shows the decisive importance of the same state power that so often made the difference in the ultimate triumph of Protestantism or reformed Catholicism.

These irreducibly different histories resist being classified as instances of some general model of religious reform, but they are nonetheless somewhat alike, if only because human beings living in very different times and places still have something in common. Living in our own time and place, we make sense of the history of any other time and place by making comparisons to what we find more familiar—implicit analogies, similar to those made explicit here. This book has been devoted to the unique features of a sixteenth-century Latin Christendom that will be vaguely familiar to some readers and quite strange to others. But analogies allow us to see that the European Christian tradition, like all others, is not completely unique. For example, it has no monopoly on the human yearning for a deeper understanding of the ultimate truths about our existence or on the human proclivity for building states that draw legitimacy from and hence demand conformity with certain religious beliefs. It is by way of such analogies that a history that must necessarily be the history of only some of us can stand for the history of all of us.

Glossary

absolute monarchy. The theory that the king's authority was subject only to God, and not to control by any human institution, such as a representative assembly (like the Estates General in France) or a court of law (like the Parlement of Paris in France). The theory of absolutism gained ground in France (and elsewhere) after the Religious Wars of the sixteenth century, but the more common view of historians is that not even a strong French king (like the imperious Louis XIV, r. 1656–1715) was ever absolute or unlimited in the practical exercise of his authority. See also constitutional monarchy.

Alba, duke of. Fernando Alvarez de Toledo (1507–1582), scion of one of Castile's greatest noble families, served as field commander for several of Charles V's campaigns. His iron-fisted rule in the Netherlands (1567–1573)—including his use of the Council of Troubles, bypassing the existing courts—helped provoke the Revolt of the Netherlands.

alchemy. Alchemy purported to investigate the hidden properties of matter, including formulas for transmuting base matter into gold.

altars. An altar was a table on which sacrifice was offered. An altar, at the center of the chancel in the east end of a church (see nave), symbolized the Catholic understanding of the mass as a representation of the sacrifice of Christ on the cross, an idea repudiated by the Protestant reformers. Under England's Edward VI, altars were to be removed. Instead, there was to be a communion table at the center of the church, not at the east end, where the altar had been. The precedent for this arrangement of the worship space was to be found in Zurich.

Alumbrados. Observant Franciscans and New Christians were prominent among Castile's "illumined ones" who, in the early decades of the sixteenth century, advocated private, meditative prayer as a means of attaining more perfect union with God. From about 1500, because of its deemphasis of church ceremonies, the movement also attracted suspicion. See inquisition.

311

Anabaptists. Agreeing on infant baptism, Catholics, Lutherans, and Reformed Protestants used the term "Anabaptist" (re-baptizer) for those who rejected it on the grounds that true baptism required faith, possible only for an adult. Among modern spiritual descendants of the sixteenth-century Anabaptists are the Mennonites, the Amish, and the Hutterites.

Angelus. A prayer originally to be recited at dusk each day, in which verses alternate with Hail Marys. The Angelus was first recommended to the faithful by Pope John XXII in 1317.

apocalyptic. From the Greek title of the last book of the New Testament, the Book of Revelation. In a broader sense, "apocalyptic" refers to expectations of an imminent end of the world, followed by God's judgment on sinful humankind.

Arianism. Arius, an Egyptian priest, taught that Christ was the highest of creatures, but not God. In response, the ecumenical council of Nicaea (325) framed the Nicene Creed, affirming that Christ is the Son of God and "consubstantial" or "one in being" with God the Father. But since "consubstantial" is not found in the New Testament many bishops opted for a halfway position, neither Arian nor Nicene. The controversy ended only when the Nicene Creed was confirmed by the Council of Constantinople (381).

Arminius. 1) Arminius (Hermann), the chieftain whose armies destroyed three Roman legions (9 A.D.) was briefly described in the *Germania* of the Roman historian Tacitus. Printed editions appeared first in Italy, then (1515) in Germany. 2) Arminius, the Latinized form of the patronymic of Jacob Hermanszoon (d. 1609), a Dutch Reformed theologian who taught at the University of Leiden, and who questioned some aspects of Calvin's doctrine of predestination.

attrition. What kind of sorrow must the penitent feel in the sacrament of confession? The more common opinion among medieval theologians was that a merciful God would forgive even those who felt sorrow for their sins only because they feared the pains of hell (this kind of sorrow was called attrition). The theological school in which Luther was trained maintained that perfect contrition—sorrow for one's sins because one had offended God—was necessary for forgiveness.

Augsburg Confession. The Augsburg Confession, authored by Philip Melanchthon, was presented to Emperor Charles V and the Diet of Augsburg (1530) as a formal statement of the beliefs of Lutheran principalities and cities. To highlight differences with the Zwinglian movement, the text stressed areas of agreement between Lutherans and Catholics, including the assertion that Christ's body and blood are present "in" the elements of bread and wine in the Lord's Supper. In 1541, as a concession to south German Protestants who were moving closer to Luther's view of the Lord's Supper (see Wittenberg Concord), Melanchthon presented a Revised Augsburg Confession affirming that Christ's body and blood are present "with" the bread and wine.

Austrian duchies. From 1276, the Habsburgs were hereditary lords of an "Austria" that came to include, among scattered other territories, six duchies that made a compact block of land. These were, with their capitals, Upper Austria (Linz) and Lower Austria (Vienna), along the Danube; to the south, Styria (Graz), Carinthia (Klagenfurt), and Carniola (Lubljana), sometimes grouped together as Inner Austria; and to the southwest, Tirol (Innsbruck), stretching from the upper Inn valley to the Alps. Modern Slovenia is roughly coterminous with Slovenian-speaking Carniola. The other five duchies, together with the then-independent episcopal principality of Salzburg, make up most of modern Austria.

Bohemia. The boundaries of the medieval kingdom of Bohemia were roughly coterminous with those of the modern Czech Republic. The king of Bohemia was one of the electoral princes of the Holy Roman Empire, but once the crown of Bohemia passed to the Habsburgs (1526), the king and the emperor were the same person.

Boleyn, Anne. Second wife of England's King Henry VIII and mother of the future Queen Elizabeth. For reasons that remain obscure, she was arrested on charges of sexual impropriety, and soon executed (1536). Ten days later Henry married Jane Seymour, who died giving birth to the future King Edward VI (1537). Henry had no children by his three subsequent wives, Anne of Cleves, Catherine Howard, and Catherine Parr.

Bourbon. According to the French monarchy's rules of inheritance, claims to the crown could pass only through a king's legitimate male heirs. The four sons of Henry II (d. 1559) and Catherine de Medici were the last males of the Valois branch of the royal family, which had come to the throne in 1328. Next in line was the Bourbon branch of the royal family, descended from a younger son of Louis IX (d. 1270, later canonized as Saint Louis). Henry of Bourbon, son of Antoine of Bourbon, became king as Henry IV (1589–1610).

bourgeois. "Bourgeois" in French means the same as "burgher" in English or "bürger" in German, that is, a citizen of a burgh or city. Only a minority of the inhabitants of cities had rights of citizenship, and, often, only a minority of citizens (burghers or bourgeois) had the right to vote or hold office in town government.

Brandenburg-Prussia. Frederick William of Hohenzollern was margrave and elector of Brandenburg (r. 1640–1688) and also duke of Prussia, a territory his family had inherited from their Hohenzollern cousins, one of whom had been Grand Master when the Teutonic Knights, a pre-Reformation military order, converted to Lutheranism. During the last phase of the Thirty Years' War Frederick William built up his army in order to stake a claim for new lands when peace was finally concluded (1648). He thus laid the foundations of future greatness for his Hohenzollern descendants. Prussia became a kingdom in 1707, and in 1870 the king of Prussia became the first emperor of a united Germany, Kaiser Wilhelm I.

canonical hours. The rules of most religious orders prescribed seven "hours" for daily prayer, based on scripture (especially the Psalms) and the writings of the Fathers. Simplified manuscript versions of the monastic "book of hours," translated into the vernacular for the laity, were often graced by beautiful miniature paintings of scenes from daily life.

canonized. In Latin as in Greek, a "canon" was a law or a rule. A person was canonized by having his or her name inserted into the canon or main part of the mass, among the saints to whom the faithful prayed for intercession. Around 1300, the process of canonization, hitherto irregular, was centralized at the papal court.

cathedral. The church where a bishop has his *cathedra*, a Greek word meaning the chair from which one exercises one's authority.

cathedral chapter. Cathedrals (and some other important churches) had chapters—colleges of priests whose members were called canons, meaning in this case priests who lived by a rule. These well-endowed clerical positions were highly sought after; in many areas membership was restricted to the sons of noble families. This was the rank of the clergy from which bishops were usually chosen, and it was also permeated by noble conceptions of caste; for example, preaching to illiterate commoners was considered beneath the dignity of a lord canon.

chancel. See nave.

chantry. In the late Middle Ages it became common to include in one's will money for endowments for masses to be said for the salvation of one's soul. Chantry was the English term for these endowments, referring to the chanting of masses for the soul of the benefactor.

church ordinances. Church ordinances enacted by Protestant (and some Catholic) governments became part of that territory's civil law, regulating the affairs of the church. Hesse's church ordinance (1526) was the first.

Codex of Justinian. The collection of ancient Roman legal texts named after Justinian (d. 565), the Byzantine emperor who ordered its compilation. The *Codex* served as the basis for civil law in much of medieval and early modern Europe, and was the subject of instruction in university faculties of civil law.

college of cardinals. The Latin *collegium* meant a corporate body of equals having its own rules (including the "colleges" of canons at cathedral churches, also the "colleges" or dormitories endowed at universities by medieval donors, etc.). In early days, "cardinals" of the church in Rome were those clerics or laymen having key administrative positions. There were cardinal-priests and cardinal-deacons, but most cardinals held the rank of bishop or archbishop. From the eleventh century, the college of cardinals was the body that elected the pope.

commandments of the church. The six commandments of the church included receiving communion once a year during the Easter season, confessing one's sins to a priest once a year, abstaining from meat on Fridays, and fasting as required during the forty days of Lent, leading up to the celebration of Christ's resurrection from the dead at Easter.

commune. From as early as the eleventh century, the Italian word *commune* denoted a sworn association of burghers claiming certain rights in the governance of their town, often in defiance of their ruler (e.g., the archbishop of Milan, who was also a prince of the Holy Roman Empire). A bit later communes began forming in the countryside as well.

conciliarism. The doctrine that supreme authority in the Catholic Church is exercised not by the pope but by an ecumenical council, or by a council acting in conjunction with the pope. This view is expressed in a decree issued by the Council of Constance (1417), convened by the Emperor Sigismund to bring an end to the Papal Schism, in which there were two, eventually three claimants to the papal throne. See also Gallican Catholicism.

congregationalism. While Calvin believed that individual churches should be governed by synods, and Luther believed they should be governed by bishops (where possible) or by temporal rulers, some other Protestant thinkers believed that each congregation should govern its own affairs. This idea had surfaced in Hesse's church ordinance (1526), which was why it was rejected by Luther. Jean Morely (1524–1594), a one-time refugee in Geneva, revived the idea in debates among French Huguenots. In seventeenth-century England, those who favored congregational autonomy were known as Independents.

consistory. When the Roman Emperor took counsel with his advisers, the meeting was called a *consistorium*. In later Church Latin, the *consistorium* was a meeting in which the Pope took counsel with his advisers, the college of cardinals. John Calvin applied the term to a meeting in which the pastor of a church took counsel with the presbyters or elders of the church. The consistory in Geneva (like parallel bodies in other Calvinist churches) took cognizance of disciplinary matters, in which parishioners were called to account for their behavior.

constitutional monarchy. Medieval monarchies were constitutional in the sense that the king was considered to act unlawfully if he failed to observe certain unwritten rules and procedures. One illustration of this idea of lawful limits on the king's freedom of action is that the Parlement of Paris insisted on scrutinizing the legality of the king's edicts before registering them as enforceable in royal courts. Another is that representative assemblies (as in England, the Low Countries, and the Spanish kingdoms of Castile and Aragon) insisted that new taxes could not be introduced without their approval. See also absolute monarchy.

contrition. See attrition.

conversos. See New Christians.

Convocation. The assembly of the clergy in England.

corporate bodies. The modern idea of the corporation dates from thirteenth-century canon law: a monastery or cathedral chapter or a university was a "corporation" in that it had a governing structure duly authorized to act on behalf of the members. Also, the "body" continued to exist even in the interim when one "head" had died and was not yet replaced by a successor. Even before the legal theory of corporations emerged, town and often village governments in some parts of Europe already had in civil law the standing of "bodies" that could act on behalf of their members; in time, so did territorial parliaments and merchant or artisan guilds.

Council of Troubles. Made up of two Spaniards and one Netherlander, the Council of Troubles was the Duke of Alba's response to heresy and sedition in the Low Countries. Between 1567 and 1573 the council condemned over twelve thousand persons (mostly in absentia) to sentences of death or lesser penalties. The most famous of its victims were the Counts of Egmont and Hornes, loyal Catholics executed in Brussels in 1568; their crime had been traveling to Spain to present Philip II with the council of state's petition for a relaxation of the heresy laws.

covenant. In the Hebrew Bible, a covenant was a solemn ritual agreement that served the function of a written contract. Circumcision was the sign of the covenant between Yahweh and his people, the descendants of Abraham (Genesis 15:10, 17:10). The idea that the Christian people had a similar covenant with God was adumbrated by some late medieval theologians, and developed in greater detail by Zwingli and especially his successor in Zurich, Heinrich Bullinger.

crucifix. A three-dimensional representation of Christ hanging on the cross. Images of the suffering Savior began to appear in Christian art during the sixth century; from the thirteenth century, large crosses or crucifixes began to be placed above the main altars in parish churches.